VISUAL QUICKSTART GUIDE

SECOND EDITION

KEVIN HOWARD GOLDBERG

Visual QuickStart Guide
XML, Second Edition
Kevin Howard Goldberg

Peachpit Press
1249 Eighth Street
Berkeley, CA 94710
510/524-2178
510/524-2221 (fax)
Find us on the Web at: www.peachpit.com
To report errors, please send a note to errata@peachpit.com

Peachpit Press is a division of Pearson Education

Production Editor: David Van Ness
Tech Editors: Chris Hare and Michael Weiss
Compositor: Kevin Howard Goldberg
Indexer: Valerie Perry
Cover Design: Peachpit Press

ISBN-13: 978-0-321-55967-8
ISBN-10: 0-321-55967-3

9 8 7 6 5

Printed and bound in the United States of America

Foreword by Elizabeth Castro

XML has come a long way since I wrote the first edition of this book in 2001. It is as widespread now as it was exotic then.

Last year, I bumped into my friend Kevin Goldberg on a visit to California. We had known each other in college, and had played a lot of Boggle together in Barcelona.

When he offered to help me revise this book, I jumped at the chance. Kevin has been working in the computer industry for more than twenty years. He started his career as a video game programmer and producer. Since 1997, Kevin has been serving as partner and chief technology officer at *imagistic*, an award-winning, Web development and services company in Southern California. In this role, he is regularly called upon to help clients clarify their business needs, and to clearly communicate the nature and applicability of potential technology solutions—in a sense, demystify technology.

Besides all of these apt credentials, Kevin is a great guy. He is smart, conscientious, creative, and—not to mention—careful with details. In addition to updating the content and examples in the book, he added chapters on XSL-FO, recent W3C recommendations (XSLT 2.0, XPath 2.0 and XQuery 1.0), and a chapter devoted to real world examples called *XML in Practice*. I am most confident that you will find this second edition of *XML: Visual QuickStart Guide* to be an excellent tutorial for learning all about XML.

Elizabeth Castro
Author of *XML for the World Wide Web: Visual QuickStart Guide*

About the Author

Kevin Howard Goldberg has been working with computers since 1976 when he taught himself BASIC on his elementary school's PDP 11/70. Since then, Kevin's career has included management consulting using commerce simulations, and lead software development for numerous video game titles in multi-million dollar divisions at Film Roman and Lionsgate (previously Trimark). In his current capacity, he runs technology operations for a world-class Internet Strategy, Marketing and Development company in Westlake Village, California.

Kevin serves on the Santa Monica College Computer Science and Information Systems Advisory Board, and was invited to speak at the ACLU Nationwide Staff Conference as a Web development and production expert.

Kevin holds a bachelor's degree in Economics and Entrepreneurial Management from the Wharton School of Business at the University of Pennsylvania, and is a candidate for a master's degree in Computer Science at the University of California, Los Angeles.

Dedication

This book is dedicated to my wife, Lainie; in exchange for harried weekends, night-time surrogates, and an overcrowded bedroom, she receives this book. I am truly blessed.

Thank You

Michael Weiss, my business partner (of more than eleven years), my brother-in-law, and my friend. His support throughout this process; uncanny ability to see things from a reader's perspective; and willingness to do what it took to get the job done, while I was, at times, preoccupied, was invaluable to me.

Chris Hare, my technical editor, for jumping into the XML deep-end and amazingly keeping everything else afloat; teaching me the subtleties of punctuation (colons, semi-colons, and parenthetical expressions, oh my!); and being so detailed that when a page came back with less than a dozen red marks, I was concerned.

The **staff at imagistic** *(Chris, Heidi, Robert, Sam, Tamara,* and *Will)*, who didn't know what was coming, but nonetheless kept all the plates spinning with grace and humor.

David Van Ness, Peachpit's production editor extraordinaire, who was so incredibly helpful, resourceful, accommodating, available, and patient.

Nancy Davis, editor-in-chief at Peachpit, for seeing all the possibilities and shepherding this complex process through to completion.

Finally, a very special thanks to **Elizabeth Castro**, whose openness, honesty, integrity, and first edition of this book made this second edition possible.

Table of Contents

Table of Contents

Part 6: Recent W3C Recommendations

Part 7: XML in Practice

Appendices

INTRODUCTION

Internet time. A phrase whose meaning has come about as fast as it suggests; *happening significantly faster than one could normally expect.* In 1991, the first Web site was put online. Now, less than twenty years later, the number of Web sites online is thought to be more than one hundred million, give or take a few.

The amount of information available through the Internet has become practically uncountable. Most of that information is written in HTML (*HyperText Markup Language*), a simple but elegant way of displaying data in a Web browser. HTML's simplicity has helped fuel the popularity of the Web. However, when faced with the Internet's huge and growing quantity of information, it has presented real limitations.

In the seven years since the first edition of this book was published, XML (*eXtensible Markup Language*) has taken its place next to HTML as a foundational language on the Internet. XML has become a very popular method for storing data and the most popular method for transmitting data between all sorts of systems and applications. The reason being, where HTML was designed to display information, XML was designed to manage it.

This book will begin by showing you the basics of the XML language. Then, by building on that knowledge, additional and supporting languages and systems will be discussed. To get the most out of this book, you should be somewhat familiar with HTML, although you don't need to be an expert coder by any stretch. No other previous knowledge is required.

What is XML?

XML, or *eXtensible Markup Language*, is a specification for *storing information*. It is also a specification for *describing the structure of that information*. And while XML is a markup language (just like HTML), XML has no tags of its own. It allows the person writing the XML to create whatever tags they need. The only condition is that these newly created tags adhere to the rules of the XML specification.

And what does all that mean? OK, enough words. Try reading through the example XML document in **Figure i.1**, and answering the following questions:

1. What information is being stored?
2. What is the structure of the information?
3. What tags were created to describe the information and its structure?

As you may have concluded, the information being stored is that of my children. The structure of the information is that each child bears a description of their name, gender, and age. Finally, the tags created to describe the information and its structure are: `my_children`, `child`, `name`, `gender`, and `age`.

So, what exactly is XML? It is a set of rules for defining custom-built markup languages. The XML specification enables people to define their own markup language. Then they, or others, can create XML documents using that markup language.

The example shown in Figure i.1 is an XML document that I created using an XML markup language that I defined. It stores information about my children using an XML structure and custom tags that I designed.

```
xml
<?xml version="1.0"?>
<my_children>
 <child>
  <name>Logan</name>
  <gender>Male</gender>
  <age>18</age>
 </child>
 <child>
  <name>Rebecca</name>
  <gender>Female</gender>
  <age>14</age>
 </child>
 <child>
  <name>Lee</name>
  <gender>Female</gender>
  <age>13</age>
 </child>
</my_children>
```

Figure i.1 *Here is an example XML document. By reading the custom tags that I created, you can tell this is an XML document about my children. In fact, you can tell how many children I have, their names, their genders, and their ages.*

What is XML?

```
xml
<?xml version="1.0"?>

<ancient_wonders>

 <wonder>

  <name language="English">
   Colossus of Rhodes</name>

  <name language="Greek">
   Κολοσσός της Ρόδου</name>

  <location>Rhodes, Greece</location>

  <height units="feet">107</height>

  <main_image file="colossus.jpg"
    w="528" h="349"/>

  <source sectionid="101"
    newspaperid="21"/>

</wonder>

 ...

</ancient_wonders>
```

Figure i.2 *At first glance, XML doesn't look so different from HTML: it is populated with tags, attributes, and values. Notice, however, that the tags are different than HTML, and in particular how the tags describe the contents that they enclose. XML is also written much more strictly, the rules of which we'll discuss in Chapter 1.*

The Power of XML

So, why use XML? What does it do that existing technologies and languages don't? For one, XML was specifically designed for data storage and transportation. XML looks a lot like HTML, complete with tags, attributes, and values **(Figure i.2)**. But rather than serving as a language for displaying information, XML is a language for storing and carrying information.

Another reason to use XML is that it is easily extended and adapted. You use XML to design your own custom markup languages, and then you use those languages to store your information. Your custom markup language will contain tags that actually describe the data that they contain. And those tags can be reused in other applications of XML, scaled back, or added to, as you deem necessary.

XML can also be used to share data between disparate systems and organizations. The reason for this is that an XML document is simply a text file and nothing more. It is well-structured, easy to understand, easy to parse, easy to manipulate, and is considered "human-readable." For example, you were able to read, and likely understand, the examples shown in both Figures i.1 and i.2.

Finally, XML is a non-proprietary specification and is free to anyone who wishes to use it. It was created by the W3C (*www.w3.org/*), an international consortium primarily responsible for the development of platform-independent Web standards and specifications. This open standard has enabled organizations large and small to use XML as a means of sharing information. And, it has supported a larger international effort to create new applications based on the XML standard, helping to overcome barriers in commerce created by independently developed standards and governmental regulations.

Extending XML

An important observation about XML **(Figure i.3)** is that while HTML is used to format data for display **(Figure i.4)**, XML describes, and is, the data itself.

Since XML tags are created from scratch, those tags have no inherent formatting; a browser can't know how to display the `<wonder>` tag. Therefore, it's your job to specify how an XML document should be displayed. You can do this using XSL, or *eXtensible Stylesheet Language*.

XSL is actually made up of three languages: XSLT, for transforming XML documents; XPath, for identifying different parts of an XML document; and XSL-FO, for formatting an XML document. XSL lets you manipulate the information in an XML document into any format you need; most frequently into HTML, or an XML document with a different structure than the original. XSL is described in detail in Part 2 *(see page 17)*.

In addition to displaying an XML document, there are ways to define the structure of an XML document. Either written with a DTD (*Document Type Definition*) or with the XML Schema language, these structural definitions (or schemas) specify the tags you can use in your XML documents, and what content and attributes those tags can contain. You'll learn about DTD in Part 3 *(see page 73)*, XML Schema in Part 4 *(see page 111)*, and I'll explain how you can use XML Namespaces to extend XML Schemas in Part 5 *(see page 161)*.

As with most technologies, even as you are reading this page, there are numerous new extensions being developed for XML. In Part 6 *(see page 181)* of the book, I'll discuss some of these recent developments, including XSLT 2.0, along with XPath 2.0 and its extension, XQuery, used for the querying of XML and databases.

```
xml
<?xml version="1.0"?>

<ancient_wonders>

...

 <wonder>

  <name language="English">
    Statue of Zeus at Olympia</name>

  <name language="Greek">
    Διας μυθολογια</name>

  <location>Olympia, Greece
    </location>

  <height units="feet">39</height>

 <main_image file="zeus.jpg"
    w="528" h="349"/>

 </wonder>

...

</ancient_wonders>
```

Figure i.3 *This XML excerpt is data describing the Statue of Zeus at Olympia, one of the seven wonders of the ancient world.*

```
html
<html>

...

  <p align="center">

   <strong>STATUE OF ZEUS AT OLYMPIA
     </strong><br/>

   <img src="zeus.jpg"
      width="528" height="349"/></p>

   The Statue of Zeus at Olympia
     (<em>Διας μυθολογια</em>) was
     located in Olympia, Greece and
     stood 39 feet tall.<br/>

</body>

</html>
```

Figure i.4 *This HTML is just one example of what you can do with the XML document in Figure i.3 using XSL transformations.*

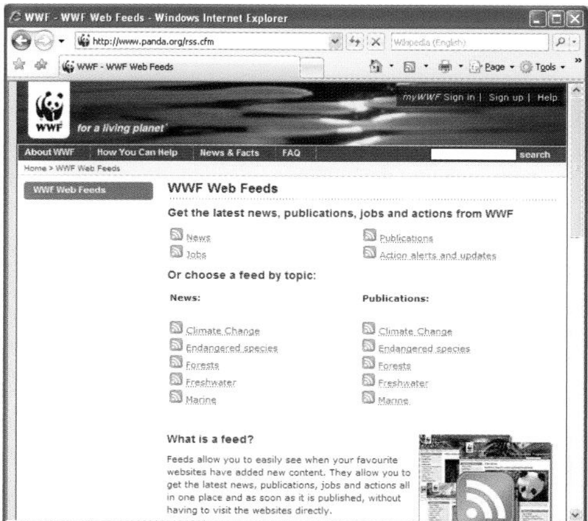

Figure i.5 *RSS* (Really Simple Syndication) *is an easy way for you to "subscribe" to news, podcasts and other content from Web sites that offer RSS feeds. Once you've subscribed to your favorite feeds, instead of needing to browse to the sites you like, information from these sites is delivered to you.*

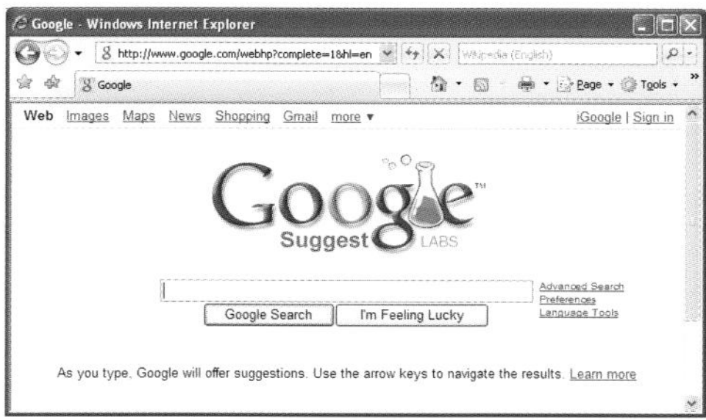

Figure i.6 *Some believe that Google Suggest was instrumental in bringing Ajax to the forefront of Web development circles. The idea is simple: as you type, Google Suggest displays matching search terms which you can choose instead of continuing to type. Try it!* www.google.com/webhp?complete=1&hl=en

XML in Practice

Since the first edition of this book, XML has been adopted in many significant ways. Not the least of which is that all standard browsers can read XML documents, use XML schemas (DTD and XML Schema), and interpret XSL to format and display XML documents.

That said, however, the once widely held notion that XML could replace HTML for serving Web pages is now more distant than ever. To accomplish this would require world-wide adoption of new browsers supporting additional XML technologies and webmasters around the world would need to undertake the gargantuan task of rewriting their sites in XML.

Since XML is not going to replace HTML, what was initially considered a temporary solution has become a well-recognized standard: use XML to manage and organize information, and use XSL to convert the XML into HTML. With this, you benefit from the power of XML to store and transport data, and the universality of HTML to then format and display it.

In addition to becoming browser readable, XML has been adopted in numerous other real world applications. Two of the most widely recognized uses are RSS and Ajax. RSS (*Really Simple Syndication*) is an XML format used to syndicate Web site content such as news articles, podcasts and blog entries **(Figure i.5)**.

Ajax (*Asynchronous JavaScript and XML*) is a type of Web programming that creates a more enhanced user experience on the Web pages that use it **(Figure i.6)**. It is the result of combining HTML and JavaScript with XML. Ajax enables Web browsers to get new data from a Web server without having to reload the Web page each time, thereby increasing the page's responsiveness and usability.

You can read about both these applications of XML, among others, in Part 7 *(see page 219)*.

About This Book

This book is divided into seven parts. Each part contains one or more chapters with step-by-step instructions which explain how to perform XML-related tasks. Wherever possible, I display examples of the concepts being discussed, and I highlight the parts of the examples on which to focus.

I often have two or more different examples on the same page, perhaps an XSL style sheet and the XML document that it will transform. You can tell what type of file the example is by looking at the example's header and the color of the text itself **(Figures i.7 and i.8)**. For example, XML uses `green text` and DTD uses `blue text`.

Throughout the book, I have used the following conventions. When I want you to type some text exactly as is, **it will display in a different font and bold**. Then, when I want you to change a placeholder in that text to a term of your own, that placeholder will appear *italicized*. Lastly, when I introduce a new term or need to emphasize something, it will also appear *italicized*.

A Guided Tour

The order of the book is intentionally designed. In Part 1 of the book, I will show you how to create an XML document. It's relatively straightforward, and even more so if you know a little HTML.

Part 2 focuses on XSL; a set of languages designed to transform an XML document into something else: an HTML file, a PDF document, or another XML document. Remember, XML is designed to store and transport data, not display it.

Parts 3 and 4 of the book discuss DTD and XML Schema, languages designed to define the structure of an XML document. In conjunction with XML Namespaces (Part 5 of the book), you can guarantee that XML documents

```
xml
<?xml version="1.0"?>

<ancient_wonders>

...

 <wonder>

  <name language="English">
    Statue of Zeus at Olympia</name>

  <name language="Greek">
    Διας μυθολογια</name>

  <location>Olympia, Greece
    </location>

  <height units="feet">39</height>

 <main_image file="zeus.jpg"
    w="528" h="349"/>

 </wonder>

...

</ancient_wonders>
```

Figure i.7 *You can tell this is an example of XML code because of the title bar and the green text color. (You'll usually be able to tell pretty easily anyway, but just in case you're in doubt, it's an extra clue.)*

```
dtd
<!ELEMENT ancient_wonders (wonder+)>

<!ELEMENT wonder (name+, location,
  height, history, main_image,
  source*)>

<!ELEMENT name (#PCDATA)>

...
```

Figure i.8 *This example of a DTD describes the XML shown in Figure i.7. Don't worry if this is not so easy to understand now, I'll go through it in detail in Part 3 of the book.*

conform to a pre-defined structure, whether created by you or by someone else.

Part 6, Developments and Trends, details some of the up-and-coming XML-related languages, as well as a few new versions of existing languages. Finally, Part 7 identifies some well-known uses of XML in the world today; some of which you may be surprised to learn.

XML2e Companion Web Site

You can download all the examples used in this book at *www.kehogo.com/xml2e*. I *strongly* recommend that you do so, and then follow along either electronically, or using a paper printout. In many cases, it's impossible to show an entire example on a page, and yet it would be helpful for you to see it all. Having an XML editor opened with the examples is ideal; *see Appendix A* for some XML editor recommendations. If not, at least having a paper printout will prove very useful.

You will also find that the Web site contains additional support material for the book, including an online table of contents, a question and answer section, and updates. I welcome your questions and comments at the Q & A section of the site. Answering questions publicly allows me to help more people at the same time (and gives you, the readers, the opportunity to help each other).

From 2001 to 2008

This book is an updated and expanded version of Elizabeth Castro's *XML for the World Wide Web* published in 2001. Liz has written many best-selling books on different technologies and I am delighted and honored to be updating her work.

I hope that you enjoy learning about XML as much as I've enjoyed writing about it.

What This Book is Not

XML is an incredibly powerful system for managing information. You can use it in combination with many, many other technologies. You should know that this book is not, nor does it try to be, an exhaustive guide to XML. Instead, it is a beginner's guide to using XML and its core tools / languages.

This book won't teach you about SAX, OPML, or XML-RPC, nor will it teach you about JavaScript, Java, or PHP, although these are commonly used with XML. Many of these topics deserve their own books (and have them). While there are numerous ancillary technologies that can work with XML documents, this book focuses on the core elements of XML, XML transformations, and schemas. These are the basic topics you need to understand in order to start creating and using your own XML documents.

Sometimes, especially when you're starting out, it's more helpful to have clear, specific, easy-to-grasp information about a smaller set of topics, rather than general, wide-ranging data about everything under the sun. My hope is that this book will give you a solid foundation in XML and its core technologies which will enable you to move on to the other pieces of the XML puzzle once you're ready.

Figure i.9 *The World Wide Web Consortium* (www.w3.org) *is the main standards body for the Web. You can find the official specifications there for all the languages discussed in this book, including XML, XSL, DTD, and XML Schema. You'll also find information on advanced and additional topics including XSL-FO, XQuery, and of course, HTML and XHTML.*

Part 1: XML

1

Writing XML

The XML specification defines how to write a document in XML format. XML is not a language itself. Rather, an XML document is written in a *custom markup language*, according to the XML specification. For example, there could be custom markup languages describing genealogical, chemical, or business data, and you could write XML documents in each one.

Every custom markup language created using the XML specification must adhere to XML's underlying grammar. Therefore, that is where I will start this book. In this chapter, you will learn the rules for writing XML documents, regardless of the specific custom markup language in which you are writing.

Officially, custom markup languages created with XML are called *XML applications*. In other words, these custom markup languages are applications of XML, such as XSLT, RSS, SOAP, etc. But for me, an application is a full-blown software program, like Photoshop. I find the term so imprecise, I usually try to avoid it.

Tools for Writing XML

XML, like HTML, can be written using any text editor or word processor. There are also many XML editors that have been created since the first edition of this book. These editors have various capabilities, such as validating your XML as you type *(see Appendix A)*.

I'll assume you know how to create new documents, open old ones for editing, and save them when you're done. Just be sure to save all your XML documents with the `.xml` extension.

An XML Sample

XML documents, like HTML documents, are comprised of tags and data. One big difference between the two documents, however, is that the tags used by an XML document are created by the author. Another big difference is that an XML document stores and describes that data; it doesn't do anything more with the data, such as display it, like an HTML document does.

XML documents should be rather self-explanatory in that the tags should describe the data they contain **(Figure 1.1)**.

```xml
<?xml version="1.0"?>
<wonder>
  <name>Colossus of Rhodes</name>
  <location>Rhodes, Greece</location>
  <height units="feet">107</height>
</wonder>
```

Figure 1.1 *An XML document describing one of the Seven Wonders of the World: the Colossus of Rhodes. The document contains the name of the wonder, as well as its location and its height in feet.*

The first line of the XML document **<?xml version="1.0"?>** is the *XML declaration* which notes which version of XML you are using. The next line **<wonder>** begins the data part of the document and is called the *root element*. In an XML document, there can be only one root element.

The next 3 lines are called *child elements*, and they describe the root element in more detail.

```
<name>Colossus of Rhodes</name>
<location>Rhodes, Greece</location>
<height units="feet">107</height>
```

The last child element, height, contains an *attribute* called **units** which is being used to store the specific units of the height measurement. Attributes are used to include additional information to the element, without adding text to the element itself.

Finally, the XML document ends with the closing tag of the root element **</wonder>**.

This is a complete and valid XML document. Nothing more needs to be written, added, annotated, or complicated. Period.

```xml
<?xml version="1.0"?>
<ancient_wonders>
 <wonder>
  <name>Colossus of Rhodes</name>
  <location>Rhodes, Greece</location>
  <height units="feet">107</height>
 </wonder>
 <wonder>
  <name>Great Pyramid of Giza</name>
  <location>Giza, Egypt</location>
  <height units="feet">455</height>
 </wonder>
</ancient_wonders>
```

Figure 1.2 *Here I am extending the XML document in Figure 1.1 above to support multiple* <wonder> *elements. This is done by creating a new root element* <ancient_wonders> *which will contain as many* <wonder> *elements as desired. Now, the XML document contains information about the Colossus of Rhodes along with the Great Pyramid of Giza, which is located in Giza, Egypt, and is 455 feet tall.*

```xml
<?xml version="1.0"?>

<wonder>

 <name>Colossus of Rhodes</name>

</wonder>
```

Figure 1.3 *In a well-formed XML document, there must be one element* (wonder) *that contains all other elements. This is called the* root element. *The first line of an XML document is an exception because it's a* processing instruction *and not part of the XML data.*

```xml
<?xml version="1.0"?>

<wonder>

 <name>Colossus of Rhodes</name>

 <main_image file="colossus.jpg"/>

</wonder>
```

Figure 1.4 *Every element must be enclosed by matching tags such as the* name *element. Empty elements like* main_image *can have an all-in-one opening and closing tag with a final slash. Notice that all elements are properly nested; that is, none are overlapping.*

```xml
<name>Colossus of Rhodes</name>
<Name>Colossus of Rhodes</Name>
```

```xml
<name>Colossus of Rhodes</Name>
```

Figure 1.5 *The top example is valid XML, though it may be confusing. The two elements (*name *and* Name*) are actually considered completely different and independent. The bottom example is incorrect since the opening and closing tags do not match.*

```xml
<main_image file="colossus.jpg"/>
```

Figure 1.6 *The quotation marks are required. They can be single or double, as long as they match each other. Note that the value of the* file *attribute doesn't necessarily refer to an image; it could just as easily say* "The picture from last summer's vacation".

Rules for Writing XML

XML has a structure that is extremely regular and predictable. It is defined by a set of rules, the most important of which are described below. If your document satisfies these rules, it is considered *well-formed*. Once a document is considered well-formed, it can be used in many, many ways.

A root element is required

Every XML document must contain one, and only one, root element. This root element contains all the other elements in the document. The only pieces of XML allowed outside (preceding) the root element are comments and processing instructions **(Figure 1.3)**.

Closing tags are required

Every element must have a closing tag. Empty elements *(see page 12)* can use a separate closing tag, or an all-in-one opening and closing tag with a slash before the final > **(Figure 1.4**, and *Nesting Elements*, later in this chapter**)**.

Elements must be properly nested

If you start element A, then start element B, you must first close element B before closing element A (Figure 1.4).

Case matters

XML is case sensitive. Elements named `wonder`, `WONDER`, and `Wonder` are considered entirely separate and unrelated to each other **(Figure 1.5)**.

Values must be enclosed in quotation marks

An attribute's value must always be enclosed in either matching single or double quotation marks **(Figure 1.6)**.

Elements, Attributes, and Values

XML uses the same building blocks as HTML: tags that define elements, values of those elements, and attributes. An XML *element* is the most basic unit of your document. It can contain text, attributes, and other elements. An element has an opening tag with a name written between less than (<) and greater than (>) signs **(Figure 1.7)**. The name, which you invent yourself, should describe the element's purpose and, in particular, its contents. An element is generally concluded with a closing tag, comprised of the same name preceded with a forward slash, enclosed in the familiar less than and greater than signs. The exception to this is called an empty element which may be "self-closing," and is discussed on page 12.

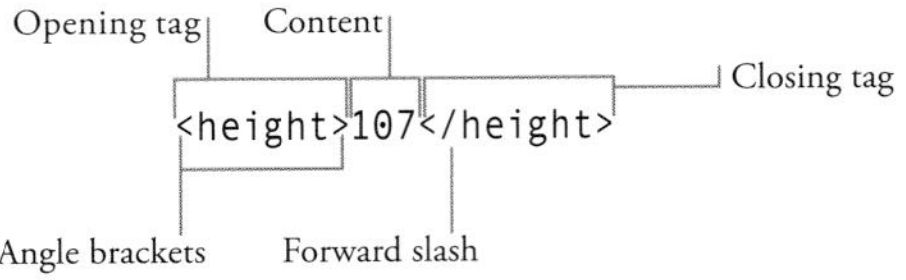

Figure 1.7 *A typical element is comprised of an opening tag, content, and a closing tag. This* height *element contains text.*

Elements may have *attributes*. Attributes, which are contained within an element's opening tag, have quotation-mark delimited *values* that further describe the purpose and content (if any) of the particular element **(Figure 1.8)**. Information contained in an attribute is generally considered metadata; that is, information *about* the data in the element, as opposed to the data itself. An element can have as many attributes as desired, as long as each has a unique name.

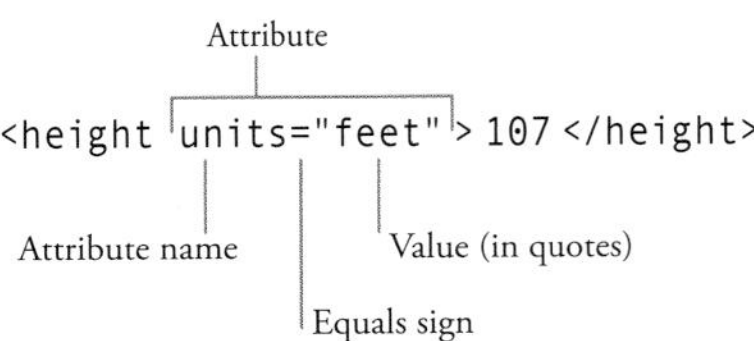

Figure 1.8 *The* height *element now has an attribute called* units *whose value is* feet. *Notice that the word* feet *isn't part of the* height *element's content. This doesn't make the value of* height *equal to* 107 feet. *Rather, the* units *attribute describes the content of the* height *element.*

The rest of this chapter is devoted to writing elements, attributes, and values.

White Space

You can add extra white space, including line breaks, around the elements in your XML code to make it easier to edit and view **(Figure 1.9)**. While extra white space is visible in the file and when passed to other applications, it is ignored by the XML processor, just as it is with HTML in a browser.

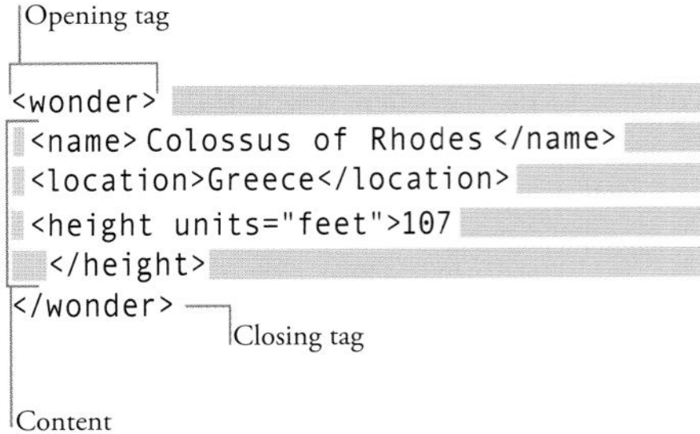

Figure 1.9 *The* wonder *element shown here contains three other elements* (name, location, and height), *but it has no text of its own. The* name, location *and* height *elements contain text, but no other elements. The* height *element is the only element that has an attribute. Notice also that I've added extra white space (green, in this illustration), to make the code easier to read.*

```
xml
<?xml version="1.0"?>
```

Figure 1.10 *Because the XML declaration is a processing instruction and not an element, there is no closing tag.*

How To Begin

In general, you should begin each XML document with a declaration that notes what version of XML you're using. This line is called the *XML declaration* (**Figure 1.10**).

To declare the version of XML that you're using:

1. At the very beginning of your document, before anything else, type **<?xml**.
2. Then, type **version="1.0"**.
3. Finally, type **?>** to complete the declaration.

✔ Tips

- The W3C released a Recommendation for XML Version 1.1 in 2006, but it has few new benefits and little to no support.
- Be sure to enclose the version number in single or double quotation marks. (It doesn't matter which you use, so long as they match.)
- Tags that begin with **<?** and end with **?>** are called *processing instructions*. In addition to declaring the version of XML, processing instructions are also used to specify the style sheet that should be used, among other things. Style sheets are discussed in detail in Part 2, *XSL*.
- This XML processing instruction can also designate the character encoding (UTF-8, ISO-8859-1, etc.), that you're using for the document. Character encodings are discussed in Appendix B.

Creating the Root Element

Every XML document must have one, and only one, element that completely contains all the other elements. This all-encompassing parent element is called the *root element*.

To create the root element:

1. At the beginning of your XML document, type **<root>**, where *root* is the name of the element that will contain the rest of the elements in the document **(Figure 1.11)**.
2. Leave a few empty lines for the rest of your XML document.
3. Finally, type **</root>** exactly matching the name you chose in Step 1.

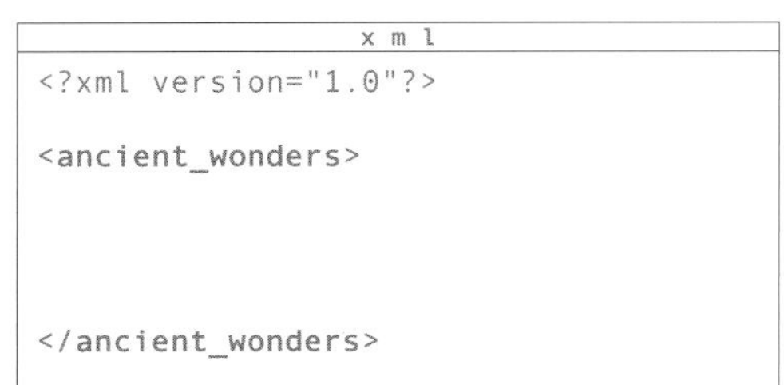

Figure 1.11 *In HTML, the root element is always* <HTML>. *In XML, you can use any valid name for your root element, including* <ancient_wonders>, *as shown here. No content or other elements are allowed before or after the opening and closing root tags, respectively.*

✔ Tips

- Case matters. <WONDER> is not the same as <Wonder> or <wonder>.
- Element (and attribute) names should be short and descriptive.
- Element and attribute names must begin with a letter, an underscore, or a colon. Names that begin with the letters *xml* (in any combination of upper- and lowercase), are reserved and cannot be used.
- Element and attribute names may contain any number of letters, digits, underscores, and a few other punctuation characters.
- Caveat: Although colons, hyphens, and periods are valid within element and attribute names, I recommend that you avoid including them, as they're often used in specific circumstances (such as for identifying namespaces, subtraction, and object properties, respectively).
- No elements are allowed outside the opening and closing root tags. The only items that are allowed are processing instructions *(see page 7)*.

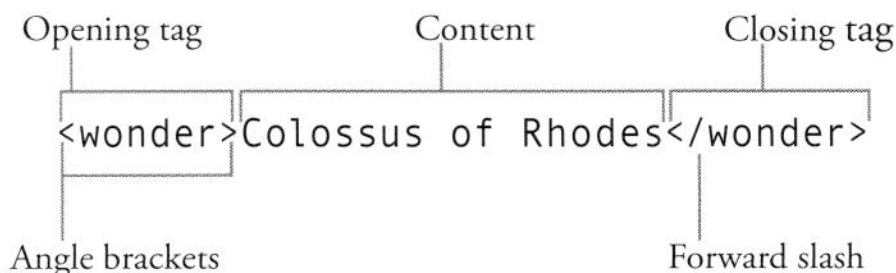

Figure 1.12 *A simple XML element is comprised of an opening tag, content (which might include text, other elements, or be empty), and a closing tag whose only difference with the opening tag is an initial forward slash.*

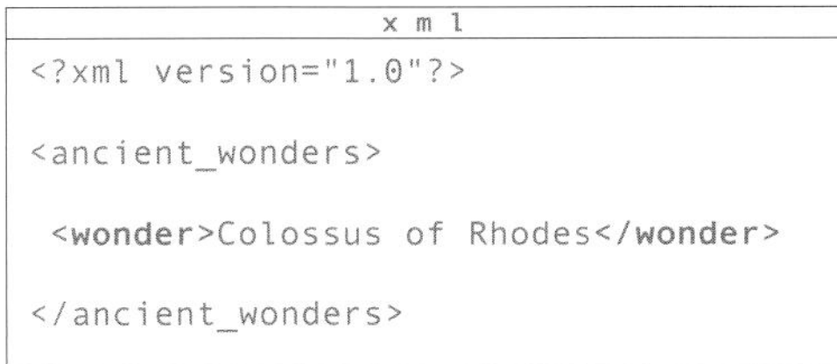

```
xml
<?xml version="1.0"?>

<ancient_wonders>

 <wonder>Colossus of Rhodes</wonder>

</ancient_wonders>
```

Figure 1.13 *Every element in your XML document must be contained within the opening and closing tags of the root element.*

Writing Child Elements

Once you have created your root element, you can create any *child element* you like. The idea is that there is a relationship between the root, or parent element, and its child element. When creating child elements, use names that clearly identify the content so that it's easier to process the information at a later date.

To write a child element:

1. Type **<name>**, where *name* identifies the content that is about to appear; the child element's name.
2. Create the content.
3. Finally, type **</name>** matching the word you chose in Step 1 **(Figures 1.12 and 1.13)**.

✔ Tips

- The closing tag is never optional (as it sometimes is in HTML). In XML, elements must always have a closing tag.
- The rules for naming child elements are the same as those for root elements. Case matters. Names must begin with a letter, underscore, or colon, and may contain letters, digits, and underscores. However, although valid, I recommend that you avoid including colons, dashes, and periods within your names. In addition, you may not use names that begin with the letters *xml*, in any combination of upper- and lowercase.
- Names need not be in English or even the Latin alphabet, but if your software doesn't support these characters, they may not display or be processed properly.
- If you use descriptive names for your elements, your XML will be easier to leverage for other uses.

Nesting Elements

Oftentimes when creating your XML document, you'll want to break down your data into smaller pieces. In XML, you can create child elements of child elements of child elements, etc. The ability to nest multiple levels of child elements enables you to identify and work with individual parts of your data and establish a hierarchical relationship between these individual parts.

To nest elements:

1. Create the opening tag of the outer element as described in Step 1 on page 9.
2. Type **<inner>**, where *inner* is the name of the first individual chunk of data; the first child element.
3. Create the content of the <inner> element, if any.
4. Then, type **</inner>** matching the word chosen in Step 2.
5. Repeat Steps 2–4 as desired.
6. Finally, create the closing tag of the outer element as described in Step 3 on page 9.

✔ Tips

- It is essential that each element be completely enclosed in another. In other words, you may not write the closing tag for the outer element until the inner element is closed. Otherwise, the document will not be considered well-formed, and will generate an error in the XML processor **(Figure 1.14)**.
- You can nest as many levels of elements as you like **(Figure 1.15)**.
- When nesting elements, best practices suggest that you indent the child element. This enables you to easily see parent, child, and sibling relationships. Most XML editors will automatically do this for you.

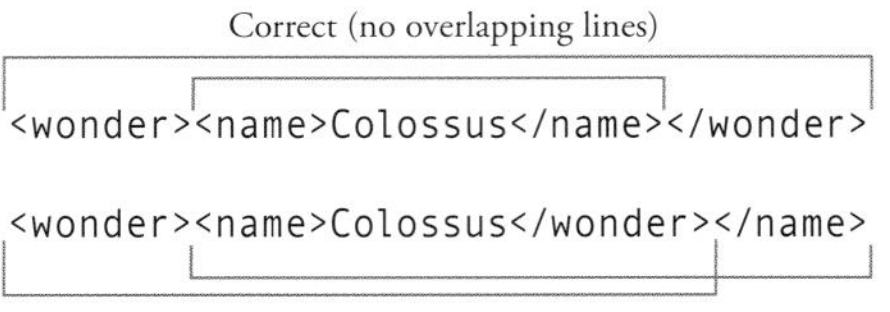

Figure 1.14 *To make sure your tags are correctly nested, connect each set with a line. None of your sets of tags should overlap any other set; each inner set should be completely enclosed within its next outer set.*

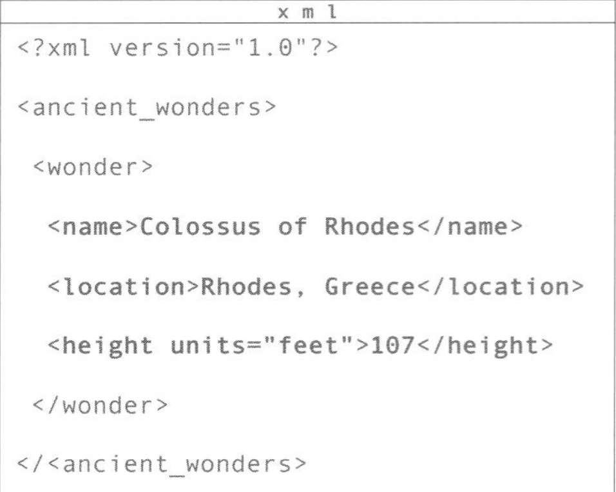

Figure 1.15 *Now the* wonder *element is nested as a child of the* ancient_wonders *element, and* name, location *and* height *are nested as child elements of the* wonder *element.*

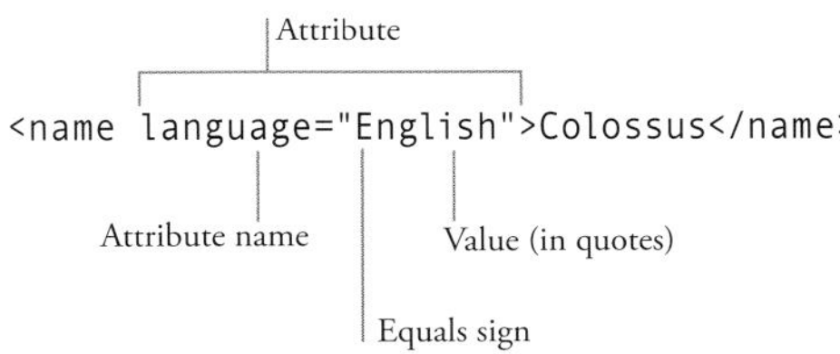

Figure 1.16 *Attributes are* name-value pairs *enclosed within the opening tag of an element. The value must be contained in matched quotation marks (either single or double).*

```
xml
<?xml version="1.0"?>

<ancient_wonders>

 <wonder>

  <name language="English">Colossus
    of Rhodes</name>

  <name language="Greek">Κολοσσός της
    Ρόδου</name>

  <location>Rhodes, Greece</location>

  <height units="feet">107</height>

 </wonder>

</ancient_wonders>
```

Figure 1.17 *Attributes let you add information about the contents of an element.*

Adding Attributes

An *attribute* stores additional information about an element, without adding text to the element's content itself. Attributes are known as "name-value pairs," and are contained within the opening tag of an element **(Figure 1.16)**.

To add an attribute:

1. Before the closing > of the opening tag, type **attribute=**, where *attribute* is the word that identifies the additional data.
2. Then, type **"value"**, where *value* is that additional data. The quotes are required.

✔ Tips

- Attribute names must follow the same rules as element names, see the Tips on page 9.
- No two attributes in a given element may have the same name.
- Unlike in HTML, attribute values must, must, **must** be in quotes. You can use either single or double quotes, as long as they match within a single attribute.
- If an attribute's value contains double quotes, use single quotes to contain the value (and vice versa). For example, **comments= 'She said, "The Colossus has fallen!"'**.
- Best practices suggest that attributes should be used as "metadata"; that is, data about data. In other words, attributes should be used to store information about the element's content, and not the content itself **(Figure 1.17)**.
- An additional way to mark and identify distinct information is with nested elements *(see page 10)*.

Using Empty Elements

Empty elements are elements that do not have any content of their own. Instead, they will have attributes to store data about the element. For example, you might have a **main_image** element with an attribute containing the filename of an image, but it has no text content at all.

To write an empty element with a single opening/closing tag:

1. Type **<name**, where *name* identifies the empty element.
2. Create any attributes as necessary, following the instructions on page 11.
3. Finally, type **/>** to complete the element (**Figure 1.18**).

To write an empty element with separate opening and closing tags:

1. Type **<name**, where *name* identifies the empty element.
2. Create any attributes as necessary, following the instructions on page 11.
3. Finally, type **>** to complete the opening tag.
4. Then, with no spaces, type **</name>** to complete the element, matching the word you chose in Step 1.

✔ Tips

- In XML, both of the above methods are equivalent (**Figure 1.19**). Which one to use is a stylistic preference; I write elements using a single opening / closing tag.
- In contrast with HTML, you are not allowed to use an opening tag with no corresponding closing tag. A document that contains such a tag is not considered well-formed and will generate an error in the XML processor.

Less than sign

```
<main_image file="colossus.jpg"/>
```

Forward slash and greater than sign

Figure 1.18 *Empty elements can combine the opening and closing tags in one, as shown here, or can consist of an opening tag followed immediately by an independent closing tag as seen in the example below.*

xml

```
<?xml version="1.0"?>

<wonders_of_the_world>

 <wonder>

  <name language="English">Colossus
    of Rhodes</name>

  <name language="Greek">Κολοσσός της
    Ρόδου</name>

  <location>Rhodes, Greece</location>

  <height units="feet">107</height>

  <main_image file="colossus.jpg"
    w="528" h="349"/>

  <source sectionid="101"
    newspaperid="21"></source>

 </wonder>

</wonders_of_the_world>
```

Figure 1.19 *Typical empty elements are those like* source *and* main_image. *Notice that these elements only contain data in their attributes; the element has no content of its own. I've used both empty element formats in this example: single opening / closing tag and separate opening and closing tags.*

Figure 1.20 *XML comments have the same syntax as HTML comments.*

```
xml
<?xml version="1.0"?>

<wonders_of_the_world>

 <wonder>

  <name language="English">Colossus
    of Rhodes</name>

  <name language="Greek">Κολοσσός της
    Ρόδου</name>

  <location>Rhodes, Greece</location>

  <height units="feet">107</height>

  <main_image file="colossus.jpg"
    w="528" h="349"/>

  <!-- the research on this wonder of
    the world came in part from the
    sectionid of the newspaper
    (identified by newspaperid) in
    the source tag below -->

  <source sectionid="101"
    newspaperid="21"/>

 </wonder>

</wonders_of_the_world>
```

Figure 1.21 *Comments let you add information about your code. They can be incredibly useful when you (or someone else) need to go back to a document and understand how it was constructed.*

Writing Comments

It's often useful to annotate your XML documents so that you know why you used a particular element, or what a piece of information specifically means. As with HTML, you can insert comments into your XML documents, and they will not be parsed by the processor **(Figure 1.20)**.

To write comments:

1. Type **<!--**.
2. Write your desired comments.
3. Finally, type **-->** to close the comment.

✔ Tips

- Comments can contain spaces, text, elements, and line breaks, and can therefore span multiple lines of XML.
- No spaces are required between the double hyphens and the content of the comments itself. In other words **<!--this is a comment-->** is perfectly fine.
- You may not use a double hyphen within a comment itself.
- You may not nest comments within other comments.
- You may use comments to hide a piece of your XML code during development or debugging. This is called "commenting out" a section. The elements within a commented out section, along with any errors they may contain, will not be processed by the XML processor.
- Comments are also useful for documenting the structure of an XML document, in order to facilitate changes and updates in the future **(Figure 1.21)**.

Predefined Entities – Five Special Symbols

Entities are a kind of autotext; a way of entering text into an XML document without typing it all out. There are many letters and symbols that can be inserted into HTML documents by using entities. In XML, however, there are only five *predefined entities.*

To write the five predefined entities:

- Type **&** to create an ampersand character (&).
- Type **<** to create a less than sign (<).
- Type **>** to create a greater than sign (>).
- Type **"** to create a double quotation mark (").
- Type **'** to create a single quotation mark or apostrophe (').

✔ Tips

- Predefined entities exist in XML because each of these characters have specific meanings. For example, if you used (<) within the text value of an element or attribute, the XML processor would think you were starting a new element **(Figure 1.22)**.
- You *may not* use (<) or (&) anywhere in your XML document, except to begin a tag or an entity, respectively. If you need to use one of these characters within the text value of an element or attribute, you *must* use one of the predefined entities.
- You may use ("), ('), or (>) within the text value of an element or attribute. However, when using (") or ('), be on the lookout for unintentionally matching existing quotes. Also, I always recommend using the predefined entity for (>) to avoid any possible confusion.
- If you want to create additional entities for your XML documents, you must explicitly declare them *(see Chapter 7).*

```
xml
<?xml version="1.0"?>

<wonders_of_the_world>

 <wonder>

  <name language="English">Colossus
    of Rhodes</name>

  <name language="Greek">Κολοσσός της
    Ρόδου</name>

  <location>Rhodes, Greece</location>

  <height units="feet">&lt; 107
    </height>

  <main_image file="colossus.jpg"
    w="528" h="349"/>

  <source sectionid="101"
    newspaperid="21"/>

 </wonder>

</wonders_of_the_world>
```

Figure 1.22 *When this document is parsed, the* < *entity will be displayed as >. So when the value of the* height *element is displayed, it will likely read something like* "< 107 ". *How it is displayed will depend on the transformation of the XML, which is discussed in Part 2,* XSL.

```
xml
<?xml version="1.0"?>

<xml_book>

 <tags>

  <appearance>

<![CDATA[
<ancient_wonders>
 <wonder>
  <name language="English">
    Colossus of Rhodes</name>
  <name language="Greek">
    Κολοσσός της Ρόδου</name>
  <location>Rhodes, Greece</location>
  <height units="feet">107</height>
  <main_image file="colossus.jpg"
    w="528" h="349"/>
  <source sectionid="101"
    newspaperid="21"/>
 </wonder>
</ancient_wonders>
]]>

  </appearance>

 </tags>

</xml_book>
```

Figure 1.23 *In this example about an example, I use CDATA to display the actual code, without the XML processor parsing it first.*

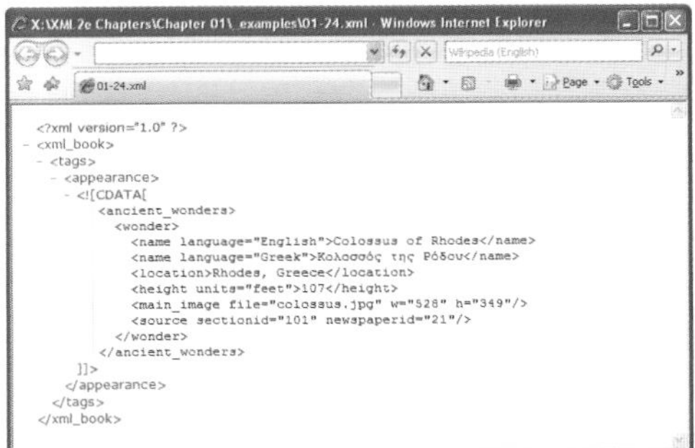

Figure 1.24 *Shown here in Internet Explorer 7 for Windows, you can see how the elements within the CDATA section are treated as text; in contrast with the* xml_book, tags, *and* appearance *elements, which are parsed by the XML processor.*

Displaying Elements as Text

If you want to write about XML elements and attributes in your XML documents, you will want to keep the XML processor from interpreting them, and instead just display them as regular text. To do this, you enclose such information in a CDATA section **(Figure 1.23)**.

To display elements as text:

1. Type **<![CDATA[**.
2. Create the elements, attributes, and content that you would like to display, but not process.
3. Finally, type **]]>** to complete the tag.

✔ Tips

- Two other common uses for the CDATA section are to enclose HTML and JavaScript so that they are not parsed by the XML processor.
- CDATA stands for (unparsed) Character Data, meaning that the CDATA content will not be interpreted by the XML processor. This is opposed to PCDATA, which stands for Parsed Character Data and is discussed in Chapter 6.
- The special meaning that symbols have is ignored in the CDATA section. To display the less than and ampersand symbols, you would write **<** and **&**. If you write **<** and **&**, that's what will display; they will not be replaced with < and &.
- You may not nest CDATA sections.
- CDATA sections can be used anywhere within the root element of an XML document.
- If, for some reason, you want to write **]]>** and you are *not* closing a CDATA section, the > must be written as **>**. See page 14 and Appendix B for more information on writing special symbols.

PART 2: XSL

2

XSLT

Now that you have an understanding of the XML language and how to create and read XML documents, the next step is to format those documents. The details for formatting XML documents was originally in a specification called XSL, which stands for *eXtensible Style Language*. However, because it was taking so long to finish, the W3C divided XSL into two pieces: XSLT (for *T*ransformations) and XSL-FO (for *F*ormatting *O*bjects).

This chapter, and the two that follow, explain how to use XSLT to transform XML documents. The end result might be another XML document or an HTML document. In reality, you can transform an XML document into practically any document type you like. *Transforming* an XML document means using XSLT to analyze its contents and then take certain actions depending on what elements are found. You can use XSLT to reorder the output according to specific criteria, display only certain pieces of information, and much more.

XSL-FO is typically used to format XML for print output, such as going directly to a PDF. It is not supported by any browsers, and requires specific parsing software to use. For more information on XSL-FO, see Chapter 5.

Most of the examples in this part of the book are based on a single XML file and a set of XSLT files, in which each often builds on the previous. I strongly recommend downloading the examples from the companion Web site (mentioned in the book's Introduction) and following along.

Transforming XML with XSLT

Let's start with an overview of the transformation process. The process starts with two documents, the XML document which contains the source data to be transformed, and the XSLT style sheet document which describes the rules of the transformation. While you can transform XML into nearly any format, I am going to use examples that return HTML.

To perform the actual transformation, you'll need an XSLT processor, or a browser that supports XSLT. Most current XML Editors have built-in XSLT support, as do most current Web browsers. See Appendix A for details.

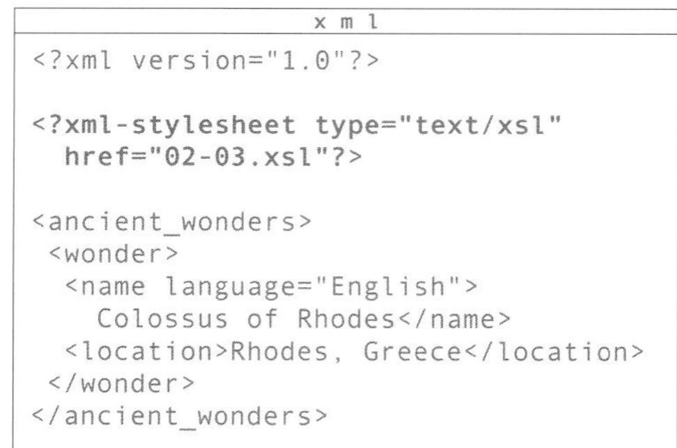

```
xml
<?xml version="1.0"?>

<?xml-stylesheet type="text/xsl"
  href="02-03.xsl"?>

<ancient_wonders>
 <wonder>
  <name language="English">
    Colossus of Rhodes</name>
  <location>Rhodes, Greece</location>
 </wonder>
</ancient_wonders>
```

Figure 2.1 *This is a very basic XML document representing a single wonder of the world. Notice the* xml-stylesheet *processing instruction linking this XML document to an XSLT style sheet.*

Analyzing the source XML

To begin, you'll need to link your XML document to your XSLT style sheet using the `xml-stylesheet` processing instruction **(Figure 2.1)**. Then, when you open your XML document in an XSLT processor or a browser, the instruction tells the processor to perform the XSLT transformation before displaying the document.

In the first step of this transformation, the XSLT processor analyzes the XML document and converts it into a *node tree*. A node tree is a hierarchical representation of the XML document **(Figure 2.2)**. In the tree, a *node* is one individual piece of the XML document (such as an element, an attribute, or some text content).

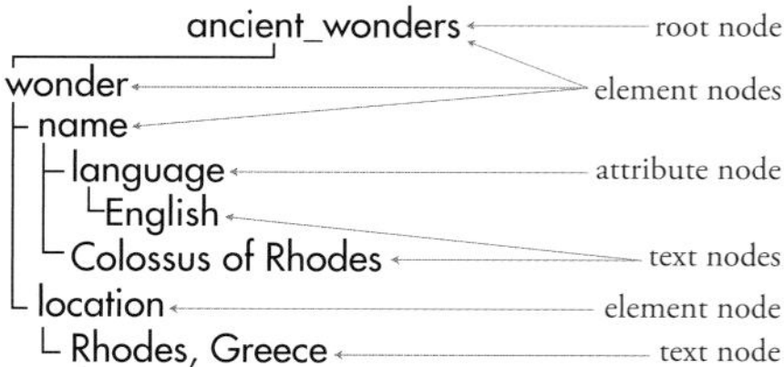

Figure 2.2 *Here is a representation of the* node tree *that corresponds to the XML document shown in Figure 2.1.*

Assessing the XSLT style sheet

Once the processor has identified the nodes in the source XML, it then looks to an XSLT style sheet **(Figure 2.3)** for instructions on what to do with those nodes. Those instructions are contained in *templates* which are comparable to functions in a programming language.

Each XSLT template has two parts: first, a label that identifies the nodes in the XML document to which the template applies; and second, instructions about the actual transformation

xslt
```
<?xml version="1.0"?>

<xsl:stylesheet xmlns:xsl="http://
  www.w3.org/1999/XSL/Transform"
  version="1.0">

 <xsl:template match="/">

  <html><head><title>Wonders of the
    World</title></head><body>
    <h1>Wonders of the World</h1>

   The <xsl:value-of select=
     "ancient_wonders/wonder/name"/>

   is located in
   <xsl:value-of select=
     "ancient_wonders/wonder
     /location"/>.

  </body></html>

 </xsl:template>

</xsl:stylesheet>
```

Figure 2.3 *A very basic XSLT document to transform the XML document shown in Figure 2.1.*

Figure 2.4 *The final transformed HTML shown in Internet Explorer 7.*

that should take place. The instructions, or rules, will either output or further process the nodes in the source document. They can also contain *literal elements* that should be output as is.

Performing the transformation

The XSLT transformation begins by processing the *root template*. Every XSLT style sheet must have a root template; this is the template that applies to the source XML document's root node. In Figure 2.3, the root template is defined with `<xsl:template match = "/">`. Within this root template, there may be other sub-templates which can then apply to other nodes in the XML document.

And the transformation continues until the last instruction of the root template is processed. The transformed document is then either saved to another file, displayed in a browser **(Figure 2.4)**, or both.

While you can use XSLT to convert almost any kind of document into almost any other kind of document, that's a pretty vague topic to tackle. In this book, I am focusing on using XSLT to convert XML into HTML. This lets you take advantage of the strengths and flexibility of XML for handling your data, as well as the compatibility of HTML for viewing it.

✔ Tips

- XSLT style sheets are text files and are saved with an `.xsl` extension.
- With some XSLT processors, you don't need an `xml-stylesheet` instruction in your XML document. Instead, you can assign your XSLT style sheet to an XML document.
- XSLT uses the XPath language to identify nodes. XPath is sufficiently complex to warrant its own chapters: Chapter 3, *XPath Patterns and Expressions,* and Chapter 4, *XPath Functions.*

Beginning an XSLT Style Sheet

Every XSLT style sheet is actually an XML document in itself, and therefore should begin with a standard XML declaration. Once that's out of the way, you define the W3C namespace for style sheets.

To begin an XSLT style sheet:

1. Type **<?xml version="1.0"?>** to indicate that the XSLT style sheet is an XML document.
2. Type **<xsl:stylesheet xmlns:xsl="http://www.w3.org/1999/XSL/Transform" version="1.0">** to specify the namespace for the style sheet and declare its prefix (`xsl`).
3. Leave a few empty lines where you will create the style sheet (with the instructions contained in this and the following two chapters).
4. Finally, type **</xsl:stylesheet>** to complete the style sheet **(Figure 2.5)**.

✔ Tips

- There are no spaces contained in the `xsl:stylesheet` tag. (It is *not* `xsl:style sheet`.) Nevertheless, I do use two words to refer to *style sheets* when talking about them in this book (as is the convention).
- The header for a style sheet is almost always the same. You can just copy and paste the two lines from one style sheet to the next.
- For more information on namespaces, see Chapters 12 and 13.

```
xslt
<?xml version="1.0"?>

<xsl:stylesheet xmlns:xsl="http://
  www.w3.org/1999/XSL/Transform"
  version="1.0">



</xsl:stylesheet>
```

Figure 2.5 *An XSLT style sheet is itself an XML document and must be well-formed.*

```
xslt
<?xml version="1.0"?>

<xsl:stylesheet xmlns:xsl="http://
  www.w3.org/1999/XSL/Transform"
  version="1.0">

<xsl:template match="/">



</xsl:template>

</xsl:stylesheet>
```

Figure 2.6 *The root template (*match="/"*) is the starting point for all XSLT processing.*

Creating the Root Template

The first thing that the XSLT processor looks for in a style sheet is the *root template*. This is the template that defines the set of rules to apply to the root node of the XML document. Specifically, it describes how to process or transform the content from the root node into some new output.

To create the root template:

1. Type **<xsl:template**.
2. Then, type **match="/"**. The forward slash matches the root node of the XML source document.
3. Next, type **>** to close the tag.
4. Leave a few lines for specifying the rules of the template, that is, what transformation should happen with the XML document (I'll get there on pages 24–34).
5. Finally, type **</xsl:template>** to complete the root template **(Figure 2.6)**.

✔ Tips

- While the XSLT processor doesn't care where the root template appears in your XSLT style sheet, it will probably be clearest to you (and the people who might need to understand your style sheet) if you put it up at the very top.
- All XSLT transformations must start with the root template. If you do not include a root template in your XSLT style sheet, a root template built in to the XSLT processor is automatically used. Usually, this built-in template simply lists all the data in the XML document in plain text (which is probably not what you want).

Outputting HTML

Now that you've created the root template, you need to define the set of rules for this template; the rules that will apply to the content in the root node. Typically, in the root template, you will start by creating the structure for the final transformed document. If your final document is HTML, you'll want to add HTML header information (`head`, `title`, `body`, etc.) at the very least. Of course, you can add more HTML, CSS, and JavaScript, as well.

To have your XSLT processor output HTML, you will need to use the `xsl:output` processing instruction **(Figure 2.7)**. You can set the output method to either `html`, `xml`, or `text`. If this instruction is omitted, processors will output XML by default.

To set the processor's output method to HTML:

1. Immediately after the `xsl:stylesheet` element, type **<xsl:output** .
2. Then, type **method="html"/>** .

Then, to add HTML to your output, you'll use *literal elements*, one of the components of an XSLT style sheet. Literals are typically HTML code and text, and they are output just as they appear in the style sheet.

To add HTML to the root template's output:

- Inside the root template rule (that is, between `<xsl:template match="/">` and its matching `</xsl:template>`), add the HTML that you'd like to output when this template is applied.

xslt

```
<?xml version="1.0"?>
<xsl:stylesheet xmlns:xsl="http://
 www.w3.org/1999/XSL/Transform"
 version="1.0">

<xsl:output method="html"/>

<xsl:template match="/">

 <html><head><title>Wonders of the
   World</title></head>
  <body>
   <p align="center"><img
     src="herodotus.jpg" width="120"
     height="171" /></p>
   <p>The famous Greek historian
     Herodotus wrote of seven great
     architectural achievements. And
     although his writings did not
     survive, he planted seeds for
     what has become the list of the
     <strong>Seven Wonders of the
     Ancient World</strong>.
   </p>
  </body>
 </html>

</xsl:template>

</xsl:stylesheet>
```

Figure 2.7 *Within the root template, anything that's not an XSLT instruction, in other words,* literal elements, *will be output as is. It's an easy way to add HTML tags and text to the output.*

```
html
<html>
 <head>
  <meta http-equiv="Content-Type"
    content="text/html;
    charset=UTF-8">
  <title>Wonders of the World</title>
 </head>

 <body>
  <p align="center"><img
    src="herodotus.jpg" width="120"
    height="171" /></p>
  <p>The famous Greek historian
    Herodotus wrote of seven great
    architectural achievements. And
    although his writings did not
    survive, he planted seeds for
    what has become the list of the
    <strong>Seven Wonders of the
    Ancient World</strong>.
  </p>
 </body>

</html>
```

Figure 2.8 *Although an XML document was processed, the XSLT processor still hasn't gotten its hands on the XML contents itself. It has only output the HTML tags and text. In the rest of this chapter, I'll show how to use XSLT to transform the XML source document to generate some of this HTML.*

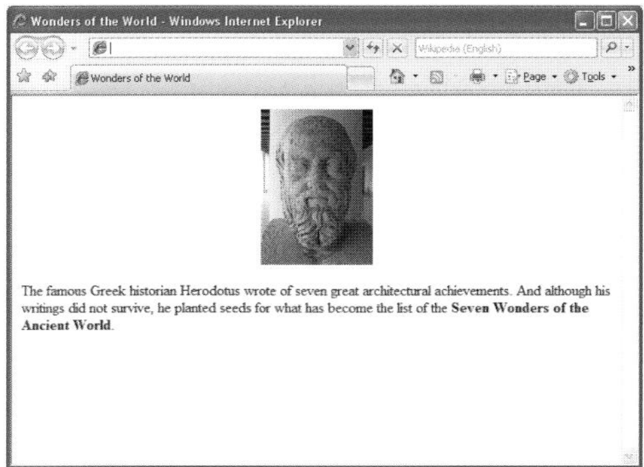

Figure 2.9 *Here's what it looks like so far in a browser. It's not very exciting yet, but it's getting somewhere.*

In templates other than the root template, you can add HTML to the output.

To add HTML to any template's output:

- Inside any other template rule (that is, between `<xsl:template match="...">` and its matching `</xsl:template>`, add the HTML that you'd like to output when this particular template is applied.

✔ Tips

- Because all XSLT documents are XML documents, they must be well-formed. Consequently, the HTML you use in the XSLT document must be well-formed as well. See Chapter 1 for more details.
- For more information about how to write HTML or XHTML, you might want to consult Elizabeth Castro's bestselling *HTML, XHTML, and CSS, Sixth Edition: Visual QuickStart Guide*. For more details see: *www.cookwood.com/html6ed/*.

Outputting Values

You've output HTML using the root template, but your XSLT style sheet still hasn't touched the XML content **(Figure 2.8)**. In order to actually output the content of an XML node (called its *string value*), you'll use the `<xsl:value-of>` element.

To output a node's content:

1. If desired, create the HTML code that will format the content *(see page 24)*.
2. Type **<xsl:value-of**.
3. Then, type **select="expression"**, where *expression* identifies the node set from the XML source document whose content should be output at this point **(Figure 2.11)**. For more information on writing expressions, consult Chapter 3, *XPath Patterns and Expressions*.
4. Finally, type **/>** to close the tag.

```xml
<?xml version="1.0"?>
<?xml-stylesheet type="text/xsl"
  href="02-10.xsl"?>

<ancient_wonders>

 <wonder>

  <name language="English">Colossus
    of Rhodes</name>

  <name language="Greek">Κολοσσός της
    Ρόδου</name>

  <location>Rhodes, Greece</location>

  <height units="feet">107</height>

...
```

Figure 2.10 *An excerpt of the XML source document shows this* wonder *element contains two* name *elements and additional contents.*

```xslt
<?xml version="1.0"?>
<xsl:stylesheet xmlns:xsl="http://
  www.w3.org/1999/XSL/Transform"
  version="1.0">

 <xsl:output method="html"/>

 <xsl:template match="/">

  <html><head><title>Wonders of the
World</title></head>
  <body>
   <h1>Seven Wonders of the Ancient
     World</h1>

   <p>The <xsl:value-of select=
     "ancient_wonders/wonder/name"/>
     is one of the wonders.</p>

  </body></html>

 </xsl:template>

</xsl:stylesheet>
```

Figure 2.11 *In this example, the* xsl:value-of *tag is requesting the value of the* name *element (within the* wonder *element within the* ancient_wonders *element).*

```
html
<html>
 <head>
  <meta http-equiv="Content-Type"
    content="text/html;
    charset=UTF-8">
  <title>Wonders of the World</title>
 </head>
 <body>
  <h1>Seven Wonders of the Ancient
    World</h1>

  <p>The Colossus of Rhodes is one
    of the wonders.</p>

 </body>
</html>
```

Figure 2.12 *When the XSLT processor applies the root template in Figure 2.11, it first outputs all the HTML header code. Then when it gets to the* xsl:value-of *element, it only outputs the value of the first node it finds, which is* Colossus of Rhodes. *I discuss how to return multiple values on page 28.*

Figure 2.13 *And now, the XSLT processor is actually using input from the XML source document.*

✔ Tips

- You can use **select="."** to output the content of the current node. This is discussed in more detail in *Determining the Current Node* on page 40.
- If the select expression matches more than one node in the XML document, only the first node's value is output. (In the example in Figure 2.12, many nodes match the XSLT select expression from Figure 2.11, but only the value of the first ("Colossus of Rhodes") is output.
- If I wanted to act on multiple nodes, I'd need a new XSLT element, discussed in *Looping Over Nodes* on page 28.
- In Figure 2.11, if I wanted to return the `name` nodes where the language attribute was equal to "Greek", I would write `xsl:value-of select="name[@language='Greek']"`. For more information, see *Processing Nodes Conditionally* on page 30.
- If the select expression matches a node, the string value of that node (the text that node contains) is output. If the node has child elements, the output includes the text contained in those child elements as well.
- If the select expression matches a node set that is empty, there is nothing to output.
- If the select expression evaluates to a number, the number is converted to a string for output.
- If the select expression evaluates to a boolean expression (evaluates to either true or false), the output will be either the text "true" or the text "false".

Outputting Values

Looping Over Nodes

As you saw in the previous topic, the `xsl:value-of` element will only act on one node, even if there are many nodes that it matches. The `xsl:for-each` element allows you to act on all nodes matched. It processes all the nodes matched by its `select` attribute, one after the other.

To batch-process nodes:

1. Within a template rule, type **<xsl:for-each**.
2. Then, type **select="expression"**, where *expression* identifies the set of nodes that will be processed.
3. Next, type **>** to close the tag.
4. Specify what processing should take place.
5. Finally, type **</xsl:for-each>** to complete the instruction **(Figure 2.14)**.

xslt

```
...
<xsl:template match="/">
...
 <table border="1"><tr><th>Wonder
   Name</th><th>Location</th>
   <th>Height</th></tr>

  <xsl:for-each select=
    "ancient_wonders/wonder">

   <tr><td><strong><xsl:value-of
     select="name[@language=
     'English']"/></strong><br/>

   (<em><xsl:value-of
     select="name[@language!=
     'English']"/></em>)</td>

     <td><xsl:value-of
       select="location"/></td>
     <td><xsl:value-of
       select="height"/></td> </tr>

    </xsl:for-each>

   </table>
...
</xsl:template>
```

Figure 2.14 *The* xsl:for-each *element contains all the things that should happen for each* wonder *node in the* ancient_wonders *node). The first* xsl:value-of *element is requesting the* name *node where the* language *attribute equals "English". The second* xsl:value-of *element is requesting the name node again where the language attribute* is not equal to *"English"* (!= means "not equal to").

Looping Over Nodes

```
html
...

<table border="1">
 <tr><th>Wonder Name</th><th>Location
   </th><th>Height</th></tr>

 <tr><td><strong>Colossus of
     Rhodes</strong><br/>(<em>Κολοσσός
     της Ρόδου</em>)</td>
   <td>Rhodes, Greece</td>
   <td>107</td></tr>

 <tr><td><strong>Great Pyramid of
    Giza</strong><br/>(<em/>)</td>
   <td>Giza, Egypt</td>
   <td>455</td></tr>

 <tr><td><strong>Hanging Gardens of
   Babylon</strong><br/>(<em/>)</td>
   <td>Al Hillah, Iraq</td>
   <td><td/></tr>
...

</table>
</body>
</html>
```

Figure 2.15 *The* xsl:for-each *instruction in Figure 2.14 creates a new row for each* wonder. *(Note: Not all the rows are shown here, due to space constraints). Once it has processed all the nodes in the selected set, it continues with the rest of the template.*

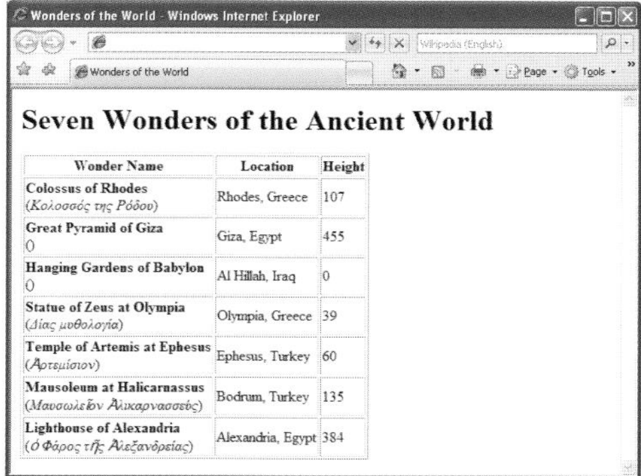

Wonder Name	Location	Height
Colossus of Rhodes (*Κολοσσός της Ρόδου*)	Rhodes, Greece	107
Great Pyramid of Giza ()	Giza, Egypt	455
Hanging Gardens of Babylon ()	Al Hillah, Iraq	0
Statue of Zeus at Olympia (*Δίας μυθολογία*)	Olympia, Greece	39
Temple of Artemis at Ephesus (*Ἀρτεμίσιον*)	Ephesus, Turkey	60
Mausoleum at Halicarnassus (*Μαυσωλεῖον Ἁλικαρνασσεύς*)	Bodrum, Turkey	135
Lighthouse of Alexandria (*ὁ Φάρος τῆς Ἀλεξανδρείας*)	Alexandria, Egypt	384

Figure 2.16 *Notice that the* name *of each wonder is written in English and then in its alternate language, if one exists.*

✔ Tips

- In general, place the `xsl:for-each` right before the rules that should be repeated for each node found. To add a table or some other container, you would do so before and after the opening and closing tags, respectively.
- The `xsl:for-each` element is often used to create HTML tables **(Figure 2.15)**. Place the opening and closing `<table>` tags before and after the `<xsl:for-each>` instruction in Figure 2.14. Then, place the `<tr>` and `<td>` tags as part of the processing that should take place as described in Step 4 on the previous page.
- Because an XSLT style sheet is also an XML document itself, when HTML is part of an XSLT file, it must follow XML's rules. For example, every opening tag must have a matching closing tag and elements may not overlap. For more details, consult Chapter 1.
- In the `select` condition of the `xsl:for-each` element, you can require a specific attribute match by using the `@[attribute='expression']`. This is the same syntax seen in the `select` attributes of both `xsl:value-of` elements in Figure 2.14.

Processing Nodes Conditionally

It's not uncommon to want to process a node or a set of nodes only if a certain condition is met. The condition is written as an expression. For example, you might want to perform a certain action if a particular node set is not empty, or if the string value of a node is equal to a particular word.

To process nodes conditionally:

1. Within a template rule, type **<xsl:if**.
2. Then, type **test="expression"**, where *expression* specifies a node set, a string, or a number. See Chapter 3, *XPath Patterns and Expressions,* for more details on writing expressions.
3. Next, type **>** to close the tag.
4. Specify what should happen if the node set, string, or number specified in Step 2 is not empty (or not equal to zero, in the case of a number).
5. Finally, type **</xsl:if>** to complete the instruction **(Figure 2.17)**.

✔ Tips

- When referring to a node set in the expression, the test returns true if the node set is not empty; that is, if it contains at least one node.
- If you want to be able to specify an alternate result when the expression is false, e.g., an else condition, use `xsl:choose` *(see page 31)*.
- You can test for all sorts of conditions. Consult Chapter 3, *XPath Patterns and Expressions,* for details on how to construct more elaborate test expressions.

```
xslt
...
<xsl:for-each select="ancient_
  wonders/wonder">
 <tr><td><strong><xsl:value-of select
  ="name[@language='English']"/>
  </strong>

  <xsl:if
   test="name[@language!='English']">
   <br/>(<em><xsl:value-of select
   ="name[@language!='English']"/>
   </em>)
  </xsl:if>
 </td>
...
```

Figure 2.17 *Here, the* xsl:if test *condition tests to see if the current node is a* name *node with a* language *attribute that is not* English. *If so, then it outputs the value of the* name *node. If not, nothing is done. This prevents displaying a set of empty parentheses when no alternate language name exists.*

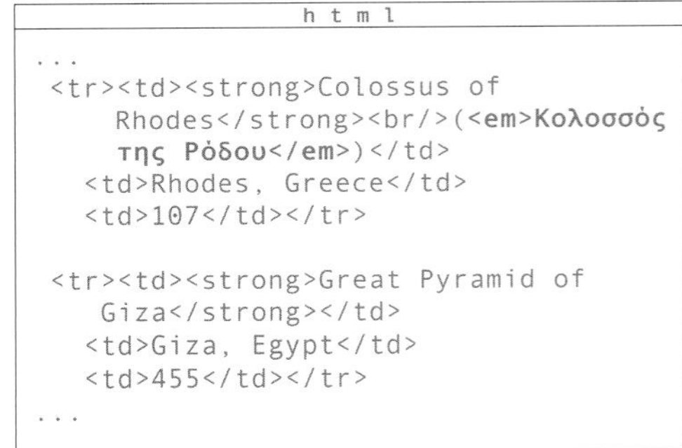

```
html
...
 <tr><td><strong>Colossus of
     Rhodes</strong><br/>(<em>Κολοσσὸς
     της Ρόδου</em>)</td>
   <td>Rhodes, Greece</td>
   <td>107</td></tr>

 <tr><td><strong>Great Pyramid of
    Giza</strong></td>
   <td>Giza, Egypt</td>
   <td>455</td></tr>
...
```

Figure 2.18 *In this output from the XSLT in Figure 2.17, the highlighted text shows an alternate language version of a* name *element. Notice that there is nothing additional output for the Great Pyramid of Giza because there isn't an alternate language* name *node.*

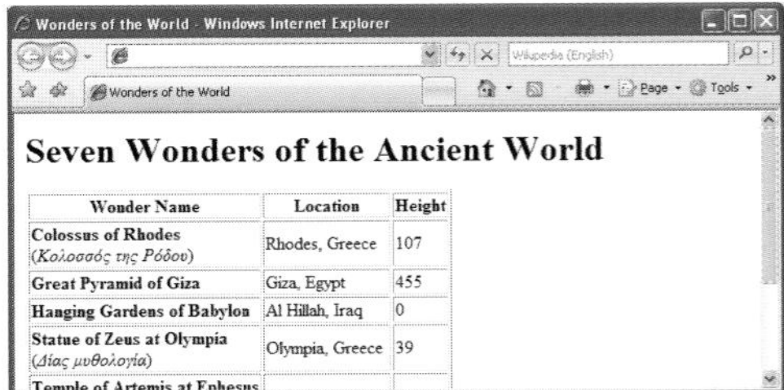

Figure 2.19 *If there is a non-English name, it is displayed; otherwise, there is no output.*

```
                    x s l t
...
<xsl:choose>
  <xsl:when test="height != 0">
    <xsl:value-of select="height"/>
  </xsl:when>

  <xsl:otherwise>
    unknown
  </xsl:otherwise>

</xsl:choose>
...
```

Figure 2.20 *In the XML document, I set the height of the Hanging Gardens of Babylon to zero. I did this because I needed a numeric value for the node but, because there are no surviving documents about the gardens, nobody knows what its dimensions may have been. (In fact, its existence is actually questioned, but that's another story altogether.)*

```
                    h t m l
...
<tr><td><strong>Great Pyramid of Giza
  </strong></td>
 <td>Giza, Egypt</td>
 <td>455</td></tr>

<tr><td><strong>Hanging Gardens of
  Babylon</strong></td>
 <td>Al Hillah, Iraq</td>
 <td>unknown</td></tr>
...
```

Figure 2.21 *By using the* xsl:choose *in Figure 2.20, instead of showing a height of zero for the Hanging Gardens of Babylon (as in Figure 2.19 on page 30), I display the word* unknown.

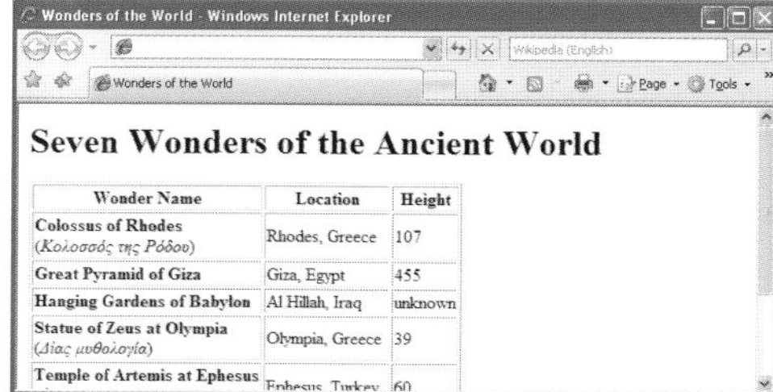

Figure 2.22 *Now the information makes more sense.*

Adding Conditional Choices

The `xsl:if` instruction described on the previous page only allows for one condition and one resulting action. You can use `xsl:choose` when you want to test for several different conditions, and react accordingly to each one. The simplest example of this is when you want to do one action when the condition is true, and another action when it's false.

To add conditional choices:

1. Within a template rule, type **<xsl:choose>**.
2. Type **<xsl:when** to begin the first condition.
3. Then, type **test="expression"**, where *expression* specifies a node set, a string, or a number. See Chapter 3, *XPath Patterns and Expressions,* for more details on writing expressions.
4. Next, type **>** to close the tag.
5. Specify the processing that should take place if the node set, string, or number tested in Step 3 is not empty (or equal to zero, in the case of numbers).
6. Type **</xsl:when>** to complete the condition.
7. Repeat Steps 2–6 for each condition.
8. If desired, type **<xsl:otherwise>**. Specify what should happen if none of the conditions specified by the `xsl:when` elements are true. Then, type **</xsl:otherwise>**.
9. Finally, type **</xsl:choose>** to complete the instruction.

✔ Tip

- In the case of multiple conditions, once a condition is found to be true, all the remaining conditions are ignored (even if there is another true condition). The action contained in this first true condition is the only one performed.

Sorting Nodes Before Processing

By default, nodes are processed in the order in which they appear in the XML source document. If you'd like to process them in some other order, you can add an `xsl:sort` element when you use `xsl:for-each`.

To sort nodes before processing:

1. Directly after an `xsl:for-each` element type **<xsl:sort**.
2. Then, type **select="criteria"**, where *criteria* is an expression that specifies the node (key) on which the source nodes should be sorted.
3. If desired, type **order="descending"**. The default is for nodes to be sorted in ascending order.
4. If desired, then type **data-type="text"** or **data-type="number"** depending on what you're sorting. The default is text.
5. Finally, type **/>** to close the instruction **(Figure 2.23)**.
6. Repeat Steps 1–5 to define as many sorting parameters as desired.

✔ Tips

- Be sure to specify the correct `data-type` in Step 4. Sorting numbers as text has such erroneous results as 100, 7, 89. Sorting text as numbers is equally ineffective.
- Descending means you go from high numbers to low, and from Z to A. Ascending means the low numbers (and letters) appear at the top.
- You can nest `xsl:sort` elements within other `xsl:sort` elements. This allows you to sort on multiple nodes (keys).

xslt

```
...
<table border="1"><tr><th>Wonder
  Name</th><th>Location</th><th>
  Height</th></tr>

<xsl:for-each select="ancient_
  wonders/wonder">

 <xsl:sort select="height"
   order="descending"
   data-type="number" />
...
```

Figure 2.23 *I've added an* xsl:sort *instruction right after the* xsl:for-each *element to sort the nodes by height, in a descending order for processing.*

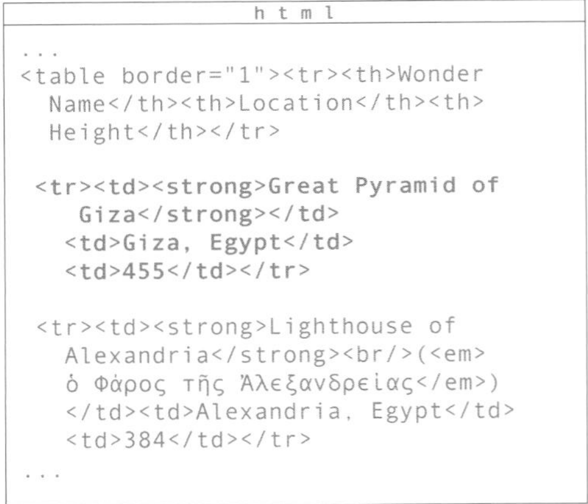

html

```
...
<table border="1"><tr><th>Wonder
  Name</th><th>Location</th><th>
  Height</th></tr>

 <tr><td><strong>Great Pyramid of
    Giza</strong></td>
   <td>Giza, Egypt</td>
   <td>455</td></tr>

 <tr><td><strong>Lighthouse of
   Alexandria</strong><br/>(<em>
   ὁ Φάρος τῆς Ἀλεξανδρείας</em>)
   </td><td>Alexandria, Egypt</td>
   <td>384</td></tr>
...
```

Figure 2.24 *Based on the XSLT in Figure 2.23, the Great Pyramid of Giza (the tallest of all the ancient wonders) is the first to be processed and thus will appear at the top of the table.*

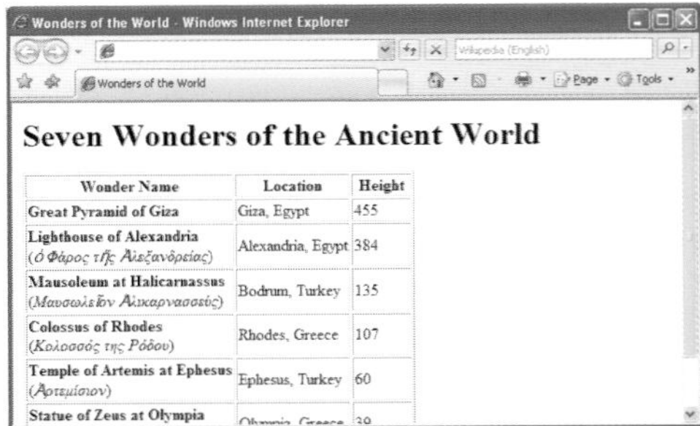

Figure 2.25 *Now the ancient wonders are listed in descending order by height, the tallest being more than 45 stories tall.*

```
xslt
...
<tr><td>
 <a>
  <xsl:attribute name="href">
    #<xsl:value-of select=
    "name[@language='English']"/>
  </xsl:attribute>

  <strong><xsl:value-of select="name[@
language='English']"/></strong>

 </a>
...
```

Figure 2.26 *Here I am using* xsl:attribute *to add an* href *attribute to an anchor element* <a>. *The* href *value will be set to # (a pound sign) and the name of the wonder being processed. In this way, each wonder will link to its own named reference on the page.*

```
html
...
<table border="1"><tr><th>Wonder
  Name</th><th>Location</th><th>
  Height</th></tr>

 <tr><td><a href="#Great Pyramid of
   Giza"><strong>Great Pyramid of
   Giza</strong></a></td>
   <td>Giza, Egypt</td>
   <td>455</td></tr>
...
```

Figure 2.27 *Now, the Great Pyramid of Giza links to an href of its own name.*

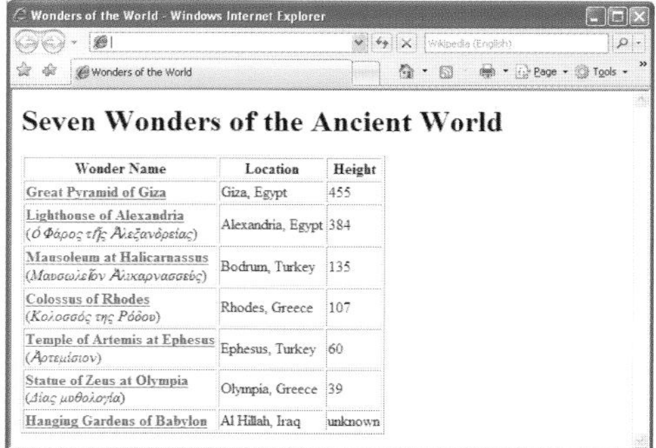

Figure 2.28 *You can see that each of the wonder's names is now a hyperlink.*

Generating Output Attributes

When you are transforming your XML source document to an HTML document (or an XML document for that matter), it's often useful to be able to add attributes and values to a given output element. For example, if you are creating an `<img>` element or an `<a>` element, you might need to include the `src`, `width`, and `height` attributes, or the `href` and `target` attributes, respectively.

To generate output attributes:

1. Directly after the opening tag of the element in which this new attribute should appear, type **<xsl:attribute**.
2. Then, type **name="att_name"**, where *att_name* is the name that the attribute should have in the element.
3. Next, type **>** to close the tag.
4. Specify the value of the new attribute using XSLT instructions or literals.
5. Finally, type **</xsl:attribute>** to complete the attribute generation **(Figure 2.26)**.
6. Repeat Steps 1–5 to define as many attributes as desired.

✔ Tip

- You will often use the `xsl:value-of` element in Step 4 to generate the value of the attribute from content that comes from your XML document.

Creating and Applying Templates

As discussed on page 20, the root template is the first thing processed in an XSLT style sheet. This template is the set of rules applied to the root node of the XML source document.

As it turns out, XSLT allows you to create more templates than just the root template. This allows you to create different sets of processing rules to apply to different parts of your XML.

While most XSLT processing can be done without using templates, one of the main benefits of using templates is the ability to reuse a template for other nodes in your document. In the same way that one can use functions in most programming languages, you would create a template, and simply apply that template whenever necessary. This eliminates the need to rewrite the exact same processing instructions each time.

To create a template:

1. Type **<xsl:template** to begin the template.
2. Then, type **match="pattern"**, where *pattern* identifies the node(s) of the XML document to which the template will be applied. The syntax for describing patterns is described in Chapter 3, *XPath Patterns and Expressions.*
3. Next, type **>** to close the tag.
4. Specify all the transformations that should happen when a node is found that matches the pattern in Step 2.
5. Finally, type **</xsl:template>** to complete the template **(Figure 2.29)**.

✔ Tips

- The root template is simply a template with a pattern that matches the root node.
- Only the root template is called automatically. All other templates must be applied manually *(see page 35)*. Otherwise, they are simply ignored.

```
xslt
...
<xsl:template match="/">
 <html><head><title>Wonders of the
   World</title></head>
  <body>
   <h1>Seven Wonders of the Ancient
     World</h1>
...
</xsl:template>

<xsl:template
 match="name[@language!='English']">

 (<em>
   <xsl:value-of select="."/>
 </em>)

</xsl:template>
...
```

Figure 2.29 *In this excerpt, I've added a new template for* name *nodes where the* language *attribute is not English. This template will output the value of the current* name *node italicized in parentheses. It does so by using* xsl:value-of select="." *which returns the value of the current node.*

```
xslt
...
<tr><td>
 <a>
  <xsl:attribute name="href">
    #<xsl:value-of select=
    "name[@language='English']"/>
  </xsl:attribute>
  <strong><xsl:value-of select="name
    [@language='English']"/></strong>
 </a><br/>

 <xsl:apply-templates select="name
   [@language!='English']"/>
</td>
...
```

Figure 2.30 *In this excerpt of the same XSLT style sheet, I have used an* xsl:apply-templates *element where the* xsl:if *element was, as seen in Figure 2.17. This* xsl:if *element was testing for a* name *node with a* language *value not equal to English. The new resulting output will be the same as before, as you will see in the figures that follow.*

```
xslt
...
<h2>History</h2>
<xsl:for-each select=
  "/ancient_wonders/wonder">
<xsl:sort select="height" order=
  "descending" data-type="number" />
 <a><xsl:attribute name="name">
   <xsl:value-of select="name
   [@language='English']"/>
   </xsl:attribute></a>
 <xsl:value-of select="name[@
language='English']"/>

 <xsl:apply-templates select=
   "name[@language!='English']"/>

 <br /><br />
</xsl:for-each>
...
```

Figure 2.31 *In this excerpt of the same XSLT style sheet, I've added a new section called History to show historical information about the ancient wonders. I am reusing the new template created in Figure 2.29 with the highlighted* xsl:apply-templates *element to display the non-English name.*

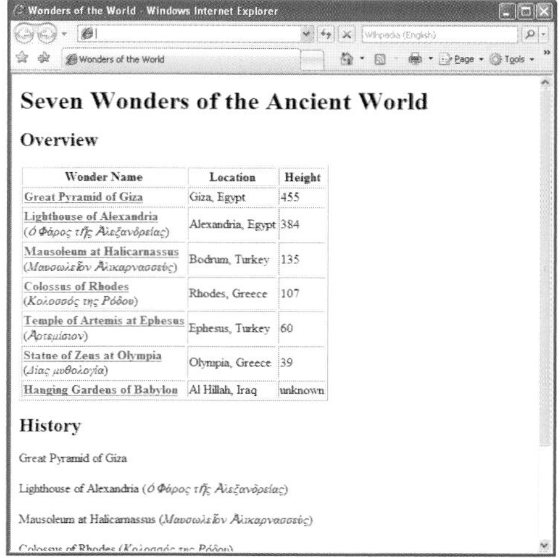

Figure 2.32 *By moving the non-English processing instructions into its own template, I am able to use the same logic and output the same information twice without having to rewrite those same instructions.*

Now that you've learned how to create templates, the next step is how to use them; in other words, how to apply a template to a specific node in your XML document. You do this by using `xsl:apply-templates`. This is how you control *where and when* the transformation described by the template is used in the final document.

To apply a template:

1. Within any template, type **<xsl:apply-templates**.
2. Then, type **select="expression"**, where *expression* identifies the node(s) of the XML document whose templates should be applied. See Chapter 3, *XPath Patterns and Expressions,* for more details on writing expressions.
3. Finally, type **/>** to complete the instruction **(Figures 2.30 and 2.31)**.

✔ Tips

- If you have multiple templates in your style sheet, the order of the `xsl:apply-templates` elements determines the order in which the templates are processed.
- If you don't specify the `select` attribute in Step 2 above, the processor will look for and apply a template to each of the current node's children.
- When using `xsl:apply-templates`, if there is no template matching the current node, a template built in to the XSLT processor is automatically used. For the root node, or an element node, it looks for a matching template for each child node. For a text or attribute node, it outputs the node value as text.
- The `xsl:apply-templates` element may contain an `xsl:sort` element *(see page 32)*.
- If you haven't already, I recommend downloading and reviewing the example files. See the book's Introduction for details.

3 XPath Patterns and Expressions

In the previous chapter, *XSLT*, you learned about creating and applying templates to transform XML documents. When you create a template, you use a pattern to specify the nodes that the template can be applied to. When you apply a template, you use an expression to specify the node set that should be processed. You write both patterns and expressions using XML Path Language (*XPath*) syntax.

XPath is a language for selecting nodes and node sets by specifying their location paths in the XML document. This chapter will describe how to specify XPath location paths in detail.

You can also use XPath in other XSLT instructions to further process given node sets to return values instead of nodes. XPath has built-in functions to do math, process strings, and test conditions in an XML document. The next chapter, *XPath Functions*, will describe these functions in detail.

Like XSLT, XQuery uses XPath expressions and is discussed in Chapter 16.

Note: The most current version of the language is XPath 2.0. However, because version 1.0 is still more widely used, these two chapters will cover XPath 1.0. XPath 2.0 is discussed in detail in Chapter 15.

Locating Nodes

At the foundation of the XPath language is the ability to use *location paths* to refer to a node or node set. Remember that a *node* is an individual piece of the XML document (such as an element, an attribute, or some text content). A location path uses relationships to describe the location of a node or set of nodes relative to a given node. When translating location paths, XPath considers all XML documents as tree structures. Specifically, they are considered node trees, which are a hierarchical structure of nodes **(Figures 3.1 and 3.2)**.

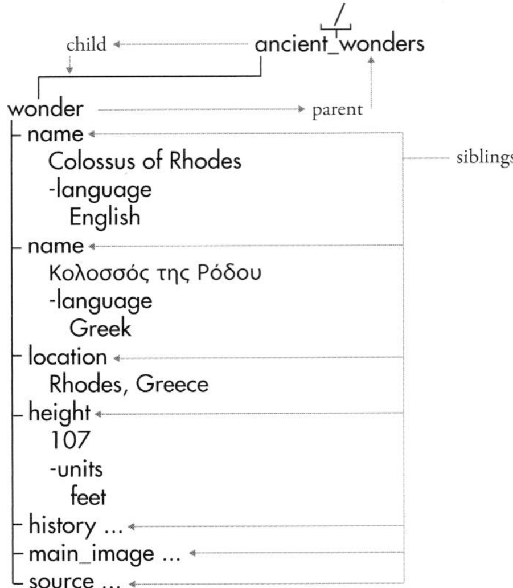

Figure 3.1 *This is an XML node tree representation of a single ancient wonder and its children.* ancient_wonders *is the* root, *or* document node. *In this example, the* ancient_wonders *element has one* child node *which is the* wonder *element. And, in turn, the* ancient_wonders *element is the* wonder *element's* parent node. *The* wonder *element has seven child nodes (*name, name, location, height, history, main_image, *and* source*), each of which are* sibling nodes *to one another. As well, each are* descendant nodes *of the* wonder *node and the* ancient_wonders *node. And this, consequently makes the* wonder *node and the* ancient_wonders *node* ancestor nodes *to these seven children.*

The XML Node Tree

In an XML node tree, *everything* in the tree is a node, and every node is in some way related to another. At the top of the node tree is the *root node*. The root node, or *document node*, can have any number of *child nodes*. To these child nodes, the root node is a *parent node*. These child nodes can have any number of child nodes themselves, and so on, and so on. Child nodes with the same parent are called *sibling nodes*. *Descendant nodes* are a node's child nodes, its children's child nodes, and so forth. *Ancestor nodes* are a node's parent node, grandparent nodes, etc. Through XPath location paths, you can access any of these nodes from any other simply by knowing the relationship between the two.

Location Paths

There are two kinds of location paths: relative location paths and absolute location paths.

A *relative location path* consists of a sequence of location steps separated by **/** (a forward slash). Each step selects a node or node set relative to the current node. Then, each node in *that* set is used as the current node for the following step, and so on.

An *absolute location path* consists of **/** (a forward slash), optionally followed by a relative location path. A **/** by itself selects the root node

```
xml
<?xml version="1.0"?>

<ancient_wonders>

 <wonder>

  <name language="English">
    Colossus of Rhodes</name>

  <name language="Greek">
    Κολοσσός της Ρόδου</name>

  <location>Rhodes, Greece</location>

  <height units="feet">107</height>

  <history> ... </history>

  <main_image ... />

  <source  ... />

 </wonder>

</ancient_wonders>
```

Figure 3.2 *This is the actual XML source that is represented by the XML node tree in Figure 3.1. As noted, the* ancient_wonders *element is the root, or document node, and is the* parent *to the* wonder *element. Continuing down the XML, the* wonder *element is the* parent *to seven children (*name, name, location, height, history, main_image, *and* source*). All seven child nodes of the* wonder *element are* siblings. *These nodes and the* wonder *element itself are* descendants *of the* ancient_wonders *node. Conversely, this makes the* ancient_wonders *node an* ancestor *to the* wonder *element and all its children.*

of the XML document. If it is followed by a relative location path, then the location path is a relative location path starting at the root node.

The choice of whether to use a relative or an absolute location path depends on the circumstance. Relative location paths are most commonly used, because they generate the resulting node set relative to the current node, and this is typically the context in which you are working.

Using Located Nodes

Often, when using location paths, you will be using the located node or node set as a container of other elements to process.

Other times, you will want to know the node's value. In XPath, there are seven different node types: root nodes (of which there is always exactly one), element nodes, text nodes, attribute nodes, comment nodes, processing instruction nodes, and namespace nodes. For each node type, there is a way of retrieving its value. For some, the value is part of the node itself; for others, the value is based on the value of its descendant nodes.

✔ Tips

- The XPath language syntax was inspired in part by the common "path/file" file system.
- The *current node* is the element, or node, that is currently being processed. The *context node* is where the XPath location path address starts. In most circumstances, these terms are interchangeable, so I use the term *current node* throughout the book.

Determining the Current Node

As the XSLT processor goes through your style sheet, it works on one node at a time. It is through the use of the `xsl:template`, `xsl:apply-templates`, and `xsl:for-each` elements that it knows which parts of your XML document to process and when.

When developing an XSLT style sheet, you will often specify what to process next with respect to what is being processed now. The node currently being processed is called the *current node*. Of course, before you can refer from the current node, you will need to know how to identify it **(Figure 3.3)**.

To determine the current node:

1. By default, the current node is the one that is specified by the current template. In other words, the current node is identified by the template's `match` attribute.
2. If there is an `xsl:apply-templates` instruction, the current node becomes the node that is matched by the corresponding template (that is, the one specified in the `match` attribute of the `xsl:template` instruction). When the processor "returns" from that `xsl:template`, the current node reverts back to one from the original template's match attribute.
3. If there is an `xsl:for-each` instruction, the current node changes to the one specified by its `select` attribute. After the `xsl:for-each` instruction, the current node reverts back to whatever it was before that instruction was processed.

✔ Tip

■ The `xsl:apply-templates` instruction may process more than one node in the case where the select expression returns a node set. In this case, each of the nodes in the set will be the current node in turn.

xslt

```
...
<xsl:template match="/">                                  1
...
 <h2>Overview</h2>

 <xsl:apply-templates select=                             1a
   "ancient_wonders/wonder">
  <xsl:sort select="height" order=
   "descending" data-type="number" />
 </xsl:apply-templates>
...
</xsl:template>

<xsl:template match="wonder">                             2
 <tr><td><a>...
   <strong><xsl:value-of select=
     "name[@language='English']"/>
   </strong></a><br/>
   <xsl:apply-templates select="
     name[@language!='English']"/>                        2a
...
</xsl:template>

<xsl:template match=
  "name[@language!='English']">                           3
 (<em>
   <xsl:value-of select="."/></em>)
</xsl:template>
...
```

Figure 3.3 *At point* 1, *the current node is / (the root node) as specified by the* xsl:template match="/" *instruction. When the processor reaches point 1a, the current node becomes the first* wonder *element in* ancient_wonders and *the processing jumps to point* 2 *where that* wonder *element is processed according to the* xsl:template match="wonder" *instruction.*

Then, when the processor reaches point 2a, *the* name *element with a language attribute not equal to* English *becomes the current node and the processing jumps to point* 3, *where that* name *element becomes the current node and is processed according to the* xsl:template match="name[@language!='English']" *instruction.*

When this instruction is complete, the processor "returns" from the name *template applied in point* 2a. *The current node then becomes the* wonder *element once again, until the processor finishes the* wonder *template and returns to the* root *template.*

After this first wonder *element is processed, the second* wonder *element becomes the current node, and so on until all the* wonder *elements have been processed (and taken their turn as the current node).*

```
xslt
...
<xsl:template match="wonder">
 <tr><td><a>...
   <strong><xsl:value-of select=
     "name[@language='English']"/>
   </strong></a><br/>
   <xsl:apply-templates select="name[@
language!='English']"/>
...
</xsl:template>

<xsl:template match=
  "name[@language!='English']">
 (<em><xsl:value-of select="."/>
   </em>)
</xsl:template>
...
```

Figure 3.4 *The current node will be the contents of some* name *element whose* language *attribute is "English." Which* name *element it is depends on where the processor is in the transformation process.*

```
html
...
<tr><td><a href="#Great Pyramid of
  Giza"><strong>Great Pyramid of
  Giza</strong></a><br/></td>
  <td>Giza, Egypt</td>
  <td>455</td></tr>

<tr><td><a href="#Lighthouse of
  Alexandria"><strong>Lighthouse of
  Alexandria</strong></a><br/>
  (<em>ὁ Φάρος τῆς Ἀλεξανδρείας</em>)
  </td><td>Alexandria, Egypt</td>
  <td>384</td></tr>

 <tr><td><a href="#Mausoleum at
  Halicarnassus">
  <strong>Mausoleum at Halicarnassus
    </strong></a><br/>
  (<em>Μαυσωλεῖον Ἁλικαρνασσεύς</em>)
  </td><td>Bodrum, Turkey</td>
  <td>135</td></tr>
...
```

Figure 3.5 *The highlighted text is output when the processor executes the* <xsl:apply-templates select="name[@language!='English']"/> *instruction in the* wonder *template. Within the template itself (*<xsl:template match="name[@language!='English']">*), the* <xsl:value-of select="."/> *instruction returns the value of the current node each time it is called.*

Referring to the Current Node

If you're currently processing the node that you want to use in a `select` attribute, there's a shortcut you can use. Instead of referencing the current node using a location path from the root node, it's much easier to use the current node shortcut **(Figure 3.4)**.

To refer to the current node:

- In a location path, type **.** (a single period).

✔ Tips

- You won't always want to select the entire node set. To get a subset of the current node, you can add a test called a *predicate*. For more details, consult *Conditionally Selecting Nodes* on page 45.
- You can also use **.** (the current node shortcut) in a predicate to refer to the *context node*. The context node is the node that is being tested by the predicate.

Referring to the Current Node

Selecting a Node's Children

If the current node contains element(s) that you want to use, you can use a shortcut to refer to these *child nodes* **(Figure 3.6)**. Instead of writing the location path from the root node, you can refer to the desired child nodes simply by using their name **(Figure 3.7)**.

To get a node's children:

1. Make sure you know what the current node is *(see page 40)*, and that the node or node set you're interested in is a child of the current node. (You can actually refer to any descendant. See Step 3 below.)
2. Then, in the desired location path, type **child** to refer to the name of the *child* element(s) within the current node.
3. If desired, you could then add **/grandchild** to refer to a node or node set contained in the child set referenced in Step 2. This enables you to dig deeper into the XML tree and reference node sets further down.
4. Repeat Step 3 until you get to the node(s) at the level you want.

✔ Tips

- Of course, before you ask for children, it's important to know which is the current node. See page 40 for details.
- Type * (an asterisk) to select all the current node's children.
- The `xsl:text` element is used to add literal text to the output. `xsl:text` cannot contain any other elements. It is often used to handle special characters such as & or >, or to control white space. Notice it is being used to add a space between the `year_built` / `year_destroyed` elements and their `eras` in Figure 3.7. Without it, there would be no space between the year and the era in the output.

xml

```
...
<history>
  <year_built era="BC">282
    </year_built>
  <year_destroyed era="BC">226
    </year_destroyed>
  <how_destroyed>earthquake
    </how_destroyed>
  <story>In 294 BC, the people of
    the island of Rhodes began
    building a colossal statue of the
    sun god Helios. They believed ...
  </story>
</history>
...
```

Figure 3.6 *Here is an excerpt from the XML document. This* history *element has four child elements. They are:* year_built, year_destroyed, how_destroyed *and* story.

xslt

```
...
<xsl:template match="history">
...
 was built in
<xsl:value-of select="year_built"/>
<xsl:text> </xsl:text>
<xsl:value-of
  select="year_built/@era"/>

<xsl:choose>
 <xsl:when
   test="year_destroyed != 0">
  and was destroyed by
  <xsl:value-of
    select="how_destroyed"/> in
  <xsl:value-of
    select="year_destroyed"/>
  <xsl:text> </xsl:text>
  <xsl:value-of
    select="year_destroyed/@era"/>.
 </xsl:when>
 <xsl:otherwise>
  is still standing today.
 </xsl:otherwise>
</xsl:choose>
<br \><br \>
</xsl:template>
```

Figure 3.7 *When the processor gets to the history template,* history *becomes the current node. With this, the processor can directly address its child nodes in XPath location paths. Notice the use of the @ symbol referring to the* era *attribute. This is discussed more on page 44.*

```
xml
...
<wonder>
 <name language="English">
   Colossus of Rhodes</name>
 <name language="Greek">
   Κολοσσός της Ρόδου</name>
...
 <history>
  <year_built era="BC">
    282</year_built>
  <year_destroyed era="BC">
    226</year_destroyed>
  <how_destroyed>
    earthquake</how_destroyed>
  <story>In 294 BC, ...</story>
 </history>
...
```

Figure 3.8 *Notice that the* history *and* name *elements are both children of (contained directly in) the* wonder *element, and thus are siblings.*

```
xslt
...
<xsl:template match="history">
...
 The <xsl:value-of select=
   "../name[@language='English']"/>
 <xsl:apply-templates select=
   "../name[@language!='English']"/>
 was built in <xsl:value-of select=
   "year_built"/>
...
```

Figure 3.9 *When the processor applies this* history *template,* history *becomes the current node. If I then want to reference the* name *element (which is its sibling), I have to use .. to go up one level (to the parent element,* wonder*). Then I use / to get to a different child, and type* name *to specify that child element.*

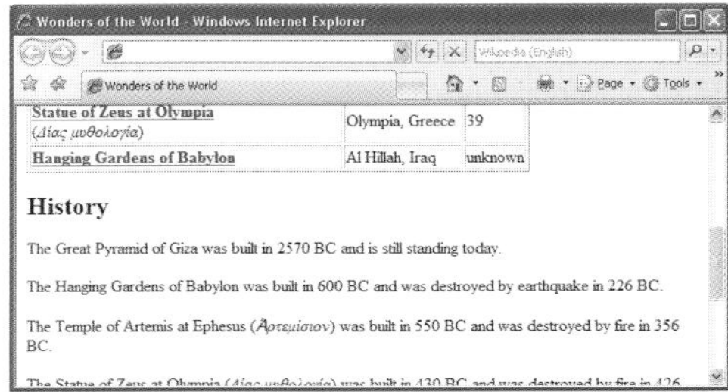

Figure 3.10 *Although the processor is now in the* history *template (not the* wonder *template), as long as I specify the new relationship, the output is correct.*

Selecting a Node's Parent or Siblings

Again, if the relationship between the current node *(see page 40)* and the desired node is quite clear **(Figure 3.8)**, it's much easier to use a shortcut than to write the complete, absolute relationship starting from the root node.

To select a node's parent:

1. Make sure you know what the current node is, and that the node set you're interested in is the parent of the current node.
2. Type **..** (two periods) to select the current node's parent.

To select a node's siblings:

1. After you've gotten to the node's parent in Step 2 above, type **/sibling**, where *sibling* refers to the name of the desired node. This sibling is therefore a child of the current node's parent, but isn't the current node itself **(Figure 3.9)**.
2. If desired, type **/niece**, where *niece* refers to a node that is the child of the sibling of the current node.
3. Repeat Step 2 as necessary to select grand-nieces, etc.

✔ Tips

- The **..** is often combined with a node's attribute to find the attribute of the parent node (**../@attribute**). More on this when I get to attributes *(see page 44)*.
- You can also use an asterisk as a wildcard within a location path. For example, **../*** would select all the child elements of the parent of the current node, including the current node itself.

Selecting a Node's Attributes

If you want the location path to return a node's attributes rather than the node itself, you can use the @ to specify that you want the attribute returned **(Figure 3.11)**.

To select a node's attribute(s):

1. Write the location path to the node, using the techniques described in this chapter.
2. Then, type **/@** to indicate that you're interested in the current node's attributes.
3. Finally, type **attribute**, to specify the name of the *attribute* you're interested in. Or type * (an asterisk) as a wildcard to select all the node's attributes.

✔ Tip

- The @ symbol is sometimes referred to as the *attribute axis*. In XPath, an axis is a set of nodes relative to the current node. In addition to the attribute axis, there are 12 other axes defined in the XPath language. They are: ancestor, ancestor-or-self, child, descendant, descendant-or-self, following, following-sibling, namespace, parent, preceding, preceding-sibling, and self. Each of these additional axes specifies a "direction" relative to the current node and represents the corresponding node set. Because each of these axes can be represented by shortcuts (specifically those defined in this chapter), the axes themselves are seldom used in practice.

```
xslt
...
<xsl:template match="history">
...
 The <xsl:value-of select=
   "../name[@language='English']"/>
 <xsl:apply-templates select=
   "../name[@language!='English']"/>
 was built in <xsl:value-of
   select="year_built"/>
 <xsl:text> </xsl:text>
 <xsl:value-of
   select="year_built/@era"/>
...
```

Figure 3.11 *To get the attribute(s) of an element, use the element's name, followed by the @ sign and then followed by the name of the attribute. Here I am requesting the* era *attribute of the* year_built *element.*

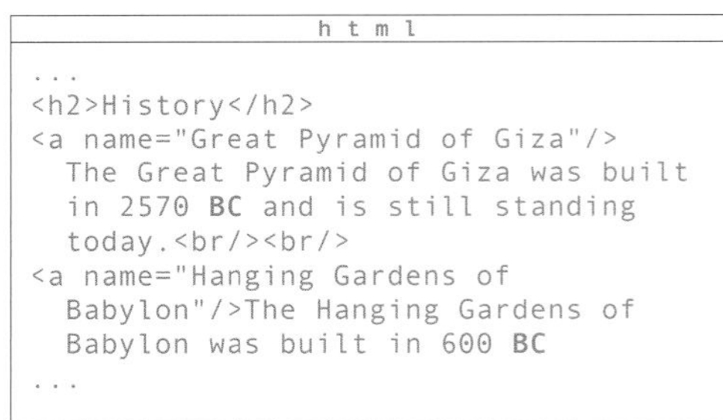

```
html
...
<h2>History</h2>
<a name="Great Pyramid of Giza"/>
  The Great Pyramid of Giza was built
  in 2570 BC and is still standing
  today.<br/><br/>
<a name="Hanging Gardens of
  Babylon"/>The Hanging Gardens of
  Babylon was built in 600 BC
...
```

Figure 3.12 *The contents of the* era *attribute (from the* year_built *element) are output.*

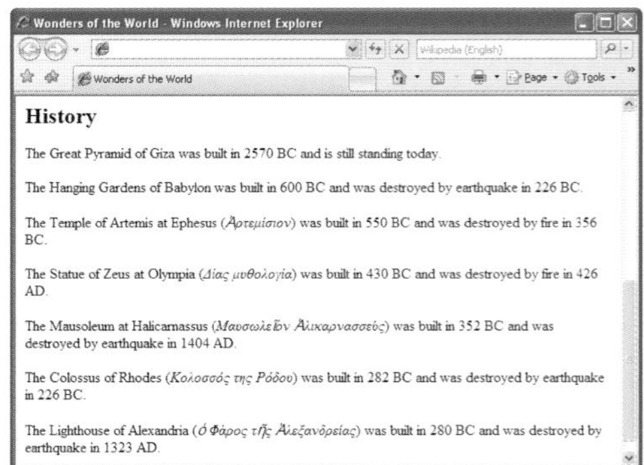

Figure 3.13 *The* era *attribute information is displayed with the* year_built *element as shown in the HTML excerpt above.*

```
xml
...
<wonder>
  <name language="English">
    Statue of Zeus at Olympia</name>
  <name language="Greek">
    Διας μυθολογια</name>
  <location>Olympia, Greece</location>
  <height units="feet">39</height>
  <history>
...
</wonder>
...
```

Figure 3.14 *Notice that in the XML document, the* wonder *element can have more than one* name *child element, each having its own* language *attribute.*

```
xslt
...
<xsl:template match=
  "name[@language!='English']">
 (<em><xsl:value-of select="."/>
   </em>)
</xsl:template>
...
```

Figure 3.15 *This template will only be applied to all* name *elements that have a* language *attribute* not *equal to* English.

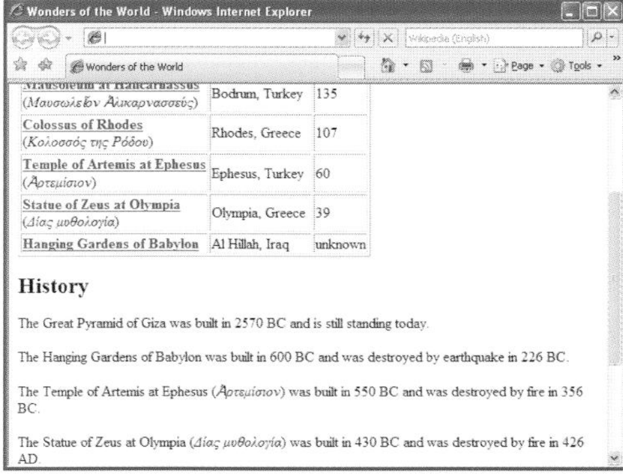

Figure 3.16 *The non-English* name *elements are displayed in italics inside parentheses, as instructed by the XSLT template.*

Conditionally Selecting Nodes

It's not always precise enough to select an entire node set from the XML document **(Figure 3.14)**. With XPath, you can create boolean expressions (called *predicates*) to test a condition and based on the results of that test, select a specific subset of the node set **(Figure 3.15)**.

Predicates can compare values, test for existence, do math, and more. You use functions to write these and more complicated conditions. For more details, see Chapter 4, *XPath Functions*.

To conditionally select nodes:

1. Create a location path to the node that contains the desired subset following the instructions in this chapter.
2. Type **[** (a left square bracket; to the right of the *p* on your keyboard).
3. Write the expression that identifies the subset.
4. Finally, type **]** (a right square bracket) to complete the predicate.

✔ Tips

- As noted above, predicates are not only for comparisons. It's enough to write **[@language]**, which would select all the current node's elements that have a `language` attribute (regardless of its value).
- You can use multiple predicates to further narrow your search. **name[@language='English'][position() = last()]** would select the `name` elements that have a `language` attribute equal to "English" and that are the last node in the set.
- You can also add an attribute selector after the predicate, if desired. For example, to get all the attributes of the last element of the current node set, type **[last ()]/@***.
- Make sure you type square brackets; not curly ones or parentheses.

Creating Absolute Location Paths

All the location paths that I've created so far have been relative location paths—ones dependent on the current node.

You can also create *absolute location paths*, ones that do not rely on the current node **(Figure 3.17)**. To do so, begin by writing the path to the desired node starting at the root node.

To create an absolute location path:

1. Type **/** to indicate that you are starting at the root node of the XML document.
2. Then type **root**, where *root* refers to the root element of your XML document.
3. Next, type **/** to go down one level in your XML document's tree hierarchy.
4. Type **container**, where *container* identifies the name of the element on the next level that contains the desired element.
5. Repeat Steps 3–4 until you have come to the parent of the node in which you are interested.
6. Finally, type **/element**, where *element* is the name of the desired node.
7. Now, you may also use a predicate, or select the node's attribute, or both.

✔ Tips

- All location path ideas and shortcuts discussed so far in this chapter can also be used when creating an absolute path.
- At any point in the location path, you can use * (an asterisk) to specify all the elements at that level.
- You may skip Steps 3–5 if the desired element is a child of the root element itself.
- Some benefits of using absolute paths are described on page 38. However, pay careful attention when doing so, as disregarding the current node may cause unforeseen consequences **(Figure 3.19)**.

xslt

```
...
<xsl:template match="wonder">
 <tr><td>
  <a><xsl:attribute name=
    "href">#<xsl:value-of select=
    "name[@language='English']"/>
    </xsl:attribute>
    <strong>

    <xsl:value-of select=
    "/ancient_wonders/wonder/name
    [@language='English']"/>
    </strong></a><br/>
...
```

Figure 3.17 *I've changed the highlighed location path (which displays the wonder's English name) from relative to absolute. I did so by adding* /ancient_wonders/wonder *to the beginning of the relative location path used in the original version* (select="name[@language='English']").

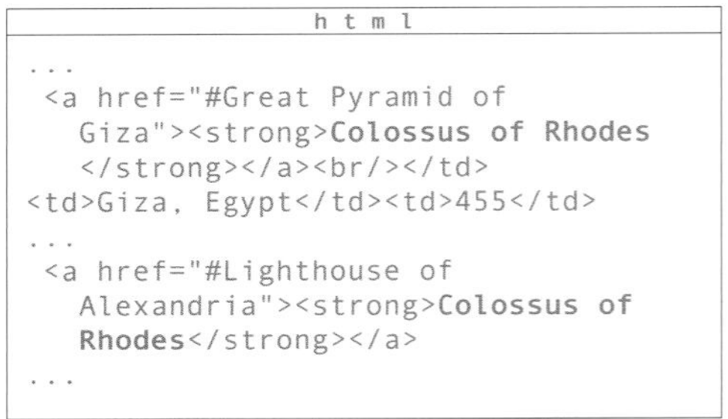

html

```
...
 <a href="#Great Pyramid of
   Giza"><strong>Colossus of Rhodes
   </strong></a><br/></td>
<td>Giza, Egypt</td><td>455</td>
...
 <a href="#Lighthouse of
   Alexandria"><strong>Colossus of
   Rhodes</strong></a>
...
```

Figure 3.18 *However, instead of getting the* current node's *English name, the absolute location path returns the first element from the* root node's *English name every time.*

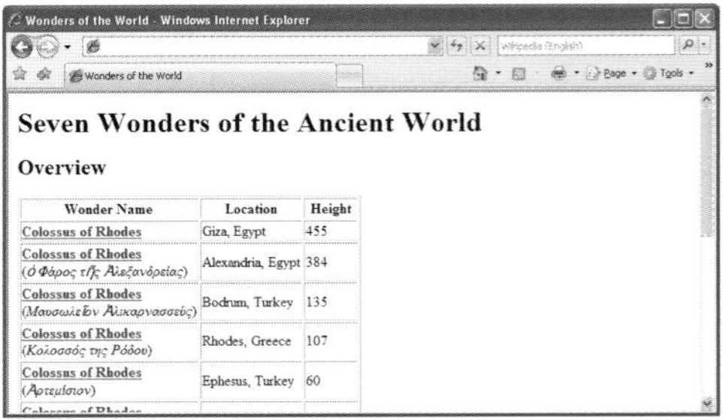

Figure 3.19 *And the point here: Make sure you know what you're doing when using absolute location paths and disregarding the current node. It may not give you what you need. Rather, you may end up with a mess.*

```
xml
...
<wonder>
 <name language="English">
   Lighthouse of Alexandria</name>
...
 <main_image file="lighthouse.jpg"
   w="528" h="349"/>
 <source sectionid="112"
   newspaperid="53"/>
</wonder>
...
```

Figure 3.20 *I know there are elements in the XML document that contain image filenames, but if I wasn't sure where they were and wanted to create a list of them all, I could use the // shortcut, see below.*

```
xslt
...
<xsl:template match="/">
 <html><head><title>Wonders of the
   World</title></head>
  <body>
   <xsl:apply-templates
     select="//*/@file" />
  </body></html>
</xsl:template>

<xsl:template match="//*/@file" >
 <xsl:value-of select="."/><br />
</xsl:template>
...
```

Figure 3.21 *The* select *and* match *attributes that are highlighted return all the nodes, no matter where they appear in the XML source, that have an* attribute *named* file. *(Note: This is a completely different XSLT file, not built upon the previous ones.)*

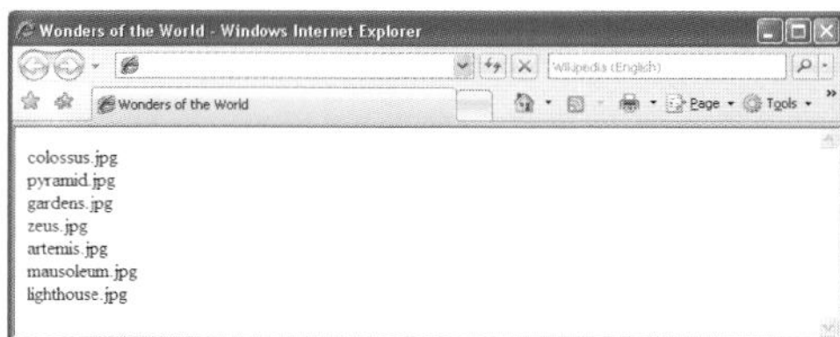

Figure 3.22 *Notice that all the filenames contained in the XML source document are displayed here, regardless of their actual location.*

Selecting All the Descendants

The **//** (double forward slash) comes in handy when you need to select all the descendants of a particular node **(Figure 3.21)**. Like most of the other shortcuts in this chapter, you can use it either in an absolute or relative location path.

To select all the descendants of the root node:

- Type **//** (two forward slashes).

To select all the descendants of the current node:

- Type **.//** (a period followed by two forward slashes).

To select all the descendants of any node:

1. Use the techniques in the previous pages to get to the node whose descendants you're interested in.
2. Then, type **//** (two forward slashes).

To select some of the descendants of any node:

1. Create the path to the node whose descendants you're interested in by using the techniques described on earlier pages.
2. Type **//**.
3. Then, type the name of the descendant elements that you're interested in.

✔ Tip

- To get to a node when you don't know (or don't care) where it is in the document, you can use the following technique. An expression like **//element_name** will output all the matching elements in the document whose name is *element_name*, wherever they may be.

XPath Functions

In the last two chapters, you learned how to use XPath location paths to specify nodes and node sets in an XML source document.

In some cases, I used location paths for further processing by templates (`xsl:template` and `xsl:apply-templates`), or in test conditions (`xsl:if` and `xsl:when`). In both of these cases, there are times that you will not need or want to use all the data in the node set returned. With XPath functions, you can apply additional logic to these node sets to return only the data you need.

In other cases, I used location paths to extract the contents of a node using `xsl:value-of`. Remember, `xsl:value-of` outputs the string value of the first node in a node set. With XPath functions, you can perform one or more operations on that string before it is output to modify the final result.

In this chapter, I will detail many common XPath functions. The official specifications for XPath Version 1.0 functions can be found at the World Wide Web Consortium site: *www.w3.org/TR/xpath#corelib*.

As noted, even though the most current version of the XPath language is 2.0, this and the previous chapter detail XPath Version 1.0. This is because version 1.0 is still the more widely used and widely supported version. XPath 2.0 is discussed in detail in Chapter 15. As well, specifications for the new version can be found at: *www.w3.org/TR/xpath20/*.

Comparing Two Values

Perhaps the most common test that you can perform on a location path is whether one value is bigger than another **(Figure 4.1)**. You can then use this answer to determine which actions should result, or simply use the resulting node set in your transformation.

To compare two values:

1. Create the path to the first node set that you want to compare.
2. Then, type **=** (equal to), **!=** (not equal to), **>** (greater than), **>=** (greater than or equal to), **<** (less than), or **<=** (less than or equal to), depending on how you want to compare the two values.
3. Finally, type a value or a path to the node set that you want to compare with the first node set identified in Step 1.

✔ Tips

- This test can be used in `xsl:template` and `xsl:apply-templates` processing, as well as condition testing using `xsl:if` and `xsl:when`.
- If you just want to test that a node set exists (regardless of its contents), skip Steps 2–3.
- String and text values in Step 3 should be enclosed in single quotes.
- Use the `and` operator to test that all of a series of multiple conditions are true. Use the `or` operator to test if at least one of a series of multiple conditions is true. Other boolean operators are not valid.
- There is also a boolean expression `not`, but it is a function, it is not an operator. For more details, see *More XPath Functions* on page 59.

```
xslt
...
<h2>Overview</h2>
 <table border="1"><tr><th>Wonder
   Name</th><th>Location</th>
   <th>Height</th></tr>

  <xsl:apply-templates
    select="ancient_wonders/
    wonder[height &gt; 100]">

  <xsl:sort select="height"
    order="descending"
    data-type="number" />
  </xsl:apply-templates>

 </table>
...
```

Figure 4.1 *In this example, I am using a comparison to refine the node set being used in the* xsl:apply-templates *instruction. Specifically, it is saying that only those* wonder *nodes that have a height greater than 100 will be used.*

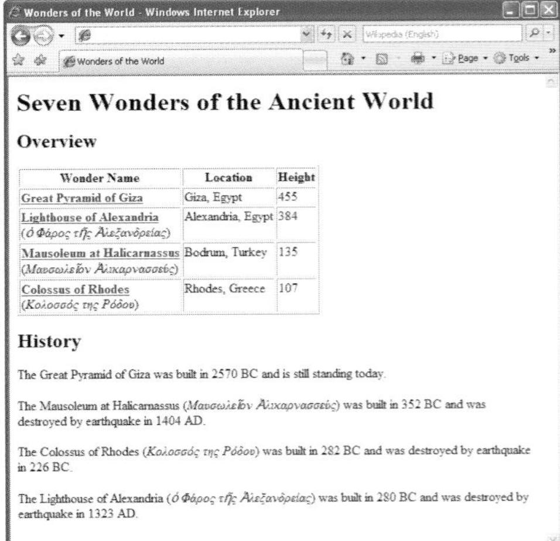

Figure 4.2 *Based on the XSLT in Figure 4.2 above, four of the seven wonders have a height greater than 100 as shown above. Notice that, in addition to the Overview section of the output, I applied the same height condition to the History section, too.*

```
xslt
...
<p>These ancient wonders are

 <xsl:for-each select=
   "ancient_wonders/wonder/name
   [@language='English']">

  <xsl:value-of select="."/>
  <xsl:choose>

   <xsl:when test=
     "position()=last()">.</xsl:when>

   <xsl:when test=
     "position()=last()-1">, and
     </xsl:when>

   <xsl:otherwise>, </xsl:otherwise>

  </xsl:choose>
 </xsl:for-each>
</p>
...
```

Figure 4.3 *Here I am using position functions to format a sentence that lists all the wonders. The wonder's name is output no matter what. If it's in the last position, a period is also output after the name. If it's in the second-to-last position (*position() = last()–1*), a comma, the word* and, *and a space are output after the name. Otherwise, if it's in any other position, only the name and a space are output.*

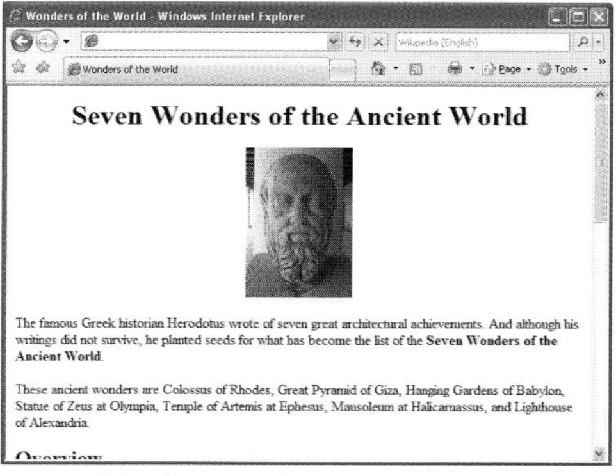

Figure 4.4 *The output from the transformation based on Figure 4.3 shows the list of the seven wonders, well-formatted with commas separating the names and a final* and *before the last wonder.*

Testing the Position

In addition to applying conditions to location paths, you can actually choose to select a specific node in the node set: the first, second, or even the last.

To test a node's position:

- Type **position() = n**, where *n* is the number that identifies the position of the node within the current node set **(Figure 4.3)**.

To find the last node in a node set:

- Type **last()** to get the last node.

✔ Tips

- You don't put anything between the parentheses in either the `position()` function or the `last()` function.
- In a predicate (a boolean expression in brackets used to test a condition), you can also use just **n** as a shortcut for **position()=n**. For example, **wonder[1]** would result in returning the first `wonder` node. (Note: You can use this shortcut in template processing, but not in `xsl:if` or `xsl:when` test expressions, or in an `xsl:value-of` instruction.)

Multiplying, Dividing, Adding, Subtracting

You can include simple arithmetic operations to your expressions. These will allow you to test for more complicated conditions or to output calculated values **(Figure 4.5)**.

To multiply, divide, add, or subtract:

1. Type the first operand. It can be a numerical constant like 12, or it can be a node set (in which case the string value of the first node is used).
2. Then, type the mathematical operator: ***** (for multiplication), **div** (for division, since / is already fraught with meaning), **+** (for addition), or **–** (for subtraction).
3. Finally, type the second operand.

✔ Tips

- Following typical math conventions, multiplication and division are performed before addition and subtraction. In other words, 4+5*3 is 19 and not 27. You can use parentheses to override the default. So, (4+5)*3 is, in fact, 27.
- To control the output of your mathematical operations (or any numeric output for that matter), you'll want to use a number formatting function *(see pages 54–55)*.
- There is a fifth operator, **mod**, for obtaining the remainder of a division. So, **20 mod 4** is 0 (since 4 divides evenly into 20), but **20 mod 3** is 2 since 20/3 is 6 with a remainder of 2.

xslt

```
...
<td valign="top">
 <xsl:choose>
 <xsl:when test="
   history/year_destroyed != 0">

  <xsl:choose>
  <xsl:when test="
    history/year_destroyed/@era =
    'BC'">
   <xsl:value-of select="
     history/year_built -
     history/year_destroyed"/>
  </xsl:when>
  <xsl:otherwise>
   <xsl:value-of select="
     history/year_built +
     history/year_destroyed - 1"/>
  </xsl:otherwise>
  </xsl:choose>

 </xsl:when>
 <xsl:otherwise>
   <xsl:value-of select="
     history/year_built + 2008 - 1"/>
 </xsl:otherwise>
 </xsl:choose>
</td>
...
```

Figure 4.5 *I added a new column to the Overview section called Years Standing. The math is pretty straightforward, but one complicated part of the logic is explained here: Since all the wonders were built in the BC era, if they were destroyed in the AD era or are still standing, I need to add, not subtract, the* year_built *and the* year_destroyed.

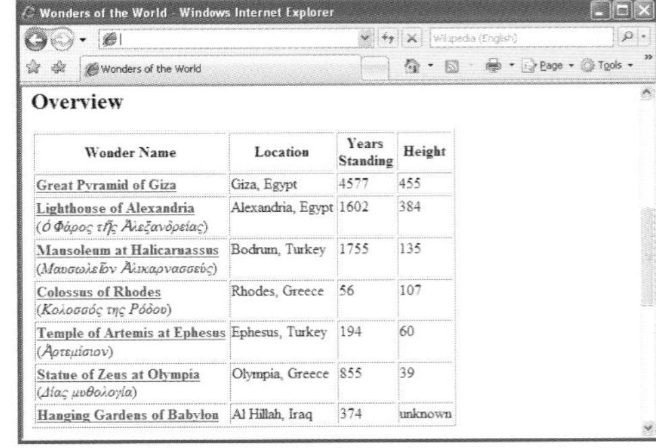

Figure 4.6 *If you do a little math using this HTML output from the XSLT in Figure 4.6, you'll see that in 260 years, the Great Pyramid of Giza will have stood longer than all the other wonders combined.*

```
xslt
...
Of these wonders,
<xsl:value-of select="
  count(ancient_wonders/wonder/
  history/how_destroyed[. =
  'earthquake'])" />
were destroyed by earthquake,

<xsl:value-of select="
 count(//how_destroyed[. = 'fire'])"/>
were destroyed by fire, and

<xsl:value-of select="
  count(//wonder) -
  count(//how_destroyed)" />
is still standing.
...
```

Figure 4.7 *In the first* count() *function I am using an absolute location path to return the number of wonders that were destroyed in an earthquake. In the last two, I used the // shortcut to return all nodes in the entire document that match the expression.*

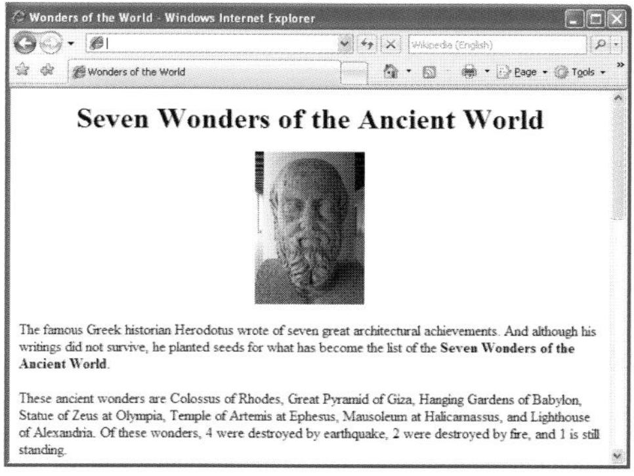

Figure 4.8 *Based on the XSLT from Figure 4.7, more than half the wonders were destroyed by earthquake.*

Counting Nodes

Often, rather than doing arithmetic on a set of nodes, you may simply want to know how many nodes there are **(Figure 4.7)**.

To count nodes:

1. Type **count(**.
2. Then, type the path to the node set whose nodes should be counted.
3. Finally, type **)** to complete the function.

✔ Tip

- The location path referenced in Step 2 can optionally include predicates. This is shown in the first two instances of `count()` in Figure 4.7.

Counting Nodes

Formatting Numbers

In XPath, arithmetic is done using floating point math which can make for long output **(Figures 4.9 and 4.10)**. Fortunately, with the `format-number` function, you can easily control the output format of numbers.

To format numbers:

1. Type **format-number(**.
2. Then, type the expression which contains the number to be formatted.
3. Next, type **, '** (a comma, a space, and a single quote).
4. Then, type **0** for each digit that should always appear, and **#** for each digit that should only appear when not zero. If desired, type **.** (a period), to separate the integer part of a number from the fractional part, and **,** (a comma), to separate groups of digits in the integer part.
5. Finally, type **')** (a single quote followed by a right parentheses) to complete the number pattern and the function **(Figure 4.11)**.

✔ Tips

- Use `#,##0.00` to output at least one digit in the number, with commas separating every three digits, and exactly two digits in the fractional part of the number (as in dollars and cents: 269.40). With `#,000.0#`, numbers with tenths (but not hundredths) would have no final zero, for example: 269.4.
- Negative numbers are preceded by a minus sign (–) by default. If you'd rather that they be surrounded by parentheses, add **;(0)** after Step 4 above.

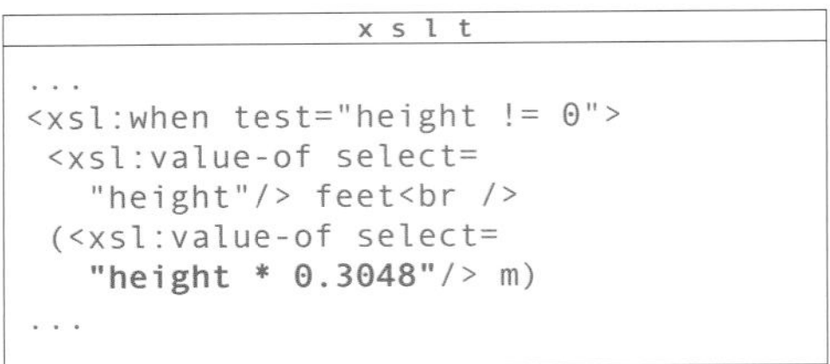

```
xslt
...
<xsl:when test="height != 0">
 <xsl:value-of select=
   "height"/> feet<br />
 (<xsl:value-of select=
   "height * 0.3048"/> m)
...
```

Figure 4.9 *In this excerpt, I am outputting the height in feet and then converting the height to meters for output as well.*

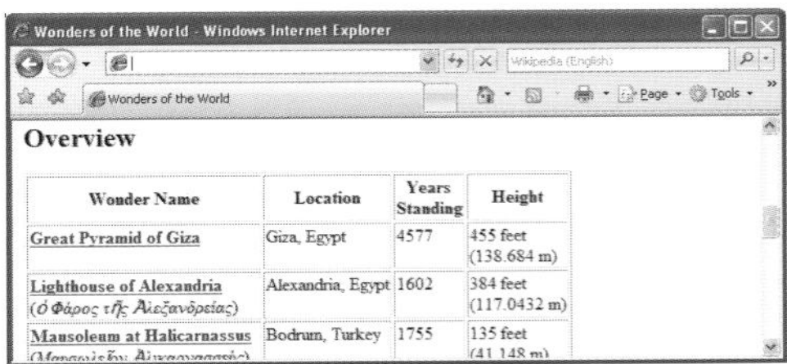

Wonder Name	Location	Years Standing	Height
Great Pyramid of Giza	Giza, Egypt	4577	455 feet (138.684 m)
Lighthouse of Alexandria (ὁ Φάρος τῆς Ἀλεξανδρείας)	Alexandria, Egypt	1602	384 feet (117.0432 m)
Mausoleum at Halicarnassus	Bodrum, Turkey	1755	135 feet

Figure 4.10 *Remember that arithmetic is done using floating point math which, as I said, can make for really ugly output.*

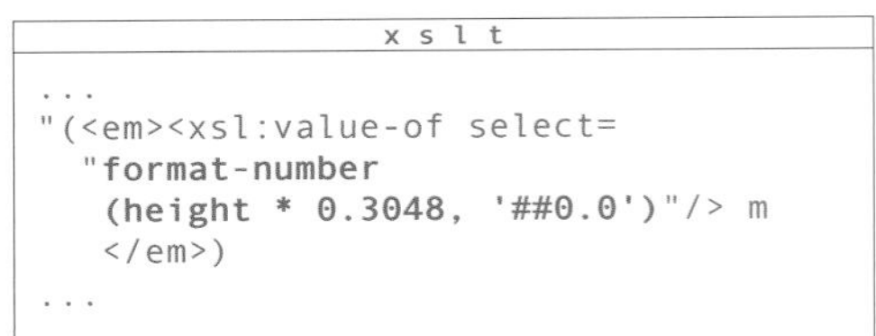

```
xslt
...
"(<em><xsl:value-of select=
  "format-number
  (height * 0.3048, '##0.0')"/> m
  </em>)
...
```

Figure 4.11 *The number being formatted is the same as in Figure 4.10 above. Now it will be formatted with at least one digit to the left of the decimal point, (but numbers are never truncated to the left) and exactly one digit to the right of the decimal point.*

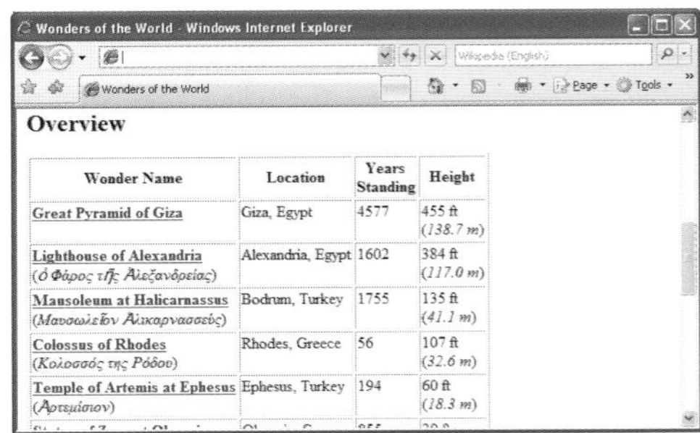

Wonder Name	Location	Years Standing	Height
Great Pyramid of Giza	Giza, Egypt	4577	455 ft (*138.7 m*)
Lighthouse of Alexandria (ὁ Φάρος τῆς Ἀλεξανδρείας)	Alexandria, Egypt	1602	384 ft (*117.0 m*)
Mausoleum at Halicarnassus (Μαυσωλεῖον Ἁλικαρνασσεύς)	Bodrum, Turkey	1755	135 ft (*41.1 m*)
Colossus of Rhodes (Κολοσσός της Ρόδου)	Rhodes, Greece	56	107 ft (*32.6 m*)
Temple of Artemis at Ephesus (Ἀρτεμίσιον)	Ephesus, Turkey	194	60 ft (*18.3 m*)

Figure 4.12 *Now, the numbers look much better without quite so many digits.*

Formatting Numbers

```
x m l
<main_image
 file="artemis.jpg" w="528" h="349"/>
```

Figure 4.13 *In this XML excerpt, you can see that the image's size is 528 pixels wide by 349 pixels tall.*

```
x s l t
...
<img>
 <xsl:attribute name="src">
   <xsl:value-of select=
     "./@file"/></xsl:attribute>
 <xsl:attribute name="width">
   <xsl:value-of select=
     "ceiling(./@w div 2)"/>
 </xsl:attribute>
 <xsl:attribute name="height">
   <xsl:value-of select=
     "ceiling(./@h div 2)"/>
   </xsl:attribute>
 </img>
...
```

Figure 4.14 *I'd like the pictures to be shown at half their regular size. Since the* width *and* height *attributes only accept integers, I use the* ceiling() *function to round the division up to the nearest integer.*

```
h t m l
...
<p align="center">
 <img src="artemis.jpg"
   width="264" height="175"/>
...
```

Figure 4.15 *After the XPath* ceiling() *function in , the* width *and* height *of the image are now half of their original values.*

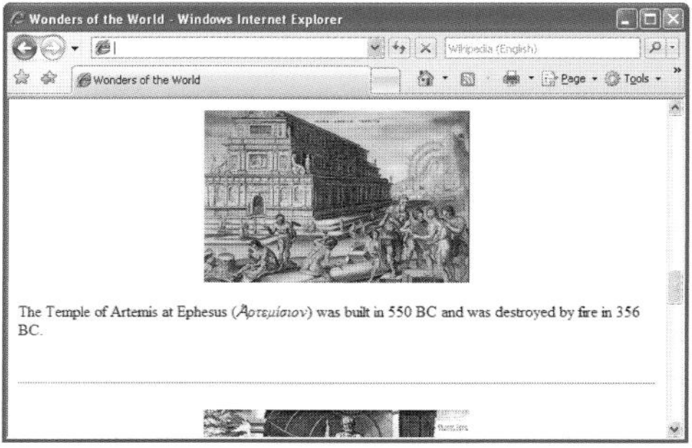

Figure 4.16 *The wonder images now display at half their normal size: 264 by 175 pixels.*

Rounding Numbers

There are three XPath functions for rounding numbers in your data source **(Figure 4.13)**. You can round to the nearest integer (round), always round up (ceiling) (), or always round down (floor).

To round numbers:

1. Type **ceiling(**, **floor(**, or **round(**, depending on whether you want to round up, down, or to the nearest integer.
2. Then, type the expression which contains the number to be formatted.
3. Finally, type **)** to complete the function.

✔ Tip

- When using the `format-number()` function, described on page 54, if there are any decimal places lost, the XSLT processor will automatically round the resulting number being output.

Extracting Substrings

When processing XML for output, it's often useful to dig into a string and take out only the bit that you need. In this example **(Figure 4.16)**, I am breaking up the `location` element into city and country by using the comma that separates them.

To extract a substring that comes before or after a particular character:

1. Type **substring-after(** or **substring-before(**, depending on whether you want to extract the part of the string that comes before or after the character.
2. Then, type the expression which contains the source string.
3. Next, type **, c**, where *c* is the character after or before the substring that will be extracted.
4. Finally, type **)** to complete the function.

✔ Tip

- You can also extract a substring in the middle of a string if you know the position of the first character you want and the total number of characters after that. You would use the `substring(s,f,n)` function, where *s* is the expression which contains the source string, *f* is the position of the first character that you want to extract, and *n* is the total number of characters you want.

```
xslt
...
<h2>Overview</h2>
<table border="1"><tr><th>Wonder Name
  </th><th>City</th><th>Country</th>
  <th>Years<br />Standing</th>
  <th>Height</th></tr>
...
<td valign="top">
 <xsl:value-of select="
   substring-before(location, ',')"/>
</td>
<td valign="top">
 <xsl:value-of select="
   substring-after(location, ',')"/>
</td>
...
```

Figure 4.17 *In the XML document, the* location *element contains both the wonder's city and country. Here, I am separating the location element into two separate outputs of city and country. I am using the string before the comma for city, and after the comma for country.*

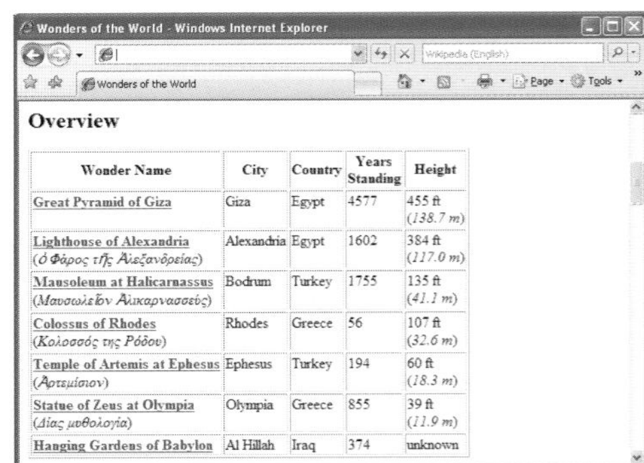

Figure 4.18 *After the XSLT in Figure 4.16, each wonder's city and country is displayed in a separate column in the Overview section.*

```
xslt
...
<p align="center">
<strong><xsl:value-of select="
translate(../name[@language='English']
,'abcdefghijklmnopqrstuvwxyz'
,'ABCDEFGHIJKLMNOPQRSTUVWXYZ')"/>
</strong><br />

<xsl:apply-templates select="
  ../main_image"/>
</p>
...
```

Figure 4.19 *In the History section, I am going to output the wonder's name above the image of the wonder. And I am going to translate the wonder's name to be all uppercase.*

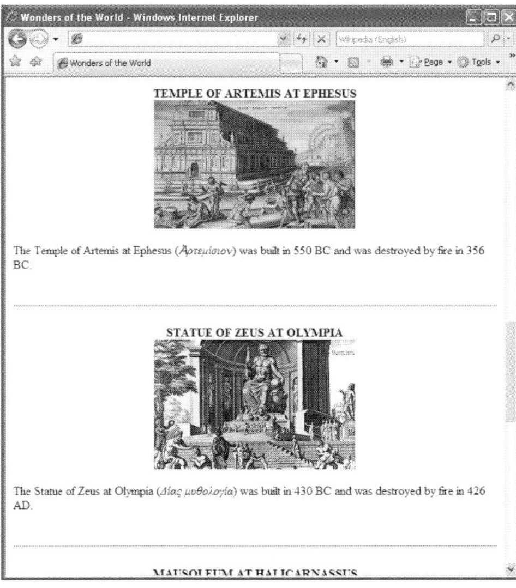

Figure 4.20 *The XSLT in Figure 4.18 capitalized each wonder's name as a header in the History section.*

Changing the Case of a String

When manipulating text, it's often important to be able to change letters from upper- to lowercase and back again.

To capitalize strings:

1. Type **translate(**.
2. Then, type the expression which contains the source string.
3. Next, type **, 'abcdefghijklmnopqrstuvwxyz'** (that is; a comma, a space, and the string which contains the letters to change).
4. Then, type **, 'ABCDEFGHIJKLMNOPQRST UVWXYZ'** (that is; a comma, a space, and the string which contains the letters that you want to replace from Step 3).
5. Finally, type **)** to complete the function **(Figure 4.18)**.

✔ Tips

- To change letters from lower- to uppercase, swap Step 3 with Step 4.
- You can use the `translate()` function to translate any character into any other character. Type the letters that should be changed in Step 3, and the letters that these should be changed into in Step 4.
- In XPath Language Version 2.0, there are many more string manipulation functions, including one to specifically convert to and from upper- and lowercase.

Totaling Values

You can use the XPath `sum()` function to add up all the values of the nodes in a node set **(Figure 4.20)**. It's great for displaying data in tables and columns **(Figure 4.21)**.

To total values:

1. Type **sum(**.
2. Then, type the path to the node set whose nodes should be totaled.
3. Finally, type **)** to complete the function.

✔ Tip

■ As shown in the example in Figure 4.20, you can combine many XPath functions together in the same output. This allows you to create very specific transformations of the XML data source.

```
xslt
...
<tr>
<td valign="top" align="right"
  colspan="4">Average Height: </td>
<td valign="top">
 <xsl:value-of select="
 format-number(
  sum(/ancient_wonders/wonder/height)
 div
  count(/ancient_wonders/wonder/
   height[.!=0]),
 '##0.0')" />
 ft</td>
</tr>
...
```

Figure 4.21 *I'm creating a row to show the average height of all the wonders. To find the average, I use the* sum() *function to add up all the values of the* height *nodes. Then I divide the total height by the number of wonders which don't have a height of zero. Finally, I format the output to show one value to the right of the decimal point.*

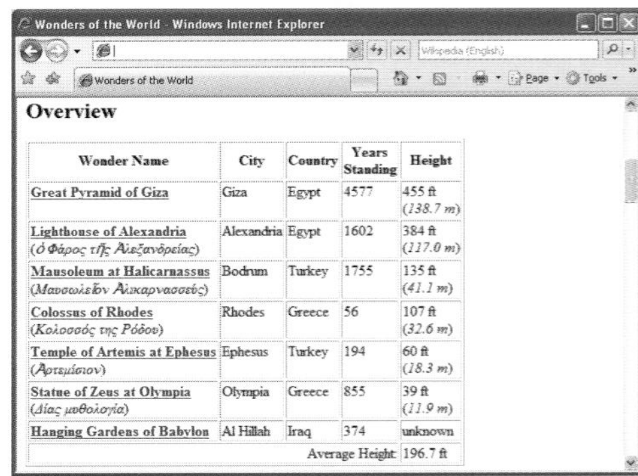

Figure 4.22 *The average height of all the wonders was nearly 20 stories high.*

```
xslt
<xsl:template match="history">
...
 <xsl:value-of select="story"/>
 <br /><br />
```

Figure 4.23 *To complete the output of the wonders-master.xml document, I add the* story *element to the History section. See Figure 4.23 below for a screenshot of the final HTML.*

Figure 4.24 *After all the XSLT and XPath work, here is screenshot of the final HTML output!*

More XPath Functions

In addition to the XPath functions detailed in this chapter, here are some additional functions you might find useful. For a full list of the functions in XPath Version 1.0, see *www.w3.org/TR/xpath#corelib*.

Node Functions:

- **name(node-set)** returns the first node in the specified node set, and **name()** returns the name of the current node.
- **id(id-str)** returns all the elements that have an ID equal to *id-str*.

String Functions:

- **contains(str1, str2)** returns True if *str1* contains *str2*, otherwise returns False.
- **string-length(str1)** returns the number of characters in *str1*, while **string-length()** returns the number of characters in the current node.
- **normalize-space(str1)** returns *str1* with all leading and trailing white space removed, and sequences of white space replaced with a single space. **normalize-space()** performs the same action on the current node.

Boolean Functions:

- **not(expression)** returns True if *expression* evaluates to False, and returns False if *expression* evaluates to True.
- **|** (a vertical bar; often located above the \ on your keyboard). Although it's technically not a function, it is used to combine two node sets into one.

✔ Tip

- While XPath 1.0 remains the most widely used version, it only provides a limited set of functions. If there is functionality you really need, you can look at XPath Version 2.0, which has a larger set of functions and operators. The specifications can be found at: *www.w3.org/TR/xpath20/*.

5

XSL-FO

As I mentioned in Chapter 2, the eXtensible Stylesheet Language (*XSL*), was originally a single specification for formatting XML documents. But before finishing it, the W3C divided XSL into two pieces: XSLT (for *T*ransformations) and XSL-FO (for *F*ormatting *O*bjects). I discussed XSLT in the last three chapters. In this chapter, I'll discuss XSL-FO.

XSL-FO is essentially a typesetting language. It enables you to easily specify page layouts, including setting margins and line spacing; creating headers, footers, and marginalia; and generating endnotes, footnotes, columnar page content, cover sheets, and tables of content.

XSL-FO is an XML-based markup language, and was designed to format XML data. You have already seen how XSLT can format XML data, transforming it into HTML. XSL-FO, however, was specifically designed to format XML data for output to print. In this chapter, the XSL-FO examples that I use will generate printable output in the Adobe PDF format.

In order to see the examples work, or to write XSL-FO yourself, you will need an XSL-FO processor. If you don't have one already, see Appendix A, *XML Tools,* for a list of options.

In 2001, XSL-FO 1.0 became an official W3C Recommendation, and was updated in 2006 to version 1.1. In March 2008, a Working Draft of version 2.0 was released. For additional information, visit the W3C's XSL Working Group site at: *www.w3.org/Style/XSL*.

The Two Parts of an XSL-FO Document

An XSL-FO document is a text-only file containing XSL-FO markup and literal content. With this document, an XSL-FO processor can generate one of many different printable outputs, including: Portable Document Format (PDF), Maker Interchange Format (MIF), PostScript (PS), and others.

Every XSL-FO document **(Figure 5.1)** can be broken into two parts, both of which are enclosed in a top-level element `fo:root`. The first part describes the *overall structure* of the final output. It does so by using XSL-FO elements and attributes to set page width / height, margins, and sidebars, as well as identify different page templates (such as those for a cover page, table of contents, odd- and even-numbered pages, or the content itself).

The overall structure part of an XSL-FO document contains an `fo:layout-master-set` element which is a container for one or more `fo:simple-page-master` child elements. These child elements describe page templates which are broken up into five region elements, such as `fo:region-body`, used for the body region of a page template.

The second part of an XSL-FO document contains and formats the *page content* of the final output. In this part, there are `fo:page-sequence` elements, each of which corresponds to an `fo:simple-page-master` element defined in the overall structure part of the document. Each page sequence contains one `fo:flow` child element for each of the regions defined within the `fo:simple-page-master` element. Finally, each `flow` element has one or more `fo:block` child elements, and each `block` element contains actual page content.

xsl-fo

```
<?xml version="1.0"?>

<fo:root xmlns:fo="http://
  www.w3.org/1999/XSL/Format">

<!-- overall structure -->
 <fo:layout-master-set>
  <fo:simple-page-master
    master-name="wonders_cover"
    page-width="8.5in"
    page-height="11in" margin="1in">
   <fo:region-body/>
  </fo:simple-page-master>
 </fo:layout-master-set>

<!-- page content -->
 <fo:page-sequence
   master-reference="wonders_cover">
  <fo:flow
    flow-name="xsl-region-body">
   <fo:block font-size="28pt"
     text-align="center">
    Seven Wonders of the Ancient
      World</fo:block>
   <fo:block font-size="14pt"
     text-align="justify"
     space-before=".25in">
     The famous Greek historian
     Herodotus wrote of seven great
     architectural achievements.
...
  </fo:flow>
 </fo:page-sequence>

</fo:root>
```

Figure 5.1 *The* overall structure *part of this XSL-FO excerpt defines a page template with* page-width, page-height, *and* margin *elements. The* page content *part contains the literal text* Seven Wonders of the Ancient World, *formatted as 28-point text, and additional text about Herodotus, formatted as 14-point justified text.*

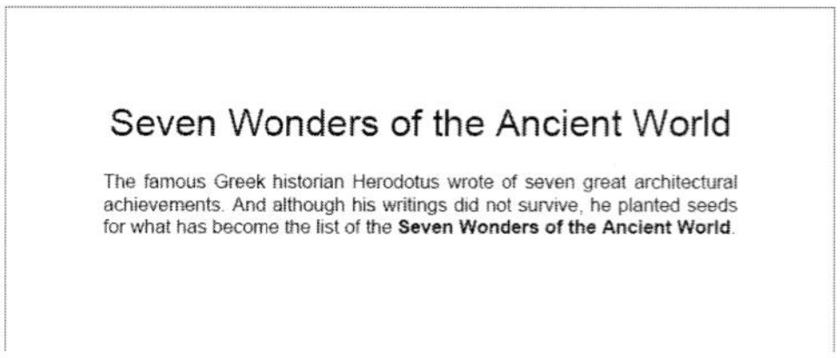

Seven Wonders of the Ancient World

The famous Greek historian Herodotus wrote of seven great architectural achievements. And although his writings did not survive, he planted seeds for what has become the list of the **Seven Wonders of the Ancient World**.

Figure 5.2 *When processed, the XSL-FO document in Figure 5.1 generates a final output document. In this case, I have created a PDF file (the top of which is shown above) from the XSL-FO document.*

```
xsl-fo
<?xml version="1.0"?>

<fo:root xmlns:fo="http://
  www.w3.org/1999/XSL/Format">

<!-- overall structure -->
 <fo:layout-master-set>
  <fo:simple-page-master
    master-name="wonders">
   <fo:region-body/>
  </fo:simple-page-master>
 </fo:layout-master-set>

<!-- page content -->
 <fo:page-sequence
   master-reference="wonders">
  <fo:flow
    flow-name="xsl-region-body">
   <fo:block>
     Colossus of Rhodes</fo:block>
  </fo:flow>
 </fo:page-sequence>

</fo:root>
```

Figure 5.3 *This is a complete XSL-FO document. The page template is named* wonders *and contains a body region, which is filled with the text* Colossus of Rhodes. *Notice that an XSL-FO document can be very sparse in content, but it still requires both the* overall structure *and* page content *parts.*

Colossus of Rhodes

Figure 5.4 *This is the top of the PDF file, which was generated by processing the XSL-FO document in Figure 5.3.*

Creating an XSL-FO Document

XSL-FO is an XML markup language, so XSL-FO documents are written using XML syntax. The first line of an XSL-FO document is the standard XML declaration, and it must contain a single root element **(Figure 5.3)**. XSL-FO documents are text-only files and are saved with an `.fo` extension.

To create an XSL-FO document:

1. Type **<?xml version="1.0"?>**.
2. Type **<fo:root** to define the root element of the XSL-FO document. Notice the `fo:` namespace prefix; it is defined next.
3. Then, type **xmlns:fo="http://www.w3.org/1999/XSL/Format"** to declare the XSL-FO namespace with the `fo:` prefix.
4. Finally, type **>** to close the tag.
5. Type **<fo:layout-master-set>** to start the overall structure part of the document.
6. Type **<fo:simple-page-master master-name="master">**, where *master* is the page template name used in Step 10.
7. Type **<fo:region-body/>** to declare that this page master will contain content in the body region.
8. Type **</fo:simple-page-master>**.
9. Type **</fo:layout-master-set>**.
10. Then, type **<fo:page-sequence master-reference="master">**, where *master* is the same name defined in Step 6. This begins the page content part of the document.
11. Type **<fo:flow flow-name="xsl-region-body">**. Here, `xsl-region-body` refers to the body region declared in Step 7.
12. Enter the page content for your final output using `fo:block` elements.
13. Type **</fo:flow>**.
14. Type **</fo:page-sequence>**.
15. Finally, type **</fo:root>** to complete the XSL-FO document.

Creating and Styling Blocks of Page Content

In XSL-FO, content such as paragraphs and headlines are contained in *blocks*. The XSL-FO processor retrieves each block's content, applies its style properties, and then stacks each block one after the other to generate the final output.

To create a block of page content:

1. As a child element to an `fo:flow` element, type **<fo:block (Figure 5.5)**.
2. Set any style properties (see below) you wish to apply to the block of page content in Step 4 below.
3. Then, type **>** to close the tag.
4. Write the literal page content, which is the text value of this `fo:block` element.
5. Finally, type **</fo:block>**.

To style a block of page content:

◆ As an attribute of an `fo:block` element, type the name of the style property and its value. For example:

font-size="f_size", where *f_size* can be a length in inches (`in`), points (`pt`), and others; an absolute size (such as `small`, `x-large`, and others); a relative size (such as `larger` or `smaller`); a percentage in numeric value or em's; or `inherit`, which uses the parent's `font-size` value.

space-after="s_after", where *s_after* can be a length in inches (`in`), points (`pt`), and others; or `inherit`, which uses the parent's `space-after` value.

✔ Tip

■ The `fo:block` element can have `fo:block` child elements, and any inheritable style properties in the parent will be applied to each child. If not automatically inherited, setting the child's style property value to `inherit` will use the parent's value.

```
xsl-fo
...
<!-- page content -->
 <fo:page-sequence
   master-reference="wonders">
  <fo:flow
    flow-name="xsl-region-body">
   <fo:block font-size="24pt"
     space-after="0.2in">
    Colossus of Rhodes
   </fo:block>
   <fo:block font-size="14pt">
    <fo:block space-after="0.1in">
     In 294 BC, the people of the
     island of Rhodes began building
...
    </fo:block>
    <fo:block space-after="0.1in">
     The Colossus was built with
     bronze, reinforced with iron,
...
    </fo:block>
   </fo:block>
  </fo:flow>
 </fo:page-sequence>

</fo:root>
```

Figure 5.5 *In this excerpt, I added more page content to the XSL-FO document shown in Figure 5.3 by using a number of additional* fo:block *elements. I also applied a few style properties to each of the blocks.*

Colossus of Rhodes

In 294 BC, the people of the island of Rhodes began building a colossal statue of the sun god Helios. They believed that it was because of his blessings that they were able to withstand a long siege on the island and emerge victorious.

The Colossus was built with bronze, reinforced with iron, and weighted with stones. While it is often depicted straddling Mandrákion harbor, this is now considered technically impossible; and therefore, it likely stood beside the harbor.

The statue was toppled by an earthquake in 226 BC. It snapped at the knees and fell over on to the land. The Oracle of Delphi suggested that it fell because the people of Rhodes had offended Helios, and they decided not to rebuild it.

The statue remained on the ground until 654 AD., and even broken, it was so impressive that many traveled to see it.

Figure 5.6 *After processing the XSL-FO document, each* fo:block *element is styled using its style properties, and stacked on top of the other in the final output.*

Look Familiar?

Many styling properties of the `fo:block` element are the same as Cascading Style Sheets (CSS) properties. If you already know CSS, that knowledge will apply to styling XSL-FO output as well.

```
xsl-fo
...
<!-- page content -->
 <fo:page-sequence
   master-reference="wonders">
  <fo:flow
    flow-name="xsl-region-body">
   <fo:block font-size="24pt"
     text-align="center"
     space-after="0.2in">
    Colossus of Rhodes
   </fo:block>
   <fo:block text-align="center"
     space-after="0.2in">
    <fo:external-graphic
      src="url('colossus.jpg')"
      content-height="3.5in"
      border-style="ridge"
      border-width="thick"/>
   </fo:block>
   <fo:block font-size="14pt">
    <fo:block space-after="0.1in">
...
```

Figure 5.7 *I added the* colossus.jpg *image to the XSL-FO document. It will display center-aligned in the final output with a thick ridge border, and be 3.5 inches tall. I also decided to center the wonder's name because I thought it looked better that way.*

Colossus of Rhodes

In 294 BC, the people of the island of Rhodes began building a colossal statue of the sun god Helios. They believed that it was because of his blessings that they were able to withstand a long siege on the island and emerge victorious.

The Colossus was built with bronze, reinforced with iron, and weighted with stones. While it is often depicted straddling Mandrákion harbor, this is now considered technically impossible; and therefore, it likely stood beside the harbor.

The statue was toppled by an earthquake in 226 BC. It snapped at the knees and fell over on to the land. The Oracle of Delphi suggested that it fell because the people of Rhodes had offended Helios, and they decided not to rebuild it.

The statue remained on the ground until 654 AD., and even broken, it was so impressive that many traveled to see it.

Figure 5.8 *The colossus.jpg image is treated like any other page content contained in a block; it is stacked, in order, and its styles are applied for the final output (in this case, being center-aligned with a 0.2-inch space after it).*

Adding Images

In addition to text content, the `fo:block` element can also contain images. The `fo:external-graphic` element, which identifies the image, can also have its own style properties defined **(Figure 5.7)**.

To add an image:

1. As a child element to an `fo:block` element, type **<fo:external-graphic**.
2. Then, type **src="graphic.uri"**, where *graphic.uri* is the path to the image file you wish to include in the final output.
3. Finally, type **/>** to close the element.

Some common style properties of the `fo:external-graphic` element include:

- **content-height="c_height"**, where *c_height* can be `auto`, which means to use the actual height of the image; `scale-to-fit`, which means to scale the image to fit in the block space provided by the XSL-FO; a length in inches (`in`), points (`pt`), and others; a percentage in numeric value or em's; or `inherit`, which uses the parent's `content-height` value. Note that when an image's `content-height` property is set, but its `content-width` property is not, the image is scaled proportionally.
- **border-style="b_style"**, where *b_style* can be `none` or `hidden`, which will not show a border; `dotted`, `dashed`, `solid`, `double`, `groove`, `ridge`, `inset`, `outset` (each of which is a specific visual style of border); or `inherit`, which uses the parent's `border-style` value.
- **border-width="b_width"**, where *b_width* can be `thin`, `medium`, `thick` (each of which is increasingly wide); a length in inches (`in`), points (`pt`), and others; or `inherit`, which uses the parent's `border-width` value.

Defining a Page Template

The root element of an XSL-FO document is fo:root. Also, as I explained, it contains two parts: One defining the final output's overall structure and one defining the final output's page content. In the last two pages, I focused on the page content part of an XSL-FO document. Now, I will focus on the overall structure.

The overall structure part is contained in a single fo:layout-master-set element, which has one or more fo:simple-page-master child elements. These elements define the page templates in which the page content is output.

To define a page template:

◆ As an attribute of an fo:simple-page-master element, type the name of the style property and the value of which to apply **(Figure 5.9)**. For example:

page-width="p_width", where *p_width* can be a length in inches (in), points (pt), and others; auto (the default setting) means the page width is determined by the XSL-FO processor; or indefinite, which means the width is determined by the size of the page content.

page-width="p_height", where *p_height* has the same options as page-width.

margin="m_value", where *m_value* is a length in inches (in), points (pt), and others.

✔ Tip

■ *Shorthand properties* are style properties that set more than one subproperty with a single attribute and value. For example, setting the margin property actually sets margin-top, margin-right, margin-bottom, and margin-left. On the previous page, border-style and border-width are also shorthand properties, setting -top, -right, -bottom and -left.

xsl-fo

```
<?xml version="1.0"?>

<fo:root xmlns:fo="http://
  www.w3.org/1999/XSL/Format">

<!-- overall structure -->
 <fo:layout-master-set>

  <fo:simple-page-master
    master-name="wonders"
    page-width="8.5in"
    page-height="11in" margin="1in">
   <fo:region-body/>
  </fo:simple-page-master>

 </fo:layout-master-set>
...
```

Figure 5.9 *The* fo:simple-page-master *element uses the* master-name *attribute to define a page template named* wonders. *By setting the style property attributes of the* fo:simple-page-master *element, I have defined that the* wonders *page template is 8.5 inches wide by 11 inches tall, and has a 1-inch margin on the top, right, bottom, and left.*

Colossus of Rhodes

In 294 BC, the people of the island of Rhodes began building a colossal statue of the sun god Helios. They believed that it was because of his blessings that they were able to withstand a long siege on the island and emerge victorious.

The Colossus was built with bronze, reinforced with iron, and weighted with stones. While it is often depicted straddling Mandrákion harbor, this is now considered technically impossible; and therefore, it likely stood beside the harbor.

The statue was toppled by an earthquake in 226 BC. It snapped at the knees and fell over on to the land. The Oracle of Delphi suggested that it fell because the people of Rhodes had offended Helios, and they decided not to rebuild it.

The statue remained on the ground until 654 AD., and even broken, it was so impressive that many traveled to see it.

Figure 5.10 *Unlike the PDF example shown in Figure 5.8, here the page content does not butt up against the top and left edges of the page; rather, there's a 1-inch margin on all sides.*

```
xsl-fo
...
<!-- overall structure -->
 <fo:layout-master-set>
  <fo:simple-page-master
    master-name="wonders"
    page-width="8.5in"
    page-height="11in">
   <fo:region-body margin="1in"/>
   <fo:region-before extent="1in"/>
  </fo:simple-page-master>
 </fo:layout-master-set>
...
```

Figure 5.11 *The header* (fo:region-before) *is defined to be 1 inch tall. To avoid overlapping content (see the Tip on this page) the body* (fo:region-body) *must have a 1-inch margin. Also, since the body now has a 1-inch margin, I removed the margin setting from the page template* (fo:simple-page-master).

```
xsl-fo
...
<!-- page content -->
 <fo:page-sequence
   master-reference="wonders">
  <fo:static-content
    flow-name="xsl-region-before">
   <fo:block font-size="18pt"
     text-align="center"
     border-bottom-width="medium"
     border-bottom-style="solid"
     margin="0.25in">
    Seven Wonders of the Ancient
    World</fo:block>
  </fo:static-content>
...
```

Figure 5.12 *The page content for the header is defined in the* <fo:static-content flow-name="xsl-region-before"> *element. This is a child element of the* fo:page-sequence *element whose* master-reference *attribute is equal to "wonders."*

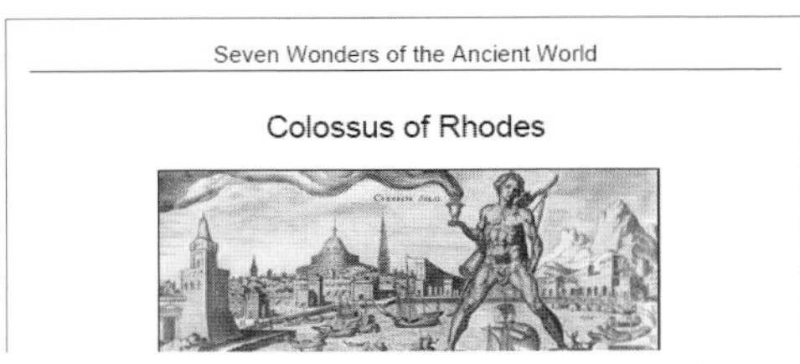

Figure 5.13 *The header content,* Seven Wonders of the Ancient World, *is output as 18 point, center-aligned text, with a medium-width, solid, bottom-aligned border.*

Creating a Page Template Header

So far, I have only used the body region of a page template defined by the `fo:region-body` element. There are four other page template regions that can be defined, which correspond to the header, footer, and left and right sidebars.

To create the structure for a header:

1. As a child element to an `fo:simple-page-master` element, and after the `fo:region-body` element, type **<fo:region-before (Figure 5.11)**. (Make note of the `master-name` attribute in the `fo:simple-page-master` element.)
2. Then, type **extent="e_value"**, where *e_value* is the height of the header region.
3. Set any style property attributes for the region, such as `background` and `border`.
4. Finally, type **/>** to close the element.

To set the page content for a header:

1. Locate the `fo:page-sequence` element whose `master-reference` attribute equals the `master-name` attribute from Step 1 above. As a child element of this element, type **<fo:static-content (Figure 5.12)**.
2. Then, type **flow-name="xsl-region-before">**. (`xsl-region-before` refers to the header region defined by the `fo:region-before` element.)
3. Write `fo:block` elements to define the page content for your header.
4. Finally, type **<fo:static-content/>**.

✔ Tip

- Although defined separately, the header region (as well as the footer, and left and right sidebar regions) is *part of* the body region. Consequently, the `margin` of the body region must be equal to (or greater than) the `extent` of the header region. If not, the body will overlap the header.

Using XSLT to Create XSL-FO

Remember, XSL-FO was designed to format XML documents, not literal text as I have shown thus far. Also, remember that XSL was originally one specification, but was split into two: XSLT and XSL-FO. By recombining these languages, you will first transform the XML source data (XSLT), and then you will format the transformed content into a final output document for publication (XSL-FO).

How to combine XSLT with XSL-FO:

1. Instead of starting with an XSL-FO document, start with an XSLT document **(Figure 5.14)**. Refer to *XSLT*, Part 2 of the book for details.
2. Within the `xsl:stylesheet` element, type **xmlns:fo="http://www.w3.org/1999/XSL/Format"** to declare the XSL-FO namespace.
3. Type **<xsl:output method="xml" indent="yes"/>** to define the output `method` to be xml (and indent this xml output which makes for easier reading).
4. Create the XSLT root template (`<xsl:template match="/">`) which will contain the entire XSL-FO document tree beginning with *its* root element, **<fo:root>**.
5. Finally, use XSLT elements, such as `xsl:apply-templates` **(Figure 5.15)**, to generate the XSL-FO page content. These XSLT elements will then call the `xsl:template` elements using the `xsl:value-of` elements **(Figure 5.16)**.

✔ Tip

- When this XSLT is processed, the output it generates is an XSL-FO document. You can then process the XSL-FO document and generate a publishable final output. Some XSLT / XSL-FO processors can even go directly from XSLT, through XSL-FO, to the final output with a single command.

xslt

```
<?xml version="1.0"?>
<xsl:stylesheet xmlns:xsl="http://
  www.w3.org/1999/XSL/Transform"
  version="1.0" xmlns:fo="http://
  www.w3.org/1999/XSL/Format">
 <xsl:output method="xml"
   indent="yes"/>

 <xsl:template match="/">
  <fo:root>
   <!-- overall layout -->
   <fo:layout-master-set>
...
```

Figure 5.14 *Here, I am using XSLT to generate the XSL-FO document shown in Figures 5.11 and 5.12. Actually, the XSL-FO being generated will include all wonders, not just the Colossus of Rhodes. This XSLT continues in the two examples below.*

xslt

```
...
<fo:flow flow-name="xsl-region-body">
 <xsl:apply-templates select=
   "ancient_wonders/wonder/name
   [@language='English']">
  <xsl:sort select="."
    order="ascending"/>
 </xsl:apply-templates>
</fo:flow>
...
```

Figure 5.15 *In the XSL-FO page templates (where the page content is entered), instead of typing literal text, I am using the XSLT* xsl:apply-templates *element. I'm calling the* name *template for each* wonder *with an English-language name, in alphabetical order.*

xslt

```
...
<xsl:template match="name">
 <fo:block font-size="24pt"
   text-align="center"
   space-after="0.2in">
  <xsl:value-of select="."/>
 </fo:block>
...
```

Figure 5.16 *This XSLT* name *template excerpt creates an XSL-FO block containing a wonder's name in 24 point, centered text, with 0.2 inches of space afterwards. This is the same styling I have used for* Colossus of Rhodes *in the previous examples.*

```
xslt
...
<xsl:template match="name">
 <fo:block font-size="24pt"
   text-align="center"
   space-after="0.2in"
   break-before="page">
  <xsl:value-of select="."/>
 </fo:block>
...
```

Figure 5.17 *This XSLT excerpt shows that a page break will be inserted before the block that outputs each wonder's name. This XSLT continues below.*

```
xslt
...
<fo:static-content
  flow-name="xsl-region-after">
 <fo:block font-size="9pt"
   text-align="right" margin="0.5in"
   margin-top="0.25in">
  Page <fo:page-number/>
 </fo:block>
</fo:static-content>
...
```

Figure 5.18 *This excerpt of XSL-FO code within the XSLT template will output in the footer the literal text* Page, *followed by the current page number.*

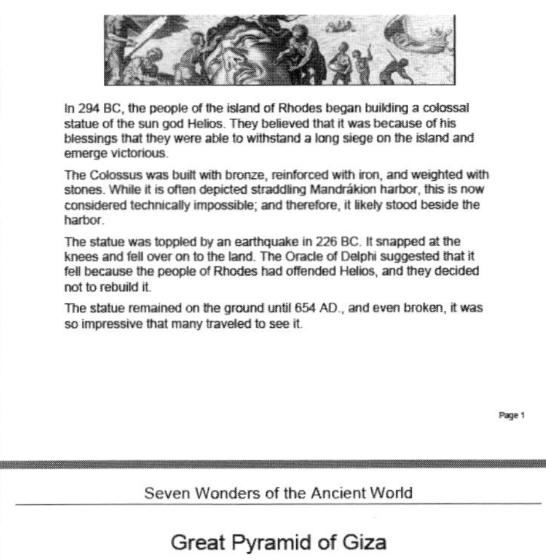
In 294 BC, the people of the island of Rhodes began building a colossal statue of the sun god Helios. They believed that it was because of his blessings that they were able to withstand a long siege on the island and emerge victorious.

The Colossus was built with bronze, reinforced with iron, and weighted with stones. While it is often depicted straddling Mandrákion harbor, this is now considered technically impossible; and therefore, it likely stood beside the harbor.

The statue was toppled by an earthquake in 226 BC. It snapped at the knees and fell over on to the land. The Oracle of Delphi suggested that it fell because the people of Rhodes had offended Helios, and they decided not to rebuild it.

The statue remained on the ground until 654 AD., and even broken, it was so impressive that many traveled to see it.

Page 1

Seven Wonders of the Ancient World

Great Pyramid of Giza

Figure 5.19 *The result of the XSLT to XSL-FO to PDF process is a seven-page document with each wonder on a separate page and page numbers in the footer.*

Inserting Page Breaks

The XSLT example on the previous page generates an XSL-FO file which, in turn, generates a final output. As you may imagine, or have seen in the example files, the final output is many pages long without any logical page breaks.

To insert a page break:

◆ As an attribute of an `fo:block` element, type **break-before="page"**. This inserts a page break before the block's content in the final output **(Figure 5.17)**.

When your final output is multiple pages, you can include XSL-FO elements to number your pages in a footer **(Figure 5.18)**.

To number each page in a footer:

1. To create the structure for a footer, the child element in the first Step 1 on page 67 should be **<fo:region-after**.
2. To set the page content for the footer, the attribute value in the second Step 2 on page 67 should be **"xsl-region-after"**. (`xsl-region-after` refers to the footer region defined by the `fo:region-after` element in Step 1.)
3. Finally, in a block of page content for the footer, type **<fo:page-number/>**, which outputs the current page number.

✔ Tips

- The `break-before` style property can take other values such as: `auto` (the default setting), where no break is forced; `even-page` or `odd-page`, where the page break is generated only for even or odd pages, respectively; `inherit`, which uses the parent's `break-before` value; or `column`, which is discussed on page 70.
- There is also a `break-after` style property which acts just like `break-before`, except the page break is inserted after the element.

Outputting Page Content in Columns

One of XSL-FO's built-in typographic capabilities is being able to define columns in which to output page content.

To output page content in columns:

1. As an attribute of a region element, type **column-count="c_count"**, where *c_count* is the number of columns to use in that region's final output **(Figure 5.20)**.
2. Within the region identified in Step 1, as an attribute of any block you wish *not* to place in the columnar layout, type **span="all" (Figure 5.21)**.
3. Within the region identified in Step 1, as an attribute of any block you wish to generate a column break, type **break-before="column"** or **break-after="column"**, as needed **(Figure 5.22)**.

✔ Tips

- Another style property attribute for columns is `column-gap`, which sets the separation width between columns. It can take be a length in inches (`in`), points (`pt`), and others; or a percentage in numeric value or `em`'s.
- Placing a column break in the last block on the last page of a final output may generate an unintentional blank page (after what should be the last page). You can avoid this problem by not including this attribute in the last block. One way to do this is to use the `xsl:if` element with the `xsl:attribute` element to only include the `break-after="column"` attribute in the second to the last block. (I have included this fix in the next set of XSLT example files.)

xslt
```
...
<!-- overall layout -->
<fo:layout-master-set>
 <fo:simple-page-master
   master-name="wonders"
   page-width="8.5in"
   page-height="11in">
  <fo:region-body margin="1in"
    column-count="2"/>
...
```

Figure 5.20 *The body region of the page template named* wonders *will be output in two columns. This XSLT continues in the two examples below.*

xslt
```
...
<xsl:template match="name">
 <fo:block span="all"
   margin-bottom="0.2in">
  <fo:block font-size="24pt"
    text-align="center"
    break-before="page">
   <xsl:value-of select="."/>
 </fo:block>
...
```

Figure 5.21 *This block element will contain the wonder name and image, and will span all columns.*

xslt
```
...
<fo:block font-size="14pt"
  text-align="justify"
  break-after="column">
 <xsl:apply-templates
   select="../history/story"/>
</fo:block>
...
```

Figure 5.22 *I added the* break-after="column" *attribute to the block that outputs the story.*

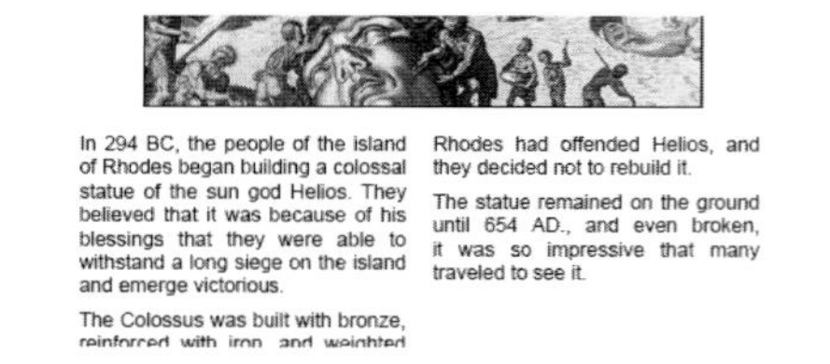

Figure 5.23 *Now the PDF shows the story text in two columns, and the image (and wonder name above it—not shown) spanning both columns.*

```
xslt
...
<!-- overall layout -->
<fo:layout-master-set>
 <fo:simple-page-master
   master-name="wonders_cover"
   page-width="8.5in"
   page-height="11in" margin="1in">
  <fo:region-body/>
 </fo:simple-page-master>
...
```

Figure 5.24 *This new page template will be a cover sheet for the PDF and is named* wonders_cover.

```
xslt
...
<!-- page content-->
<fo:page-sequence
  master-reference="wonders_cover">
  <fo:flow
    flow-name="xsl-region-body">
   <fo:block font-size="28pt"
     text-align="center">
    Seven Wonders of the Ancient World
...
```

Figure 5.25 *An initial version of the cover sheet was shown in Figures 5.1 and 5.2.*

Seven Wonders of the Ancient World

The famous Greek historian Herodotus wrote of seven great architectural achievements. And although his writings did not survive, he planted seeds for what has become the list of the **Seven Wonders of the Ancient World**.

Submitted by: Kevin Howard Goldberg

Figure 5.26 *The cover sheet uses a different page template with no header or footer.*

Adding a New Page Template

On page 66, I defined a page template that I have used for my final output in all the examples thus far. Now, I want to create a cover page for my output with a different overall layout and different page content.

To add a new page template:

1. As a child element of the `fo:layout-master-set` element, type **<fo:simple-page-master (Figure 5.24)**.
2. Then, type **master-name="master"**, where *master* is the page template name used in the `fo:page-sequence` element below.
3. Include any style properties as desired, see *Defining a Page Template* on page 66.
4. Finally, type **>** to close the tag.
5. Type **<fo:region-body/>** to declare that this page master will contain content in the body region, and include any style properties you would like for the region.
6. Include any other region declaration elements *(see page 67)*.
7. Finally, type **</fo:simple-page-master>**.

To define page content for a new page template:

1. In the page content part of your XSL-FO document, type **<fo:page-sequence master-reference="master">**, where *master* is the name of the page template from Step 2 above **(Figure 5.25)**.
2. Type **<fo:flow flow-name="xsl-region-body">** to create the container for blocks of content for the body region.
3. Enter page content blocks for the region.
4. Type **</fo:flow>** to complete the element.
5. Repeat Steps 3 and 4 for other regions defined in Step 6 above.
6. Finally, type **</fo:page-sequence>**.

Part 3: DTD

CREATING A DTD

In Part 1 of the book, you learned XML's underlying grammar, which forms the rules for writing an XML document. In Part 2, you learned how to transform an XML document into another form, in this case HTML. Now, in Part 3, you'll learn how to define a custom markup language in XML.

To define such a language, you will first identify its elements and their attributes, declaring which are required, and which are not. This information is called a *schema*. For example, an historian might create WowML, the (fictitious) Wonders of the World Markup Language, as a system for cataloging data about the wonders of the world. WowML might have elements like `wonder`, `name`, `year_built`, and `story`.

Schemas, while not required, are exceptionally important for keeping XML documents consistent. In fact, you can compare any XML document to its corresponding schema to *validate* whether it conforms to the rules specified in the schema *(see Chapter 8)*. And, if an XML document is deemed valid, then its data is in the proper form as specified by the schema.

There are two principal systems for writing schemas: DTD and XML Schema. A DTD, or *Document Type Definition*, is an older, but widely used system with a peculiar and limited syntax. The next three chapters are devoted to writing DTD-style schemas. The other primary system, XML Schema, is described in detail in Part 4 of the book. For some reasons why you might choose one over the other, consult *Pros and Cons of DTDs* on page 110.

Working with DTDs

A DTD, or *Document Type Definition*, is a set of rules that defines a custom markup language in XML. A DTD, at its core, simply identifies elements and their attributes. If an XML document does not adhere to the rules defined by the DTD, it is not considered valid for that particular custom language. With this validation test, you can quickly discern if a given XML document follows the rules you set forth for your language or not.

As I've mentioned, XML uses the same building blocks as HTML: Elements, attributes, and values. Elements are the foundational units of an XML document **(Figure 6.1)**. They can contain values, have attributes, and they can contain other elements. A DTD for a given custom markup language will define a list of elements and any child elements that each element can have **(Figure 6.2)**. It will define any attributes that each element can have, and it will define whether these elements and attributes are optional or required. In this way, the DTD defines the legal structure of the custom markup language, and therefore, any valid XML document that is part of this language.

A DTD is a text-only document and is customarily saved with a `.dtd` extension. It is not an XML document itself and therefore does not begin with the standard XML declaration.

✔ Tips

- DTDs are a great way to insure the consistency of XML data shared between different people and companies. You can use a DTD to validate that the XML documents you receive from others are in the proper format before using them.
- You will need to use an XML Editor or some type of DTD processor to validate an XML document against a given DTD. You can find details about both in Appendix A.

```xml
<?xml version="1.0"?>
<wonder>
  <name>Colossus of Rhodes</name>
  <location>Greece</location>
  <height>107</height>
</wonder>
```

Figure 6.1 *Here is one of the first XML documents you saw in this book. This XML document has four elements: the root element,* wonder, *and its three child elements:* name, location, *and* height.

```dtd
<!ELEMENT wonder
          (name, location, height)>

<!ELEMENT name     (#PCDATA)>
<!ELEMENT location (#PCDATA)>
<!ELEMENT height   (#PCDATA)>
```

Figure 6.2 *This DTD excerpt defines the structure of the XML document in Figure 6.1. It reads as follows: the* wonder *element contains three child elements:* name, location, *and* height*; the* name *element is of type PCDATA, the* location *element is of type PCDATA and the* height *element is of type PCDATA. PCDATA is defined more on page 77; but, for now, I'll say that PCDATA is simply text.*

```
xml
<?xml version="1.0"?>
<ancient_wonders>
 <wonder>
  <name language="English">
    Colossus of Rhodes</name>
  <name language="Greek">
    Κολοσσὸς της Ρόδου</name>
  <location>Rhodes, Greece</location>
  <height units="feet">107</height>
  <history>
   <year_built era="BC">
     282</year_built>
   <year_destroyed era="BC">
     226</year_destroyed>
   <how_destroyed>
     earthquake</how_destroyed>
   <story>In 294 BC, the people of
     the island of Rhodes ...</story>
  </history>
 </wonder>
</ancient_wonders>
```

Figure 6.3 *Notice in this pared-down version of the master XML document, most of the elements contain text. (Some also contain attributes which I discuss on page 84.) The* history *child elements also contain text, while* history *itself does not. Elements with children are discussed on page 79.*

```
dtd
<!ELEMENT name            (#PCDATA)>
<!ELEMENT location        (#PCDATA)>
<!ELEMENT height          (#PCDATA)>
<!ELEMENT year_built      (#PCDATA)>
<!ELEMENT year_destroyed  (#PCDATA)>
<!ELEMENT how_destroyed   (#PCDATA)>
<!ELEMENT story           (#PCDATA)>
```

Figure 6.4 *Almost every DTD will have elements that are defined as PCDATA. In this DTD excerpt, I am showing all the elements from Figure 6.3 that are defined to contain text.*

Defining an Element That Contains Text

To define the structure of your custom markup language in a DTD, you define the structure and content of the elements that a valid XML document would have.

Many elements in your XML document will contain just text **(Figure 6.3)**. While an `address` element may contain child elements for `street`, `city`, `state`, and `zip`, these elements themselves will likely just contain text.

To define an element that only contains text:

1. Type **<!ELEMENT tag** where *tag* is the name of the element you wish to define.
2. Then, type **(#PCDATA)** (*include* the parentheses!). This defines the element as one that should only allow text content.
3. Finally, type **>** to complete the element definition **(Figure 6.4)**.

✔ Tips

- PCDATA stands for *parsed character data*, and it refers to the text value of an element. This character data will be parsed, or analyzed, by an XML processor.
- Text (also called a string) can be any series of letters, numbers, and symbols, such as "Hello," or "4 Privet Dr.," or "99811."
- An element that is defined to contain PCDATA can't contain any other element.
- Everything is case-sensitive in XML. The word **<!ELEMENT** must be typed just so. **<!Element** just doesn't cut it. And don't forget the exclamation point. You can choose a mixed-case *name* for the element, as long as you always refer to it and use it in exactly the same way. Many XML applications use all lowercase. This way you don't have to spend time remembering what case anything should be.

Defining an Empty Element

In addition to elements that contain text, DTDs must also be able to define *empty elements*. As discussed in Chapter 1, an empty element is an XML element that does not have any content value of its own. Instead, it uses its attributes to store data **(Figure 6.5)**.

To define an empty element:

1. Type **<!ELEMENT tag**, where *tag* is the name of the element you wish to define.
2. Then, type **EMPTY** to indicate that the element will not contain a text value of its own.
3. Finally, type **>** to complete the element definition **(Figure 6.6)**.

✔ Tips

- Notice that when writing `EMPTY`, you do not use parentheses as is required when writing `(#PCDATA)`.
- As mentioned above, empty elements will have attributes which are discussed on page 84.

```
xml
...
<main_image file="lighthouse.jpg"
  w="528" h="349"/>
<source sectionid="112"
  newspaperid="53"/>
...
```

Figure 6.5 *In this XML excerpt, the* main_image *and* source *elements are both empty elements. It doesn't matter whether they use a single or separate opening and closing tags, they are both empty.*

```
dtd
<!ELEMENT main_image   EMPTY>
<!ELEMENT source       EMPTY>
```

Figure 6.6 *This is the DTD excerpt that defines the elements in Figure 6.5. Defining their attributes will be discussed on page 84.*

```
x m l
<?xml version="1.0"?>
<ancient_wonders>
 <wonder>
  <name language="English">
    Colossus of Rhodes</name>
  <name language="Greek">
    Κολοσσὸς της Ρόδου</name>
  <location>Rhodes, Greece</location>
  <height units="feet">107</height>
  <history>
   <year_built era="BC">
     282</year_built>
   <year_destroyed era="BC">
     226</year_destroyed>
   <how_destroyed>
     earthquake</how_destroyed>
   <story>In 294 BC, the people of
     the island of Rhodes ...</story>
  </history>
  <main_image file="lighthouse.jpg"
    w="528" h="349"/>
  <source sectionid="112"
    newspaperid="53"/>
 </wonder>
</ancient_wonders>
```

Figure 6.7 *In this pared-down version of the XML master document, the* ancient_wonders *element has a single child element, the* wonder *element.*

```
d t d
<!ELEMENT ancient_wonders (wonder)>
```

Figure 6.8 *This DTD definition defines that the* ancient_wonders *element can contain a single element named* wonder *as shown in Figure 6.7. Note: The* wonder *element's contents depend on its definition only (and are not affected by the* ancient_wonders *definition in the least).*

Defining an Element That Contains a Child

Now that you understand how to define basic XML elements in a DTD, you need to be able to define parent elements: elements that contain other elements **(Figure 6.7)**.

To define an element to contain one child element:

1. Type **<!ELEMENT tag**, where *tag* is the name of the element you wish to define.
2. Then, type **(child)**, where *child* is the name of the element that will be contained in the element you're defining.
3. Finally, type **>** to complete the element definition **(Figure 6.8)**.

✔ Tips

- A tag that is defined to contain one other element may not contain anything except that element. It may not contain additional elements, nor may it contain text.
- You can make a child element optional, or have it appear multiple times. For more details, consult *Defining How Many Occurrences* on page 81.
- You can also control the order in which elements must appear in an XML document *(see page 80)*.
- Once you define that an element contains another element, it must contain that element every time it appears in the XML document. If not, the XML document will not be considered valid.

Defining an Element That Contains Children

Oftentimes, an XML element contains a sequence of child elements **(Figure 6.9)**. In a DTD, you can define a sequence of child elements that must be contained in the parent element. This sequence also defines the order in which the children must appear.

To define an element with children:

1. Type **<!ELEMENT tag**, where *tag* is the name of the element you wish to define.
2. Then, type **(child1**, where *child1* is the first element that should appear in the parent element.
3. Next, type **, child2**, where *child2* is the next element that should appear in the parent element. Separate each child element from the next with a comma and space.
4. Repeat Step 3 for each child element that should appear in the parent element.
5. Then, type **)** to complete the sequence.
6. Finally, type **>** to complete the element definition **(Figure 6.10)**.

✔ Tips

- The most important thing in a sequence is the comma. The comma is the character that separates elements (or groups of elements) in a sequence.
- You may not use `(#PCDATA)` in any part of a sequence; sequences must only contain elements.
- The elements contained in a sequence may of course contain their own child elements. The `history` element defined in Figure 6.10 actually contains four individual child elements (as seen in Figure 6.12 on the next page).

xml

```
<?xml version="1.0"?>
<ancient_wonders>
 <wonder>
  <name language="English">
    Colossus of Rhodes</name>
  <location>Rhodes, Greece</location>
  <height units="feet">107</height>
  <history>
   <year_built era="BC">
     282</year_built>
   <year_destroyed era="BC">
     226</year_destroyed>
   <how_destroyed>
     earthquake</how_destroyed>
   <story>In 294 BC, the people of
     the island of Rhodes ...</story>
  </history>
  <main_image file="lighthouse.jpg"
    w="528" h="349"/>
  <source sectionid="112"
    newspaperid="53"/>
 </wonder>
</ancient_wonders>
```

Figure 6.9 *The* wonder *element has many child elements. Notice, that many of the elements have attributes which I discuss in more detail on page 84.*

dtd

```
<!ELEMENT wonder (name, location,
  height, history, main_image,
  source)>
```

Figure 6.10 *This DTD definition which validates the XML in Figure 6.9 says that the* wonder *element must contain each one of the listed elements, in order. And, it may not contain anything else.*

```
dtd
<!ELEMENT ancient_wonders (wonder+)>

<!ELEMENT wonder (name+, location,
  height, history, main_image,
  source*)>
```

Figure 6.11 *The special symbols (sometimes called* quantifiers*), make the definition much more flexible. Now, the* ancient_wonders *element must contain at least one (and an unlimited number of)* wonder *elements. In addition, the* wonder *element must contain at least one (and an unlimited number of)* name *elements, and there may be any number of* source *elements (including none). The* location, height, history, *and* main_image *elements must all appear exactly once (which is the default).*

```
dtd
<!ELEMENT history (year_built,
  year_destroyed?, how_destroyed?,
  story)>
```

Figure 6.12 *This definition of the* history *element says that it must contain exactly one each of the* year_built *and* story *elements. The* year_destroyed *and* how_destroyed *elements may be omitted (or may appear at most one time).*

Defining How Many Occurrences

So far, parent elements can only contain one instance of each of their child elements. But DTDs do allow more than just one instance of a child element in an XML document. There are three special symbols in DTDs that can be used to define how many times a child element can appear within a parent element **(Figures 6.11 and 6.12)**.

To define the number of occurrences:

1. In the contents portion of the element definition, type the child element's name.
2. Then, type ***** to indicate that the child element can appear as many times as necessary, or not at all, in the parent element being defined *(zero or more times)*.

   Or type **+** to indicate that the child element must appear at least once, and as many times as desired in the parent element being defined *(one or more times)*.

   Or type **?** to indicate that the child element can appear at most once, if at all, in the parent element being defined *(zero or one time)*.

✔ Tips

- To reiterate:
  - * means zero or more times
  - \+ means one or more times
  - ? means zero or one time only.
- It's important to remember that an element without a quantifier must appear exactly once.
- You can also use quantifiers to define the number of occurrences for a sequence *(see page 80)*.
- There's no special way to define a specific quantity of an element (for example, three). The one rather long-winded way is to write: **(element, element, element)**.

Defining How Many Occurrences

Defining Choices

Sometimes you might need an XML element to contain one thing or another **(Figure 6.13)**.

To define choices for the content of an element:

1. Type **<!ELEMENT tag**, where *tag* is the name of the element you wish to define.
2. Then, type **(child1**, where *child1* is the first child element that may appear.
3. Next, type **|** to indicate that if the first child element appears, the following one may not (and vice versa).
4. Then, type **child2**, where *child2* is the second child element that may appear.
5. Repeat Steps 3–4 for each additional choice.
6. Then, type **)** to complete the list of choices.
7. Finally, type **>** to complete the element definition **(Figure 6.14)**.

✔ Tips

- You can add the * quantifier after Step 6 to allow the element to have any number of any of the choices *(see page 81)*.
- When an asterisk quantifier is applied to a list of choices, it means that the element can contain any number of the individual choices, in any order, effectively creating an unordered list of the choices.
- In some cases, you may want an element to contain both content and child elements. This is referred to as *mixed content* as seen in Figure 6.13. In this case, you must add the asterisk quantifier as described in the tips above. *Note*: This is not something you will use often when writing your own custom language. Rather, it is something that you might use when writing a DTD to support multiple XML documents from multiple sources.

```xml
<ancient_wonders>
 <wonder>
  <name>Colossus of Rhodes</name>
  <location>Rhodes, Greece</location>
 </wonder>
 <wonder>
   Great Pyramid of Giza, Giza, Egypt
 </wonder>
 <wonder>
   Temple of Artemis at Ephesus
  <city>Ephesus</city>
  <country>Turkey</country>
 </wonder>
</ancient_wonders>
```

Figure 6.13 *Imagine that the information for the ancient wonders came from three different sources, each having a different* wonder *element structure.*

```dtd
<!ELEMENT ancient_wonders (wonder+)>
<!ELEMENT wonder
  (#PCDATA | name | location | city
    | country)*>
<!ELEMENT name        (#PCDATA)>
<!ELEMENT location    (#PCDATA)>
<!ELEMENT city        (#PCDATA)>
<!ELEMENT country     (#PCDATA)>
```

Figure 6.14 *This DTD uses choices to support the different structures of the* wonder *element shown in Figure 6.13. It declares that the* wonder *element can contain zero or more occurrences of PCDATA,* name, location, city, *or* country *elements.*

```dtd
<!ELEMENT history
  ((year_built, year_destroyed,
   how_destroyed, story)
  |
  (year_built, story))>
```

Figure 6.15 *This is another way to write the DTD logic from Figure 6.12. Here the DTD is defining the* history *element to either contain the* year_built, year_destroyed, how_destroyed, *and* story *elements; or, only the* year_built *and* story *elements.*

```
xml
<ancient_wonders>
 <wonder>
  <name>Colossus of Rhodes</name>
  <location>Rhodes, Greece</location>
 </wonder>
 <wonder>
   Great Pyramid of Giza, Giza, Egypt
 </wonder>
 <wonder>
   Temple of Artemis at Ephesus
  <city>Ephesus</city>
  <country>Turkey</country>
 </wonder>
 <wonder>
 <name>
   Mausoleum at Halicarnassus</name>
  <location>
   <city>Bodrum</city>
   <country>Turkey</country>
  </location>
 </wonder>
</ancient_wonders>
```

Figure 6.16 *Here, I've added another* wonder *element (from a new unexpected source) to the XML document in Figure 6.13. This new* wonder *element has yet another structure to it. Notice that in this new element, the* location *element does not contain any PCDATA; rather, it is a parent element to the* city *and* country *elements.*

```
dtd
<!ELEMENT ancient_wonders (wonder+)>
<!ELEMENT wonder
  (#PCDATA | name | location | city
    | country)*>
<!ELEMENT name        (#PCDATA)>
<!ELEMENT location     ANY>
<!ELEMENT city        (#PCDATA)>
<!ELEMENT country     (#PCDATA)>
```

Figure 6.17 *Instead of adding to the DTD in Figure 6.14 to define the new* location *structure, I have defined the element to contain anything. It's not as clear as defining* location *to contain specific content, but it does work.*

Defining an Element That Contains Anything

While not ideal for creating a structured set of rules, in a DTD you can define an element to contain anything; meaning, it can contain any combination of elements and text. As with mixed content, this is useful if you are creating a DTD to support XML documents from different sources. It may be the only way to define elements you know *and* allow for element structures you can't anticipate **(Figure 6.16)**.

To define an element that can contain anything:

1. Type **<!ELEMENT tag**, where *tag* is the name of the element you wish to define.
2. Then, type **ANY** to allow the element to contain any combination of elements and parsed character data.
3. Finally, type **>** to complete the element definition **(Figure 6.17)**.

✔ Tips

- You should be judicious with your use of `ANY`. The point of a DTD is to set up rules for what an element can and cannot contain. If you're going to allow every element to contain anything, you might as well skip the DTD altogether. DTDs aren't required; they simply help keep data consistent.
- `ANY` defines that an element may contain any structure. However, if the element contains child elements, those children must still be defined in the DTD. In other words, `ANY` does not allow an element to contain child elements that are not defined in the DTD; all elements that appear in a valid XML document must still be defined.
- Every element must be defined exactly once in a DTD and no more. Even if an element can appear in many different places in a valid XML document, it must only be defined once.

About Attributes

Attributes are useful to provide additional data *about* an element. Information contained in attributes tends to be *about* the content of the XML document, as opposed to *being* the content itself.

For example, in the Wonders of the World XML master document, the `name` element contains a `language` attribute which *describes* the language that the `name` element content is in. You could easily restructure the XML so that the same information is in two individual child elements. The `name` element could contain two elements, a `language` element and a `local_name` element.

Either way is fine, but general best practices suggest that elements are better used for information you want to display; and attributes are better used for information about information. Some of the reasons for this are: Attributes cannot describe data relationships like child elements can, their values are not as easily validated by a DTD, and they cannot contain multiple values whereas child elements can.

Attributes are, of course, often used with empty elements where they describe information about the element. For example, they are often used to store IDs, as attributes are not the data, but information about the data *(see page 88)*.

✔ Tip

- How you choose to craft your XML should be based on its usage. If you are not going to "do" much with a particular piece of information, then having it as an attribute is fine. If you are going to use that information in a more significant way, then having it be the content value of an element is more appropriate **(Figure 6.18)**.

```xml
<how_destroyed year="426">
  fire</how_destroyed>
```

```xml
<year_destroyed>426</year_destroyed>

<how_destroyed>fire</how_destroyed>
```

Figure 6.18 *Both of these bits of XML contain the same information: The Statue of Zeus at Olympia was destroyed in 426 by fire. The difference lies in how the information is organized. In the top example, 426 is an attribute's value. In the bottom example, both 426 and fire are content, enclosed in individual elements.*

```
dtd
<!ELEMENT height (#PCDATA)>
<!ATTLIST height
          units CDATA #IMPLIED>
```

Figure 6.19 *This attribute definition says that the* height *element can contain an optional* units *attribute (because of the #IMPLIED status) that contains text (because of the CDATA attribute type).*

```
xml
<height>39</height>
```

```
xml
<height units="feet">39</height>
```

```
xml
<height units="39">feet</height>
```

Figure 6.20 *According to the DTD in Figure 6.19, all three of these XML excerpts are valid, since the* units *attribute is optional (#IMPLIED), and its contents may be any combination of characters.*

```
dtd
<!ELEMENT height (#PCDATA)>
<!ATTLIST height
          units CDATA #REQUIRED>
```

Figure 6.21 *This version of the definition says that in the* height *element, the* units *attribute is required.*

```
xml
<height>39</height>
```

```
xml
<height units="feet">39</height>
```

```
xml
<height units="39">feet</height>
```

Figure 6.22 *These examples are the same as those shown in Figure 6.20 above. When validated against the DTD in Figure 6.21, however, only the last two excerpts are valid. The first excerpt is not valid because the* height *element does not contain a* units *attribute.*

Defining Attributes

An attribute may not appear in a valid XML document unless it has been declared in the DTD. An attribute definition consists of four parts: *element name*, *attribute name*, *attribute type*, and an *optional status*.

To define an attribute:

1. Type **<!ATTLIST tag**, where *tag* is the element name in which the attribute will appear.
2. Then, type **att_name**, where *att_name* is the name of the attribute.
3. Next, type **CDATA** to indicate that the attribute type is text. And, unlike (#PCDATA), CDATA, or *character data*, will not be parsed by the processor.
4. Then, for the attribute's optional status, type **#IMPLIED** to indicate that the attribute may be omitted, if desired **(Figure 6.19)**.

   Or type **#REQUIRED** to indicate that the attribute may not be omitted and must contain a value **(Figure 6.21)**.
5. Finally, type **>** to complete the attribute definition.

✔ Tips

- Note that all the parts of an attribute definition are case-sensitive. Type them as I have them here. Something like **#Required** doesn't mean a thing in a DTD.
- You can define all the attributes for a given element in a single attribute definition. Before completing the attribute definition in Step 5 above, repeat Steps 2–4 for each attribute that the element should contain. This is the most common way of defining multiple attributes for a single element.

Defining Default Values

Instead of having an attribute's optional status be either #REQUIRED or #IMPLIED, you can set an attribute to have default values.

To define an attribute with default values:

1. Follow Steps 1, 2, and 3 on page 85 to define the element name, attribute name, and attribute type.
2. Then, type **"default"** (the opening and closing quotes are required), where *default* will be the value for the attribute if none is set in the XML document **(Figure 6.23)**.

   Or type **#FIXED "default"**, where *default* will be the value for the attribute if none is explicitly set. *And*, if set, the attribute must be set to this value for the XML document to be valid **(Figure 6.25)**.
3. Finally, type **>** to complete the attribute definition.

✔ Tips

- If you define an attribute with a default value, the XML parser will automatically add the default value if the attribute is not set in the XML document **(Figure 6.24)**.
- If you define an attribute with **#FIXED "default"**, the value of the attribute in the XML document *must* be set to the *default* value, if it is set at all. If the attribute is not set, then the parser will automatically set it to the value of the default **(Figure 6.26)**.
- You may not combine a default value with either **#REQUIRED** or **#IMPLIED**. In fact, since there is a default value already being set, neither optional status would actually make sense.

dtd
```
<!ELEMENT height (#PCDATA)>
<!ATTLIST height
          units CDATA "feet">
```

Figure 6.23 *This time, I am adding a default value of* feet *for the* height *attribute.*

xml
```
<height units="feet">39</height>
```

xml
```
<height units="meters">39</height>
```

xml
```
<height>39</height>
```

Figure 6.24 *All these XML excerpts are valid. The* units *attribute can be set to any value and may even be omitted. If the* units *attribute is omitted, as in the third example, the parser will act as if the attribute is actually present and that its value is* feet.

dtd
```
<!ELEMENT height (#PCDATA)>
<!ATTLIST height
          units CDATA #FIXED "feet">
```

Figure 6.25 *A fixed value can be useful for ensuring that an attribute has a given value, whether or not it actually appears in the XML document.*

xml
```
<height units="feet">39</height>
```

xml
```
<height units="meters">39</height>
```

xml
```
<height>39</height>
```

Figure 6.26 *These examples are the same as those in Figure 6.24 above. When validated against the DTD in Figure 6.25, though, the middle example is no longer valid; if the attribute is set, it must contain a value of* feet *(and not* meters, *or any other characters). Note that in the bottom example, the parser acts as if the* units *attribute is actually set to* feet.

```
dtd
<!ELEMENT height (#PCDATA)>
<!ATTLIST height
       units (inches|feet) #REQUIRED>
```

Figure 6.27 *In this example, I only want to allow two possibilities for the value of the* units *attribute in the* year *element:* inches *or* feet. *The list of choices appears between parentheses, separated by a vertical bar. Note that the attribute must be set (because of the* #REQUIRED *value).*

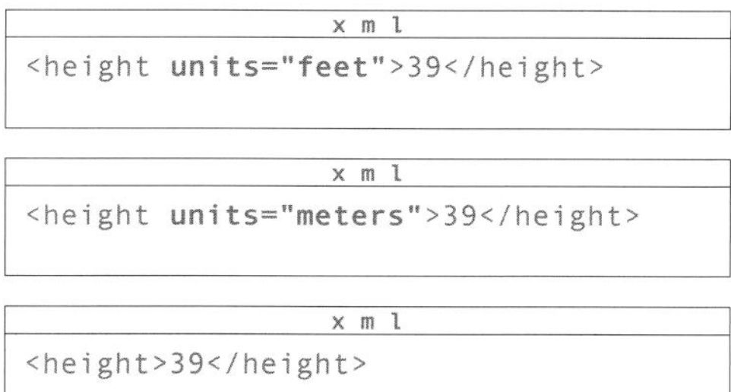

```
xml
<height units="feet">39</height>
```

```
xml
<height units="meters">39</height>
```

```
xml
<height>39</height>
```

Figure 6.28 *Of these three XML excerpts, only the top is valid with respect to the bit of DTD in Figure 6.27. The middle example is invalid because* meters *is not one of the allowed choices for the content of the attribute. The bottom example is invalid because the* units *attribute is missing despite being* #REQUIRED.

Defining Attributes with Choices

DTDs support attribute types that allow much more than just character data. One such type allows you to define an attribute that supports different pre-defined choices **(Figure 6.27)**.

To define an attribute with choices:

1. Follow Steps 1 and 2 on page 85 to begin the attribute definition.
2. Type **(choice_1 | choice_2)**, where *choice_n* represents each possible value for the attribute, and each attribute in the XML document can use any one of the listed choices. Each choice should be separated by a vertical bar, and the full set should be enclosed in parentheses.
3. Identify any optional attribute statuses as described in Step 4 on page 85 and in Step 2 on page 86.
4. Finally, type **>** to complete the attribute definition.

✔ Tips

- Each choice in a list must follow the rules for valid XML names *(see page 8)*.
- There are several other kinds of attribute types: ID, IDREF, and IDREFS, which are explained on pages 88–89; NMTOKEN and NMTOKENS, which are described on page 90, and ENTITY, which is described in Chapter 7.

Defining Attributes with Unique Values

There are a few special kinds of attribute types. ID attributes are defined to have a value that is unique (not repeatable) throughout the XML document. An ID attribute is ideal for keys and other identifying information (product codes, customer codes, etc).

To define ID attributes:

1. Follow Steps 1 and 2 on page 85 to begin the attribute definition.
2. Type **ID** to define that the value of the attribute will be unique and non-repeatable throughout the XML document. In other words, no other element may have an attribute with the same value.
3. Identify any optional attribute statuses as described in Step 4 on page 85. (Note: ID attributes can only be #REQUIRED or #IMPLIED, they cannot use the default values defined on in Step 2 on page 86.)
4. Finally, type **>** to complete the attribute definition **(Figure 6.29)**.

✔ Tips

- An XML document is not considered valid if two elements with ID attributes have the same value, regardless of whether the element or attribute names are the same or different.
- The one exception to this rule is that there can be an unlimited number of omitted ID attributes, each implying a null value.
- The value of an ID attribute must follow the same rules as valid XML names *(see page 8)*. (That means an ID attribute cannot contain only numerical values, like many database ID fields, Social Security numbers, etc., unless you prefix them with a letter or underscore.)

dtd

```
<!ELEMENT wonder (name)>

<!ATTLIST wonder
        code ID #REQUIRED>
```

Figure 6.29 *If you're going to create an ID attribute, it's a good idea make it required. If not, it must be implied since ID attributes cannot have default values.*

xml

```
<wonder code="w_143">
  <name language="English">
   Hanging Gardens of Babylon</name>
</wonder>

<wonder code="w_284">
  <name language="English">
    Statue of Zeus at Olympia</name>
</wonder>
```

xml

```
<wonder code="w_284">
  <name language="English">
   Hanging Gardens of Babylon</name>
</wonder>

<wonder code="w_284">
  <name language="English">
    Statue of Zeus at Olympia</name>
</wonder>
```

Figure 6.30 *As defined by the DTD in Figure 6.29, the* code *attribute must contain a unique value throughout the XML document. Given this, the first excerpt is valid, but the second is not.*

```
dtd
<!ELEMENT special_site (title, url)>

<!ATTLIST special_site
        wonder_focus IDREF #REQUIRED>
```

Figure 6.31 *The* special_site *element will keep track of Web sites dedicated to each wonder. Its* wonder_focus *attribute is defined as an IDREF type, enabling it to contain the ID of the wonder on which it focuses.*

```
xml
<special_site wonder_focus="w_143">
 <title>The Lost Gardens</title>
 <url>www.lost-gardens.com</url>
</special_site>

<special_site wonder_focus="w_143">
 <title>Herodotus in Babylon</title>
 <url>www.herodotus.com/babylon</url>
</special_site>

<special_site wonder_focus="w_284">
 <title>Zeus at Olympia</title>
 <url>www.olympiaszeus.com</url>
</special_site>
```

Figure 6.32 *Given the DTD in Figure 6.31, the* wonder_focus *attribute must contain a value from an existing ID attribute in the document. (Note: This excerpt is from an XML file that also contains the XML excerpt in the top example of Figure 6.30 on page 88).*

```
dtd
<!ELEMENT general_site (title, url)>

<!ATTLIST general_site
        contents IDREFS #REQUIRED>
```

Figure 6.33 *The* general_site *element has an IDREFS attribute called* contents. *This attribute can contain a list of the IDs of the wonders on which the* general_site *element focuses.*

```
xml
<general_site
  contents="w_143 w_284">
 <title>Wonders of the World</title>
 <url>
   www.wonders_of_the_world.com</url>
</general_site>
```

Figure 6.34 *This XML excerpt is valid when using the DTD in Figure 6.33.*

Referencing Attributes with Unique Values

An attribute whose value is the same as any existing ID attribute (defined on page 88) in the XML document is called an IDREF attribute **(Figure 6.31)**.

An attribute whose value is a white-space-separated list of existing ID attribute values is called an IDREFS attribute (notice that this attribute ends in an "S") **(Figure 6.33)**.

To reference attributes with unique values:

1. Follow Steps 1 and 2 on page 85 to begin the attribute definition.
2. Type **IDREF** to define an attribute that can contain a value matching any existing ID attribute's value (such as one that you defined with the instructions on page 88).

   Or type **IDREFS** (*with* an "s") for an attribute that can contain several white-space-separated values which match any existing ID attribute's value.
3. Identify any optional attribute statuses as described in Step 4 on page 85 and Step 2 on page 86.
4. Finally, type **>** to complete the attribute definition.

✔ Tips

- Note that there may be several IDREF attributes that refer to the same ID **(Figure 6.32)**. That's fine. It's just the ID itself that must be unique to one element.
- There's nothing that keeps repeated items out of an IDREFS attribute. Something like **contents="w_143 w_143 w_143"** is perfectly valid for the parser, whether or not it's what you want. For more control over element and attribute contents, you have to abandon DTDs in favor of XML Schema *(see Part 4)*.

Restricting Attributes to Valid XML Names

DTDs don't allow for much data typing, but there is one restriction that you can apply to attributes. The value of an attribute defined as the NMTOKEN type, must be a valid XML name. That is, a value that begins with a letter or an underscore and contains only letters, numbers, underscores, hyphens, and periods.

To ensure attribute values follow the rules for valid XML names:

1. Follow Steps 1 and 2 on page 85 to begin the attribute definition.
2. Type **NMTOKEN** if you want the attribute value to be a valid XML name as defined on page 8.

   Or type **NMTOKENS** if you want the attribute value to be a white-space-separated list of valid XML names.
3. Identify any optional attribute statuses as described in Step 4 on page 85 and Step 2 on page 86.
4. Finally, type **>** to complete the attribute definition **(Figure 6.35)**.

✔ Tips

- NMTOKEN attributes may not contain any white space, which may be one good reason to use this particular type.
- If you want the value of an attribute to not only be a valid XML name, but also to be unique throughout the XML document, use ID instead of NMTOKEN *(see page 88)*.

```
dtd
<!ELEMENT w_visit EMPTY`>

<!ATTLIST w_visit
   primary_keyword NMTOKEN #REQUIRED>
```

Figure 6.35 *In this rather contrived example, I need a single word for each wonder to use as the primary keyword in a special online application called Wonderful Visit. I created an element called* w_visit *with a* primary_keyword *attribute. To keep the value of the* primary_keyword *attribute to just one word (with no white space), I can define it to be the NMTOKEN type.*

```
xml
<wonder>
 <w_visit
   primary_keyword="colossus"/>
 <name language="English">
   Colossus of Rhodes</name>
...
<wonder>
 <w_visit
   primary_keyword="great pyramid"/>
 <name language="English">
   Great Pyramid of Giza</name>
...
```

```
xml
<wonder>
 <w_visit
   primary_keyword="colossus"/>
 <name language="English">
   Colossus of Rhodes</name>
...
<wonder>
 <w_visit
   primary_keyword="great_pyramid"/>
 <name language="English">
   Great Pyramid of Giza</name>
...
```

Figure 6.36 *Only the second example above would be considered valid against the DTD in Figure 6.35. In the first, the* primary_keyword *attribute* "great pyramid" *has a space in its value, and spaces are not allowed in an NMTOKEN attribute.*

7 Entities and Notations in DTDs

Entities are just like autotext entries or shortcuts. With an entity, you define its name and the text it should expand into when referenced in your document. Then, when you type the entity reference in an XML document or DTD, it is replaced with text you defined.

There are several types of entities, but they all work in the same way, and they are all defined through a DTD. The differences lie in where the entity can be expanded, and what kind of data it contains.

Entities can be divided into two main types: *general entities* and *parameter entities*. General entities can be expanded only in XML documents; parameter entities can be expanded only in DTDs.

General entities can be further subdivided into internal and external, parsed or unparsed. Parameter entities can also be further subdivided into internal and external, but parameter entities are always parsed.

Creating a General Entity

The simplest kind of entities are defined in a DTD, and they simply represent text. Officially, they are called *internal general entities*. I often just call them shortcuts.

To create an internal general entity:

1. In the DTD, type **<!ENTITY**.
2. Then, type **ent_name**, where *ent_name* specifies the name of the entity; the name you'll refer to when using the entity in your XML document.
3. Next, type **"content"**, where *content* is the shortcut text that will appear when you use the entity in your XML document.
4. Finally, type **>** to complete the entity definition **(Figure 7.1)**.

✔ Tips

- For details on using these shortcuts, see *Using General Entities* on page 93.
- The entity name reference (in Step 2 above) must follow the rules for valid XML names *(see page 8)*.
- In XML, there are five built-in general entities: **&** , **<** , **>** , **"** , **&apost;** *(see page 14)*. All other entities must be declared in the DTD before being used.
- Many common entities have been defined and are easily available to include in your own DTDs. For more details, see the Tips on page 95.

```
dtd
<!ENTITY wow "Wonders of the World">
```

Figure 7.1 *You can use internal general entities for quickly typing long phrases; ones that you might use frequently in your XML document.*

```
xml
<story>
  The first and most interesting fact
  about the gardens is that there is
  significant controversy about
  whether the gardens existed at all.
 ...
  Regardless of the final outcome,
  it is interesting to note that the
  imagination of the poets and
  ancient historians have created one
  of the &wow;.
</story>
```

Figure 7.2 *It's easier and faster to type* &wow; *than* Wonders of the World.

```
html
...
<p align="center">
 <strong>HANGING GARDENS OF BABYLON
   </strong><br>
 <img src="gardens.jpg"
   width="264" height="175"></p>
 The Hanging Gardens of Babylon was
   built in 600 BC and was destroyed
   by earthquake in 226 BC.

 The first and most interesting fact
   about the gardens is that there
   is significant controversy about
   whether the gardens existed at all.
   <br><br>
  ...
 Regardless of the final outcome, it
   is interesting to note that the
   imagination of the poets and
   ancient historians have created
   one of the Wonders of the World.
   <br><br>
...
```

Figure 7.3 *The entity created in Figure 7.2 "expands" when the XML is parsed.*

Using General Entities

Once you have defined an entity in your DTD, you can use it in any XML document that references that DTD.

To use general entities:

1. In the XML document, type **&** (an ampersand).
2. Then, type **ent_name**, where *ent_name* identifies the name of your entity (the one you used in Step 2 on page 92.
3. Finally, type **;** (a semicolon) **(Figure 7.2)**.

✔ Tips

- You may only use a general entity after it has been defined in the DTD referred to by your XML document. If not, the parser will return an error that the entity has not been defined.
- Character references are used for adding special symbols to a document, such as writing **&246;** to generate the **ö** symbol, etc. They look rather similar to entities, but they are not entities, and do not need to be declared in the DTD *(see Appendix B)*.
- General entities are used in XML documents only; they cannot be used in XSLT documents. (There are ways around this, but they are advanced and cumbersome.)
- You may use an entity within another entity's definition as long as there is no circular reference.

Creating an External General Entity

If you have a larger entity, or one that could be reused in multiple DTD documents, it is often more convenient to save it in a separate, external document.

To create an external general entity:

- Create the content for the entity in an external file. Save the file as text-only using an extension of `.ent` **(Figure 7.4)**.

To define an external general entity:

1. In your DTD where you want to use the content, type **<!ENTITY** to begin the entity definition.
2. Then, type **ent_name**, where *ent_name* specifies the name of the external entity; the name you'll refer to when using the entity in your XML document.
3. Next, type **SYSTEM** to indicate that the entity is defined externally in another document.
4. Then, type **"entity.uri"**, where *entity.uri* is the location of the file containing the entity content.
5. Finally, type **>** to complete the entity definition **(Figure 7.5)**.

✔ Tips

- The **"entity.uri"** in Step 4 above can refer to a file on your computer, a local area network, or on the Internet.
- Using the `.ent` file extension for your external general entity is not required (any extension will work fine), but `.ent` is most common.
- Using external entities, you can actually create a single DTD from several others.

dtd

```
<story>
  The first and most interesting fact
  about the gardens is that there is
  significant controversy about
  whether the gardens existed at all.
 ...
  Regardless of the final outcome,
  it is interesting to note that the
  imagination of the poets and
  ancient historians have created one
  of the &wow;.
</story>
```

Figure 7.4 *This time, I'll define the entity to be the entire chunk of XML code. Notice that it includes the* wow *general entity defined in Figure 7.1. I'll save it as a text file called* gardens.ent.

dtd

```
<!ENTITY
  gardens_story SYSTEM "gardens.ent">
```

Figure 7.5 *The* gardens_story *entity points to the URI of the file that contains the entity's contents shown in Figure 7.4.*

```
xml
<?xml version="1.0" standalone="no"?>
...
<wonder>
 <name language="English">
   Hanging Gardens of Babylon</name>
 <location>Al Hillah, Iraq</location>
 <height units="feet">0</height>
 <history>
  <year_built era="BC">
   600</year_built>
  <year_destroyed era="BC">
   226</year_destroyed>
  <how_destroyed>
   earthquake</how_destroyed>
  &gardens_story;
 </history>
...
```

Figure 7.6 *First, be sure to add* standalone="no" *to the XML declaration. Then, you can use the external general entity in the document, as* &gardens_story; *is used here.*

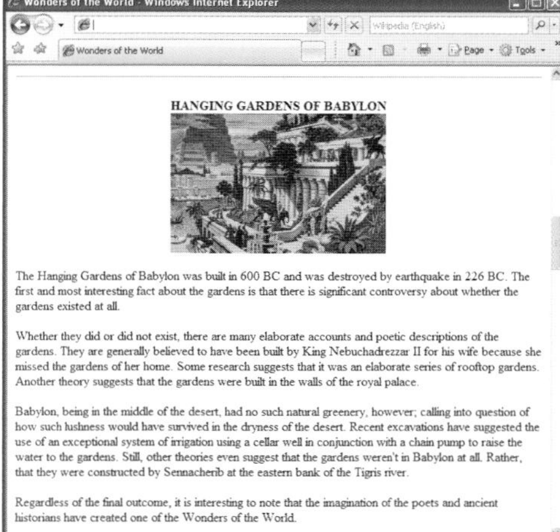

Figure 7.7 *The entity (defined in Figure 7.5) contains an element, text, and another entity. And the idea is the same: You type something short, and the parser replaces it with the referenced content. Note that any elements coming from an external general entity must still be defined in the DTD for the document to be valid.*

Using External General Entities

Once created, you can use your entity, share your entity with others, and borrow entities from others (provided they've created external general entities, too).

To use external general entities:

1. In the XML document that will refer to the DTD, add **standalone="no"** to the initial XML declaration *(see page 7)*. This tells the XML parser that the document will rely on an external file; in this case, the one that contains the entity definition.
2. Then, in the XML document, type **&** (an ampersand).
3. Next, type **ent_name**, where *ent_name* identifies the name of your entity (the one you used in Step 2 on page 94.
4. Finally, type **;** (a semicolon) **(Figure 7.6)**.

✔ Tips

- A URI (*Uniform Resource Identifier*) is a string of characters used to identify and locate a resource. It is often used interchangeably with URL (*Uniform Resource Locator*). Technically, a URI can be either a URL or a URN (*Universal Resource Name*), but for purposes this book, I will use URI and URL to mean the same thing.
- You could link to a standardized list of entities, like the ones available at: *www.w3.org/TR/xhtml1/#h-A2*. This would let you use the easy-to-remember entity references for accented characters without having to manually define each one.
- A general entity (like those described on pages 92 and 94) are defined as part of a DTD and used in the body of an XML document. There is another kind of entity used to add content to the DTD itself. It is called a *parameter entity* and has a slightly different syntax *(see page 100)*.

Creating Entities for Unparsed Content

So far, I've only talked about entities whose content is text. Entities that contain text are called *parsed entities* because the XML parser looks at them and analyzes them in the course of going through the XML document. *Unparsed entities*, which I'll describe here, don't usually contain text (but can), but most importantly are completely bypassed by the XML parser. They can be used to embed non-text or non-XML content into an XML document.

To create unparsed content:

- Create the data that you want to embed in the XML document. It may be, or contain, virtually anything; including plain text, an image file, a video file, a PDF file, or anything else **(Figure 7.8)**.

In order to create an entity for unparsed content, you must first identify how to process the unparsed content using a *notation*.

To create a notation about the unparsed content:

1. In the DTD where you want to embed the content, type **<!NOTATION n_name**, where *n_name* will be used to identify the unparsed content.
2. Then, type **SYSTEM**.
3. Next, type **"notation.instr"**, where *notation.instr* is usually information (such as a URI), that defines how to process the unparsed content. (Note, however, that there is no official format for this information, so consult your XML processor for more details.)
4. Finally, type **>** to complete the notation. **(Figure 7.9)**

Figure 7.8 *Here is a typical chunk of unparsed data: A JPEG image. It's called* lighthouse.jpg.

dtd

```
<!ELEMENT ancient_wonders (wonder*)>
<!ELEMENT wonder (name+, photo)>
<!ELEMENT name (#PCDATA) >
<!ATTLIST name
          language CDATA #REQUIRED>

<!NOTATION jpg SYSTEM "image/jpeg">
```

Figure 7.9 *The identifying name of the notation element* jpg *will be used when creating the entity for the unparsed content.*

Creating Entities for Unparsed Content

```
                    dtd
<!ELEMENT ancient_wonders (wonder*)>
<!ELEMENT wonder (name+, photo)>
<!ELEMENT name (#PCDATA) >
<!ATTLIST name
          language PCDATA #REQUIRED>

<!NOTATION jpg SYSTEM "image/jpeg">

<!ENTITY lighthouse_pic SYSTEM
        "lighthouse.jpg" NDATA jpg>
```

Figure 7.10 *The entity's name,* lighthouse_pic, *refers to an external* SYSTEM *file called* lighthouse.jpg, *and I can get more information about the file by looking at the notation identifier* NDATA jpg.

To define an entity for the unparsed content:

1. On a new line in the same DTD, after the corresponding notation for the unparsed content, type **<!ENTITY** to begin the unparsed entity definition.
2. Then, type **ent_name**, where *ent_name* specifies the name for the external entity; the name you'll refer to when using the entity in your XML document.
3. Next, type **SYSTEM** to indicate that the entity is defined in a separate document.
4. Then, type **"entity.uri"**, where *entity.uri* is the location of the file with the unparsed content.
5. Next, type **NDATA n_name**, where *n_name* is the unparsed content's identifying name you created in Step 1 on page 96.
6. Finally, type **>** to complete the entity definition **(Figure 7.10)**.

✔ Tips

- The **"notation.instr"** in Step 3 on the previous page can be a MIME type (an Internet standard describing content types), a URI indicating a local or external application that can handle the unparsed content, or practically anything else. According to the specification, there is no required format for this information, and each XML application can use the information as it chooses.
- Unparsed entities are inherently general entities because they become part of the body of an XML document.
- The contents of an unparsed entity can be just about anything. Often, it's an image file, audio file, video file, or some other kind of multimedia file. It could also be plain text. It doesn't matter what it is because the XML parser won't look at it.

Embedding Unparsed Content

Once you've defined an entity for your unparsed content, as described on page 96, you can then embed it into your XML document. Unparsed entities do not have entity references (like the parsed entities I described earlier). Instead, unparsed entities are referred to through a special ENTITY attribute type.

To declare the attribute that will contain the reference to the unparsed entity:

1. In the DTD, first define an element. It is this element that will contain the attribute referencing the unparsed entity.
2. Type **<!ATTLIST tag**, where *tag* is the element you defined in Step 1.
3. Then, type **att_name**, where *att_name* identifies the name of the attribute defined in Step 1. It will contain the reference to the unparsed entity.
4. Next, type **ENTITY** to indicate that the attribute can contain references to an unparsed entity.

   Or, type **ENTITIES** if you want the attribute to be able to contain multiple white-space-separated references to unparsed entities.
5. Then, you may define a status or default value for the attribute. For more details, consult *Defining Attributes* on page 85 and *Defining Default Values* on page 86.
6. Finally, type **>** to complete the attribute definition **(Figure 7.11)**.

```
dtd
<!ELEMENT ancient_wonders (wonder*)>
<!ELEMENT wonder (name+, photo)>
<!ELEMENT name (#PCDATA) >
<!ATTLIST name
        language CDATA #REQUIRED>

<!NOTATION jpg SYSTEM "image/jpeg">

<!ENTITY lighthouse_pic SYSTEM
        "lighthouse.jpg" NDATA jpg>

<!ELEMENT photo EMPTY>
<!ATTLIST photo
        source ENTITY #REQUIRED>
```

Figure 7.11 *First, I define the* photo *element that will contain the attribute referencing the unparsed data. Then, I define the entity's attribute* source *using the ENTITY attribute type.*

```
xml
<?xml version="1.0" standalone="no"?>
...
<ancient_wonders>
 <wonder>
  <name language="English">
   Lighthouse of Alexandria</name>
  <name language="Greek">
   ὁ Φάρος τῆς Ἀλεξανδρείας</name>
  <photo source="lighthouse_pic" />
 </wonder>
</ancient_wonders>
```

Figure 7.12 *The value of the* photo *element's* source *attribute corresponds to the name of the entity referencing the unparsed data.*

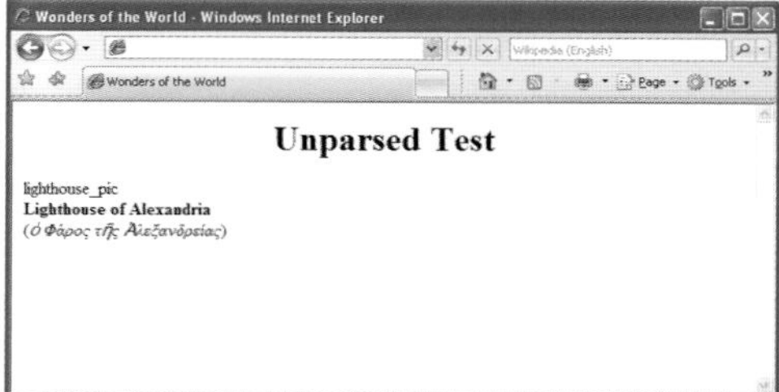

Figure 7.13 *After using XSLT to transform the XML, the results are disappointing in Internet Explorer 7 (shown here), and actually in most other current browsers.*

To embed an unparsed entity in an XML document:

1. In the XML document that will refer to the DTD, add **standalone="no"** to the initial XML declaration. This tells the XML parser that the document will rely on an external file; in this case, the one that contains the unparsed entity.
2. In the body of the XML document, within the attribute declared with an ENTITY type (on the preceding page), type **att_name="ent_name"**, where *att_name* identifies the attribute and *ent_name* is the name of the unparsed entity you created in Step 2 on page 96 **(Figure 7.12)**.

✔ Tips

- While XML parsers are supposed to be able to use the notation information to help them to view/play/display the unparsed entity, current browsers cannot. In short, they won't show the embedded data **(Figure 7.13)**.
- In fact, there is a general consensus that using unparsed entities is complicated and confusing. Instead, you could set an element's value to a URL that points to any file of your choosing, and use attributes to clarify additional information if you desire.

Creating and Using Parameter Entities

The entities that I've talked about so far all reference text or files that will be used in an XML document. In a DTD, you can also create entities for the DTD itself. These kinds of shortcuts are called *parameter entities.*

To create a parameter entity:

1. In the DTD, type **<!ENTITY** to begin the entity definition.
2. Then, type **%** followed by a space to note that the entity is a parameter entity.
3. Next, type **ent_name**, where *ent_name* specifies the name of the entity; the name you'll refer to when using the entity in your DTD.
4. Then, type **"content"**, where *content* is the shortcut text that will appear when you use the entity in your DTD.
5. Finally, type **>** to complete the entity definition **(Figure 7.14)**.

Once you've created the parameter entity, you can use it.

To use a parameter entity:

1. In the DTD, type **%** (with no following space).
2. Then, type **ent_name**, where *ent_name* is the identifying name of your entity (the one you used in Step 3 above).
3. Finally, type **;** (a semicolon) **(Figure 7.15)**.

✔ Tips

- Parameter entities must be created in the DTD before they're used in the DTD. In this case, the order does matter.
- Parameter entities can only be used within the DTD, and are distinguished from general entities by the percent sign (%).

```
dtd
<!ENTITY % p "(#PCDATA)">
```

Figure 7.14 *Here is very simple example. I have created a parameter entity named* p *for something that is quite frequently typed in most DTDs:* (#PCDATA).

```
dtd
<!ENTITY % p "(#PCDATA)">

<!ELEMENT ancient_wonders (wonder+)>
<!ELEMENT wonder (name+, location,
  height, history, main_image,
  source*)>
<!ELEMENT name %p;>
<!ATTLIST name
          language CDATA #REQUIRED>
<!ELEMENT location %p;>
<!ELEMENT height %p;>
<!ATTLIST height
          units CDATA #REQUIRED>
<!ELEMENT history (year_built,
  year_destroyed?, how_destroyed?,
  story)>
<!ELEMENT year_built %p;>
<!ATTLIST year_built
          era (BC | AD) #REQUIRED>
<!ELEMENT year_destroyed %p;>
<!ATTLIST year_destroyed
          era (BC | AD) #REQUIRED>
<!ELEMENT how_destroyed %p;>
<!ELEMENT story (#PCDATA | para)*>
<!ELEMENT para EMPTY>
<!ELEMENT main_image EMPTY>
<!ATTLIST main_image
          file CDATA #REQUIRED
          h CDATA #REQUIRED
          w CDATA #REQUIRED>
<!ELEMENT source EMPTY>
<!ATTLIST source
          sectionid CDATA #REQUIRED
          newspaperid CDATA #REQUIRED>
```

Figure 7.15 *In my master DTD, I am using the* %p; *parameter entity to mean* (#PCDATA).

Creating an External Parameter Entity

As with general entities, parameter entities can also be created in external files.

To create an external parameter entity:

- Create the entity's content in an external file and save it as *text only* using an `.ent` extension **(Figure 7.16)**.

```
d t d
<!ELEMENT main_image EMPTY>
<!ATTLIST main_image
          file CDATA #REQUIRED
          w CDATA #REQUIRED
          h CDATA #REQUIRED>
```

Figure 7.16 *Here is a bit of DTD that I have saved in a separate file called* pic.ent. *I want to use it in several other DTDs, as it contains the declarations for the* main_image *element and its attributes.*

To define an external parameter entity:

1. In your DTD, type **<!ENTITY** to begin the entity definition.
2. Then, type **%** to indicate that this is for a parameter entity.
3. Next, type **ent_name**, where *ent_name* specifies the name of the external entity; the name you'll refer to when using the entity in your XML document.
4. Then, type **SYSTEM** to indicate that the entity is defined externally in another document.
5. Next, type **"entity.uri"**, where *entity.uri* is the location of the file with the entity content.
6. Finally, type **>** to complete the entity definition **(Figure 7.17)**.

```
d t d
<!ENTITY % full_pic SYSTEM "pic.ent">
```

Figure 7.17 *In this DTD, and any in which I want to declare the* main_image *element and its attributes, I have to first define the entity (as shown here).*

✔ Tips

- Use this external parameter entity **(Figure 7.18)** in the same way you would an internal parameter entity, see *Creating and Using Parameter Entities* on page 100.
- If you are using an internal DTD *(see page 106)*, then in the XML document containing the DTD, add **standalone="no"** to the initial XML declaration. This tells the XML parser that the document will rely on an external file.

```
d t d
<!ENTITY % full_pic SYSTEM "pic.ent">

<!ELEMENT ancient_wonders (wonder+)>
<!ELEMENT wonder (name+, location,
  height, history, main_image,
  source*)>
...
<!ELEMENT story (#PCDATA | para)*>
<!ELEMENT para EMPTY>
%full_pic;
<!ELEMENT source EMPTY>
<!ATTLIST source
          sectionid CDATA #REQUIRED
          newspaperid CDATA #REQUIRED>
```

Figure 7.18 *Once the entity is defined, it can be used by typing its reference; in this case,* %full_pic;.

```
x m l
...
<main_image file="gardens.jpg"
  w="528" h="349"/>
<source sectionid="11"
   newspaperid="24"/>
 <source sectionid="18"
   newspaperid="151"/>
</wonder>
...
```

Figure 7.19 *When the DTD in Figure 7.18 is parsed, the processor replaces the* %full_pic *parameter entity reference with the contents of the file shown in Figure 7.16. Now the* main_image *element in the XML file is considered valid against the DTD.*

8 Validation and Using DTDs

In the previous two chapters, you learned how to create DTDs. In this chapter, you'll learn how to use them.

Specifically, a DTD defines rules for every element and attribute that can appear in an XML document. However, you must declare the DTD in your XML document in order to use it. Once this declaration is made, you can use various tools to validate the XML document against the DTD. This is the reason for creating a DTD in the first place, to insure that a given XML document is constructed in a specific way as defined by the DTD.

DTDs can be written and saved as separate files, or they can be written entirely inside an XML document. A benefit of writing internal DTDs is that there is only one file to manage that contains both the DTD structure and the XML content. A benefit of writing external DTDs is that they can easily be used to validate many XML documents. In fact, they can be used by other people and companies who are generating XML documents to validate their documents before sending them to you, and vice versa. In this way, the validation process enables the sharing of XML documents, as well as the verification that these documents are all consistently structured.

Creating an External DTD

If you have a set of related XML documents, you may want them all to use the same DTD. Instead of copying the DTD into each document, you can create an external file that contains the DTD **(Figure 8.1)**, and then reference the DTD from each of the XML documents that needs it.

To create an external DTD:

1. Define the rules for the DTD in an external file, as described in Chapters 6 and 7.
2. Save the file as *text only* using an extension of `.dtd`.

✔ Tips

- As you may have noticed in the previous two chapters, all the DTD examples that were used by the XML documents were external DTDs. This is the most common way of using DTDs.
- For details on how to use this external DTD, see *Declaring an External DTD* on page 105.

```
dtd
<!ELEMENT wonder (name, location,
                  height)>
<!ELEMENT name     (#PCDATA)>
<!ELEMENT location (#PCDATA)>
<!ELEMENT height   (#PCDATA)>
```

Figure 8.1 *This DTD has been saved as* 08-01.dtd *(the filename has no special meaning, except that it corresponds to the Figure 8.1). Notice that it has no relationship to any XML document, yet. It simply contains DTD definitions and was saved as* text only *with the* .dtd *extension.*

```
xml
<?xml version="1.0" standalone="no"?>
<!DOCTYPE wonder SYSTEM "08-01.dtd">
<wonder>
 <name>Colossus of Rhodes</name>
 <location>Greece</location>
 <height>107</height>
</wonder>
```

```
xml
<?xml version="1.0" standalone="no"?>
<!DOCTYPE wonder SYSTEM "08-01.dtd">
<wonder>
 <name>Colossus of Rhodes</name>
 <location>Greece</location>
 <height units="feet">107</height>
</wonder>
```

```
xml
<?xml version="1.0" standalone="no"?>
<!DOCTYPE wonder SYSTEM "08-01.dtd">
<wonder>
 <name>Colossus of Rhodes</name>
 <name language="Greek">
   Κολοσσός της Ρόδου</name>
 <location>Greece</location>
 <height>107</height>
</wonder>
```

Figure 8.2 *According to the DTD referred to in each of these XML documents' document type declarations (*08-01.dtd*, shown in Figure 8.1), only the first XML document is valid. In the second, the* height *element has a* units *attribute that is not defined. In the third, there are two* name *elements, but only one is allowed.*

Declaring an External DTD

Now that you've created an external DTD, you need to refer to it within your XML document. You do this using a *document type declaration* (see the last Tip on this page) which declares the DTD **(Figure 8.2)**.

To declare an external DTD:

1. Type **<!DOCTYPE root**, where *root* corresponds to the name of the root element in this XML document.
2. Then, type **SYSTEM** to indicate that the DTD is defined in an external document.
3. Next, type **"dtd.uri"**, where *dtd.uri* is the location of the file with the DTD content.
4. Finally, type **>** to complete the document type declaration.
5. Then, in the XML declaration at the top of the document, add **standalone="no"**. This tells the XML parser that the document will rely on an external file; in this case, the one that contains the DTD.

✔ Tips

- As discussed, for an XML document to be *valid*, it must conform to the rules of the corresponding DTD.
- The **"dtd.uri"** in Step 3 above can refer to a file on your computer, a local area network, or the Internet.
- The default value of the `standalone` attribute in the XML declaration in Step 5 is `no`. Consequently, in the examples in Figure 8.2, the attribute was not needed.
- Here's some terminology fun. The collection of element and attribute rules is called a DTD, or *document type definition*. The lines of code that refer to the DTD are called a *document type declaration*. To distinguish them, think of the document type declaration as the instruction that refers to, or declares, the document type definition.

Declaring and Creating an Internal DTD

For individual XML documents (ones that you won't be sharing with others, or at least a very little), it is simplest to declare and create the DTD within the XML document itself.

The rules for creating a DTD, whether internal or external, are the same. The difference between the two is the way the *document type declaration* is written; in other words, how the DTD is declared.

To declare and create an internal DTD:

1. At the top of your XML document, after the XML declaration *(see page 7)*, type **<!DOCTYPE root [**, where *root* corresponds to the name of the root element in your XML document.
2. Then, create your DTD by defining its elements and attributes using the information you learned in the previous two chapters.
3. Finally, type **]>** to complete the document type declaration **(Figure 8.3)**.

✔ Tips

- Even though internal DTD declarations are part of the XML document itself, they are not XML elements, and thus do not require a closing slash before the final **>**.
- In fact, although the DTD schema specification is part of the XML specification, DTDs use a specific syntax that is not XML compliant at all.
- You can use both an internal and external DTD in the same XML document **(Figure 8.4)**. When doing so, the internal DTD rules override those from the external DTD. Unfortunately, however, most XML processors treat conflicts between an internal and external DTD as errors **(Figure 8.5)**.

```
xml
<?xml version="1.0"?>
<!DOCTYPE wonder [
 <!ELEMENT wonder
 <!ELEMENT wonder (name, location,
   height)>
 <!ELEMENT name (#PCDATA)>
 <!ELEMENT location (#PCDATA)>
 <!ELEMENT height (#PCDATA)>
]>
<wonder>
 <name>Colossus of Rhodes</name>
 <location>Greece</location>
 <height>107</height>
</wonder>
```

Figure 8.3 *Here is a simple internal DTD. It goes right after the XML declaration and before the actual tags in the body of the XML document. This corresponds to the first example in Figure 8.2.*

```
xml
<?xml version="1.0"?>
<!DOCTYPE wonder SYSTEM "08-01.dtd"[
 <!ATTLIST height
           units CDATA #REQUIRED>
]>
<wonder>
 <name>Colossus of Rhodes</name>
 <location>Greece</location>
 <height units="feet">107</height>
</wonder>
```

Figure 8.4 *Combining both an internal and external DTD can sometimes be beneficial. Here, I have updated the second example in Figure 8.2 with an internal DTD which declares a* units *attribute for the* height *element. It is now a valid XML document.*

```
xml
<?xml version="1.0"?>
<!DOCTYPE wonder SYSTEM "08-01.dtd"[
<!ELEMENT wonder (name*, location,
                  height)>
<!ATTLIST name
         language CDATA #IMPLIED>
]>
<wonder>
 <name>Colossus of Rhodes</name>
 <name language="Greek">
   Κολοσσός της Ρόδου</name> ...
```

Figure 8.5 *Unfortunately, while the third example from Figure 8.2 now appears to be valid, most XML processors will return an error stating that it is not legal to redefine the* wonder *element.*

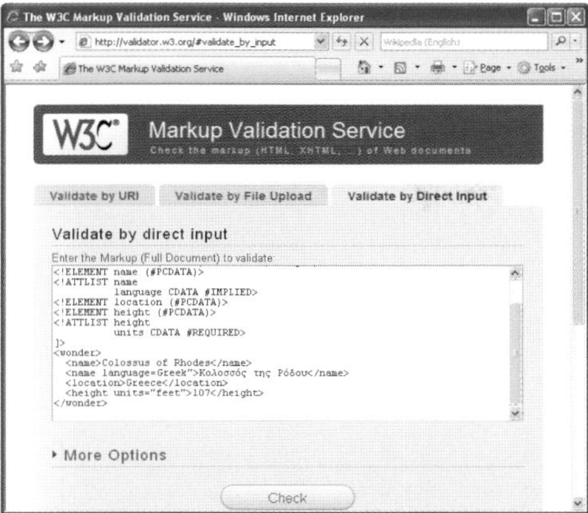

Figure 8.6 *I copied and pasted the XML from my editor into the text box labeled* "Validate by direct input." *(Can you see the error?)*

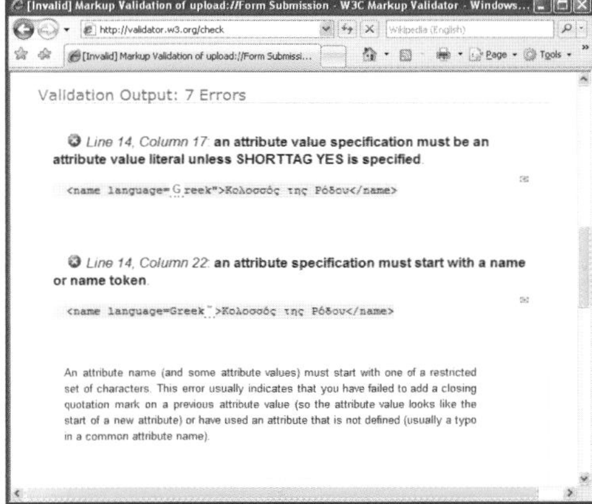

Figure 8.7 *The validator tells me that I've forgotten the opening quotation mark before the attribute value* "Greek". *Also notice that this problem caused seven total errors. However, once the quotation mark error is fixed, all the additional "ghost" errors will disappear.*

Validating XML Documents Against a DTD

Now that you have created your DTD and have declared it in your XML document, you will want to validate your XML against it. Every XML parser is required to return an error if your XML document is not well-formed; however, not all have the ability to validate your XML against a DTD.

If the XML parser you are using cannot validate XML against a DTD, there are several validators available online. I like the W3C's Markup Validation Service.

To use an online validator:

1. Make sure you've declared the DTD in your document.
2. With your browser, go to: *http://validator.w3.org/* **(Figure 8.6)**.
3. You can choose to "Validate by URI," "Validate by File Upload," or "Validate by Direct Input" (that is, copying your XML document into the text box on the page).
4. Click "Check". The validator gives you a useful report of any errors it may find **(Figure 8.7)**.

✔ Tips

- If you use an external DTD, it must be publicly available as well, otherwise an online validator won't be able to get to it.
- Often, one error can cause *ghost errors*, where most of the code below this first error is misunderstood, see Figure 8.7. Usually, if you correct the first error in the list and then revalidate, many additional errors (the ghost errors) will disappear.
- Another online validator is Brown University's Scholarly Technology Group's XML Validator at: *www.stg.brown.edu/service/xmlvalid/*.

Naming a Public External DTD

If your DTD will be used by others, you should name your DTDs in a standard way: using a *formal public identifier*, or FPI. An XML parser could then use the FPI to find the latest version of the DTD on a public Web server.

To name an external DTD:

1. Type

   -//, if your DTD is not a recognized standard (this is most common), or

   +//, if your DTD is an approved non-ISO standard, or

   ISO//, if your DTD is an approved ISO standard.
2. Then, type **owner//**, where *owner* identifies the person or organization who wrote and will maintain the DTD.
3. Next, type **DTD description//**, where *description* is a reference to the DTD and should contain a unique element, such as a version number.
4. Finally, type **XX**, where *XX* is the two-letter abbreviation for the language the DTD uses. Use **EN** for English (and see Tip for more on other languages).

✔ Tips

- You can find the complete, official list of two-letter language abbreviations in ISO 639 online at: *www.unicode.org/unicode/onlinedat/languages.html.*
- ISO is the International Organization for Standardization. It is an international standards organization similar to the W3C.

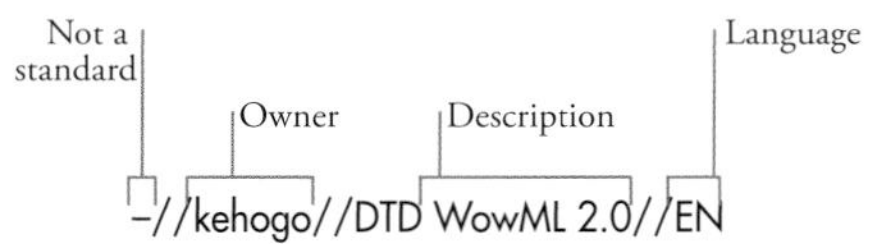

Figure 8.8 *Here is the official public name for the DTD that will describe my Wonders of the World XML documents.*

```xml
<?xml version="1.0"?>
<!DOCTYPE ancient_wonders PUBLIC
  "-//kehogo//DTD WowML 2.0//EN"
  "http://www.kehogo.com/dtd
   /wonders-master.dtd">

<ancient_wonders>
 <wonder>
  <name language="English">
    Colossus of Rhodes</name>
...
 </wonder>
</ancient_wonders>
```

Figure 8.9 *This time, the XML parser will use the public identifier to try and find the DTD, perhaps in a public repository. If that proves unsuccessful, it will use the DTD referenced by the given URI.*

Declaring a Public External DTD

If my Wonders of the World DTD becomes very popular, and there are copies of it distributed far and wide, I would want it to be possible for the public to declare it in their own XML documents using its formal public identifier (the name I just created for it on page 108).

To declare a public external DTD:

1. Type **<!DOCTYPE root**, where *root* is the name of the root element in the XML document to which the DTD will apply.
2. Then, type **PUBLIC** to indicate that the DTD is a standardized, publicly available DTD.
3. Next, type **"FPI"**, where *FPI* is the formal public identifier for the DTD *(see page 108)*.
4. Then, type **"dtd.uri"**, where *dtd.uri* is the location of the DTD, indicating its location on a public server.
5. Finally, type **>** to complete the document type declaration.
6. Then, in the XML declaration at the top of the document, add **standalone="no"**. This tells the XML parser that the document will rely on an external file; in this case, the public external DTD.

✔ Tip

- When an XML parser sees a formal public identifier, it will usually try to get a copy of the DTD from the best possible server; perhaps one that's closer on the Internet or one that has the latest version of the DTD. If it can't find the DTD by using the FPI, it can then resort to using the URI.

Pros and Cons of DTDs

DTDs are schemas. They specify the elements, attributes, and relationships that a valid XML document can contain.

DTDs are very powerful and very useful; however, there are other schema languages for XML. The most recognized and most used alternative is called XML Schema, and each schema language has its costs and benefits. I will discuss XML Schema in the next part of the book.

Some pros of using DTDs:

- They are compact and easily comprehended with a little direction.
- They can be defined inline (internal DTDs) for quick development.
- They can define entities (see Chapter 7).
- They are likely the most widely accepted and are supported by most XML parsers.

Some cons of using DTDs:

- They are not written using XML syntax, and require parsers to support an additional language.
- They do not support Namespaces (see Chapters 12 and 13).
- They do not have data typing (requiring data to be an integer, a string, or a date, etc.), thereby decreasing the strength of the validation.
- They have limited capacity to define how many child elements can nest within a given parent element.

Part 4: XML Schema

9

XML Schema Basics

The specifications for XML include the syntax for a schema language: A way to define what a valid XML document could contain. This language, known as a DTD (Document Type Definition), enables users to define elements, attributes, and their relationships for any application of XML needed *(see Part 3)*.

In 2001, the W3C developed a new schema language to address many of the shortcomings of DTD *(see page 110)*. This schema language was named XML Schema, which is admittedly confusing because DTDs are a type of XML schema (lower case "s"). Even still, it's most often called XML Schema, though it is occasionally called XML Schema Definition (XSD). And now, with version 1.1 of the language, it is known as XML Schema Definition Language (XSDL). However, for this book, I will use the name XML Schema, which is still the most widely recognized name of them all.

XML Schema, written in XML itself, is deeper and more powerful than a DTD. A few examples of its strength include its system of data types that let you specify when an element should, for example, contain an integer, or a period of time, or a string. It supports namespaces, which are discussed in Chapters 12 and 13. It also lets you define both local and global elements, thereby allowing two elements to have different definitions, even though they have the same name. In short, XML Schema gives you much more control over the contents of an XML document, and will likely supplant DTDs as the most widely accepted schema language in the near future.

Working with XML Schema

An XML Schema specifies the structure of valid XML documents **(Figure 9.1)** by defining a set of elements, their relationships to each other, and the attributes that they can contain. In a DTD, all XML elements are defined using one element type. In XML Schema, an XML element can be defined as either a simple type or a complex type. Essentially, a *simple type* is an XML element that only contains text, whereas a *complex type* is an XML element that contains child elements and/or attributes.

Let's take a closer look at simple types. Again, in XML Schema, a simple type element is one that contains only text. In a DTD, a text-only element is defined as #PCDATA, meaning its contents might be a name, number, date, or practically anything. In XML Schema, you can (and must) specify exactly what kind of content you want an element to contain. You do this by assigning it a *data type*. There are many built-in data types; like string, integer, and date **(Figure 9.2)**. You can also create custom data types to have even more control over an element's content.

Where simple type elements describe the text of an XML document, complex type elements describe its structure **(Figure 9.3)**. There are four kinds of complex type elements: those that contain child elements; those that contain both child elements and text; those that contain only text; and those that are empty. You'll find more detailed information in Chapter 11, *Defining Complex Types*.

```xml
<?xml version="1.0"?>
<wonder>
 <name>Colossus of Rhodes</name>
  <location>Greece</location>
  <height>107</height>
</wonder>
```

Figure 9.1 *Here is one of the first XML documents I used in the book.*

```xsd
<element name="name"
  type="string"/>

<element name="location"
  type="string"/>

<element name="height"
  type="integer"/>
```

Figure 9.2 *These elements are defined using XML Schema's built-in simple data types. The* name *and* location *elements must be strings, and the* height *element must be an integer.*

```xsd
<element name="wonder">
  <complexType>
    <sequence>
...
    </sequence>
  </complexType>
</element>
```

Figure 9.3 *This complex type definition using XML Schema defines the* wonder *element as containing a sequence of elements (the sequence of child elements is not shown here).*

Working with XML Schema

```
xsd
<?xml version="1.0"?>
<element name="wonder">
 <complexType>
  <sequence>
   <element name="name"
     type="string"/>
   <element name="location"
     type="string"/>
   <element name="height"
     type="string"/>
  </sequence>
 </complexType>
</element>
```

Figure 9.4 *Put Figures 9.2 and 9.3 together and you get most of an XML Schema that defines the XML document shown in Figure 9.1. The rest of the XML Schema is explained on the next page.*

✔ Tips

- One of the benefits of XML Schema is that it uses XML syntax, which you probably already know by now!
- Because an XML Schema is an XML document, it must begin with an XML declaration, have one root element, and be well-formed, just like all other XML documents **(Figure 9.4)**.
- Interestingly, when the first version of this book was being published, XML Schema was still a working draft. Now, the W3C is working towards the completion of XML Schema Version 1.1. It is being developed to fix bugs and make improvements where possible, while maintaining the same basic scope as (and remaining mostly compatible with) version 1.0. You can find up-to-date information at the W3C's XML Schema Working Group site at: *www.w3.org/XML/Schema.*

Beginning a Simple XML Schema

An XML Schema is a text-only document, and begins with a standard XML declaration. It is customarily saved with an `.xsd` extension, and its root element must be `schema`.

To begin an XML Schema:

1. At the top of your document, type **<?xml version="1.0"?>**.
2. Type **<xs:schema** to define the root element. The `xs:` is a namespace prefix *(see Tip on namespaces below)*.
3. Then, type **xmlns:xs="http://www.3.org/2001/XMLSchema"** to declare the XML Schema namespace (*xmlns*). This also declares that the elements and data types that are part of this namespace should be prefixed with `xs:` as you saw in Step 2 above.
4. Type **>** to complete the root element's tag.
5. Leave a few empty lines for your XML Schema's rules.
6. Finally, type **</xs:schema>** to complete the root element, and the XML Schema document itself **(Figure 9.5)**.

✔ Tips

- A *namespace* is a "space" in which names reside. Names that are part of one namespace are not the same as names that are part of another namespace (even if they are spelled the exact same way).
- The W3C created a namespace which contains all XML Schema elements and data types. This namespace is declared in Step 3 above. Once declared, in order to indicate that a particular element or data type should be considered part of the W3C's XML Schema namespace, it must start with the `xs:` namespace prefix **(Figure 9.6)**. Namespaces are discussed at length in Chapters 12 and 13.

xsd

```
<?xml version="1.0"?>
<xs:schema xmlns:xs=
  "http://www.w3.org/2001/XMLSchema">

...

</xs:schema>
```

Figure 9.5 *An XML Schema is an XML document itself. The root element must be* schema, *and its namespace is declared to be the W3C's XML Schema namespace.*

xsd

```
<?xml version="1.0"?>
<xs:schema xmlns:xs=
  "http://www.w3.org/2001/XMLSchema">

<xs:element name="wonder">
 <xs:complexType>
  <xs:sequence>
   <xs:element name="name"
     type="xs:string"/>
   <xs:element name="location"
     type="xs:string"/>
   <xs:element name="height"
     type="xs:string"/>
  </xs:sequence>
 </xs:complexType>
</xs:element>

</xs:schema>
```

Figure 9.6 *Here, I've combined the XML Schema excerpt in Figure 9.4 with the correct XML declaration, an* xs:schema *root definition. I have also started all the XML Schema elements with the XML Schema namespace prefix* xs:.

```
xml
<?xml version="1.0"?>
<wonder xmlns:xsi="http://
  www.w3.org/2001/XMLSchema-instance"
  xsi:noNamespaceSchemaLocation=
  "09-06.xsd">
...
```

Figure 9.7 *In order to associate an XML Schema with an XML document, you must declare the XML Schema document location within the root element of the XML document.*

```
xml
<?xml version="1.0"?>
<wonder xmlns:xsi="http://
  www.w3.org/2001/XMLSchema-instance"
  xsi:noNamespaceSchemaLocation=
  "09-06.xsd">

 <name>Colossus of Rhodes</name>
 <location>Greece</location>
 <height>107</height>

</wonder>
```

Figure 9.8 *Here, I've added the XML Schema association to the XML document from Figure 9.1. Then, when checked, this XML document is valid against the XML Schema in Figure 9.6.*

Associating an XML Schema with an XML Document

To validate an XML document against an XML Schema, you must specify the location of the XML Schema in the XML document itself.

To declare the XML Schema and its location:

1. Inside the definition of the root element of your XML document, type **xmlns:xsi= "http://www.w3.org/2001/XMLSchema"**. This allows you to define the location of your XML Schema in the next two steps.
2. Type **xsi:noNamespaceSchemaLocation=**
3. Finally, type **"xsd.uri"**, where *xsd.uri* is the location of the XML Schema file against which you want to validate your XML file **(Figure 9.7)**.

✔ Tips

- Most XML parsers can validate XML documents against a declared XML Schema **(Figure 9.8)**. If the XML parser you are using cannot, there are validators available online that can. The W3C has a validator at: *www.w3.org/2001/03/webdata/xsv*. There are other validators listed at: *www.w3.org/XML/Schema*.
- The **"xsd.uri"** in Step 3 above can refer to a file on the Internet, local area network, or your local computer.
- Step 1 above declares the *XML Schema Instance* namespace which includes the `xsi:noNamespaceSchemaLocation` attribute used in Step 2, along with a few other namespace attributes. Namespaces are discussed in Chapters 12 and 13.

Annotating Schemas

Since an XML Schema is an XML document, you can include standard XML comments in your XML Schema documents *(see page 13)*.

In addition to these standard comments, XML Schema offers the ability to add more structured comments to your document. Whereas XML comments are readable by people, they are ignored by parsers, and often not passed through during XML transformations. XML Schema comments (*annotations*, as they are called), can be parsed and processed, because they are elements themselves **(Figure 9.9)**.

To annotate XML Schemas:

1. Type **<xs:annotation>**.
2. Next, type **<xs:documentation>** to begin the comment.
3. Type the comment.
4. Type **</xs:documentation>** to complete the comment.
5. Finally, type **</xs:annotation>** to complete the annotation.

✔ Tips

- Whether you use XML comments, XML Schema annotations (or both), commenting your XML Schema makes it much easier to work with your documents.
- You can create annotations anywhere in the XML Schema, after the root element. They can be placed just after the `xs:schema` root element (to comment on the entire schema), or just after individual element definitions (to give more information about them), or both.

xsd

```
<?xml version="1.0"?>
<xs:schema xmlns=
  "http://www.w3.org/2001/XMLSchema">

<xs:annotation>
 <xs:documentation>This XML Schema
   will be used to validate the set
   of XML documents for the Wonders
   of the World project.
 </xs:documentation>
</xs:annotation>
...
```

Figure 9.9 *An annotation helps you document the XML Schema. It can facilitate future revisions.*

10

Defining Simple Types

In XML Schema, an element defined as a simple type can contain only text. In other words, it cannot have attributes or child elements. However, it's a little misleading to say it can only contain text. Rather, it's more accurate to say that it can only contain a value, because with XML Schema, you can declare that it can contain a particular kind of text. In other words, you can declare that an element contain only numbers, or only dates, or only boolean values, etc.

XML Schema includes a large collection of built-in simple types for the most common kinds of text. These include strings, boolean values, URLs, various date and time formats, and numbers of all kinds.

You can also apply restrictions, or *facets*, to these simple types in order to limit them further. In doing so, you actually can create your own custom simple types. For example, you might want to define that an element contain a string that matches a certain pattern (like a telephone number or product code). Or, you might want to define that an element can only contain one of a specific set of dates. This feature allows you to more specifically and effectively define the acceptable element values that make up a valid XML document.

Defining a Simple Type Element

As stated, in XML Schema, a simple type element can only contain a value; it may not contain any child elements, and it may not have any attributes.

With simple types, you can define that an XML element be a string, integer, boolean value **(Figure 10.1)**, or one of the other simple data types that are built into the XML Schema language *(see pages 122–124)*.

To define a simple type element:

1. Type **<xs:element** to begin the definition.
2. Then, type **name="label"**, where *label* is the name of the XML element that you are defining. (In other words, the name of the element for which you are writing the XML Schema should replace the word "label".)
3. Next, type **type="**.
4. Then, to identify your XML element's simple data type:

   Type **xs:string** if the element will contain a string of characters.

   Or type **xs:decimal** if the element will contain a decimal number. For other possible number types, see page 124.

   Or type **xs:boolean** if the element will contain the values *true* or *false* (or, *1* or *0*).

   Or type **xs:date** if the element will be a date. For other possible date types, see page 122.

   Or type **xs:time** if the element will be a time of day. For other possible time types, see page 122.

   Or type **xs:anyURI** (as in *URI* and not *URL*) if the element will contain a reference to a file on the Internet, a local area network, or even your computer.
5. Next, type **"** to complete the data type.
6. Finally, type **/>** to complete the definition.

```
xsd
<xs:element name="height"
            type="xs:string"/>

<xs:element name="year_built"
            type="xs:integer"/>
```

Figure 10.1 *When defining an element in an XML Schema, you identify the XML document's element name and what kind of content it should contain (its simple data type). In this case, the content of the* height *element is defined to be a string, and* year_built *is defined to be an integer.*

```
xml
<height>39 feet</height>

<year_built>430</year_built>
```

Figure 10.2 *A* string *is a series of letters, numbers, and/or symbols. An* integer *is any whole number. Therefore, both the* height *and* year_built *elements are valid when compared against the XML Schema definition in Figure 10.1.*

```
xml
<height>39</height>

<year_built>long ago</year_built>
```

Figure 10.3 *In this XML excerpt, the* height *element looks like it might not be valid based on the XML Schema in Figure 10.1; but in fact, it is valid since a number is a string (though, conversely, not all strings are numbers). The* year_built *element, however, is invalid. The phrase "long ago" is not an integer.*

```
xsd
<xs:element name="last_modified"
            type="xs:date"/>
```

Figure 10.4 *In this XML Schema excerpt, the XML element* last_modified *is defined to contain date values. This is done by using the built-in XML Schema simple type:* date.

```
xml
<last_modified>2008-05-23
  </last_modified>
```

Figure 10.5 *The* last_modified *element in this XML excerpt is valid based on the XML Schema definition in Figure 10.4. It is valid because it contains a date, and is in the proper format. In XML Schema, the date format is* YYYY-MM-DD. *(That is, a four-digit year, followed by a dash, followed by two digits representing the month, another dash, and then two digits representing the day.) With all built-in simple type formats, it's important to know the format in which the data should be written.*

```
xml
<last_modified>May 23, 2008
  </last_modified>
```

Figure 10.6 *Although this* last_modified *element contains a date, it is actually not valid because the date is not in the proper format.*

✔ Tips

- There are many other built-in simple types. You can find the entire list at: *www.w3.org/TR/xmlschema-2/#built-in-datatypes.*
- Built-in simple types always begin with the XML Schema namespace prefix, which is typically declared as `xs:` **(Figure 10.4)**. Namespaces are discussed in more detail in Part 5 of the book.
- You can also create custom simple types by extending the built-in simple types. For more details, consult *Deriving Custom Simple Types* on page 126.
- Attributes themselves are also simple types (since they can only contain values, not child elements or attributes of their own), and they are declared in much the same way as simple type elements. I'll discuss them in the next chapter, see *Defining Attributes* on page 154.
- To reiterate, a simple type element cannot contain child elements or attributes. If an element needs to contain child elements or attributes, it will be defined as a complex type. For more details, see Chapter 11, *Defining Complex Types.*

Using Date and Time Types

In addition to the simple data types I just discussed, XML Schema has several more refined data types for dates and times. To define an XML element using one of these types, replace Step 4 on page 120 with the one below that suits your purpose.

To use date and time types:

- Use **xs:date** to require that an element's content be a date **(Figure 10.7)**. It must be formatted **YYYY-MM-DD**. That is, May 23, 2008 would be written: 2008-05-23.
- Use **xs:time** to require that an element's content be the time of day **(Figure 10.8)**. It must be formatted **hh:mm:ss**. That is, 4:21 p.m. is written: 16:21:00. (Time is written in "military" or universal format.)
- Use **xs:dateTime** to require that an element's content be a date and a time **(Figure 10.9)**. It should be formatted **YYYY-MM-DDThh:mm:ss**. That is, 4:21 p.m. on May, 23, 2008 would be written: 2008-05-23T16:21:00.
- Use **xs:duration** to require that an element's content be an amount of time **(Figure 10.10)**.

  The duration must be formatted as **PnYnMnDTnHnMnS**, where **P** is always required (it stands for Period), and **T** is only required if you have any time units. Each *n* indicates how many of the following units there are: **Y**ears, **M**onths, **D**ays, **H**ours, **M**inutes, **S**econds, and is a non-optional, non-negative integer. For example, 3 months, 4 days, 6 hours, and 17 minutes would be written: P3M4DT6H17M, and 90 days would be written: P90D.

  You can also add an optional leading hyphen to indicate that the duration goes back in time (not forward). For example, –P90D would mean 90 days ago.

xsd
```
<xs:element name="birth"
  type="xs:date"/>
```

xml
```
<birth>1879-03-14</birth>
```

Figure 10.7 *Albert Einstein was born on March 14, 1879. (In 1921, Einstein received the Nobel Prize for his work in Theoretical Physics, and in 1999 he was named "Person of the Century" by* Time *magazine.)*

xsd
```
<xs:element name="time_painted"
  type="xs:time"/>
```

xml
```
<time_painted>21:08:00</time_painted>
```

Figure 10.8 *Initially thought to be the setting sun, it is now believed that Vincent van Gogh's Expressionist painting "*Moonrise,*" depicts the night sky in Saint-Rémy at 9:08 p.m., on July 13, 1889. (Notice that the time is written in "military" or universal format.)*

xsd
```
<xs:element name="when_shot"
  type="xs:dateTime"/>
```

xml
```
<when_shot>
  1968-04-04T18:01:00-05:00</when_shot>
```

Figure 10.9 *The assassination of Martin Luther King, Jr., a well-known leader in the American Civil Rights movement, took place at 6:01 p.m. on April 4, 1968. His assassination happened in Tennessee, so the time is written with –05:00, indicating a –5 hour offset from UTC (see first Tip on the next page).*

xsd
```
<xs:element name="strike_length"
  type="xs:duration"/>
```

xml
```
<strike_length>P5D</strike_length>
```

Figure 10.10 *Mohandas Gandhi was a world-renowned leader who made famous the idea of resistance through civil disobedience. In 1939, while in prison, he went on a 5-day hunger strike for peace.*

```
xsd
<xs:element name="tribute_year"
  type="xs:gYear"/>
```

```
xml
<tribute_year>1995</tribute_year>
```

Figure 10.11 *Marie Curie's work in radioactivity won her Nobel Prizes in 1903 and 1911. In 1995, her ashes were transferred to the Panthéon in Paris, making her the first woman ever honored in that way.*

```
xsd
<xs:element name="birth_month"
  type="xs:gMonth"/>
```

```
xml
<birth_month>--12</birth_month>
```

Figure 10.12 *Nostradamus was an apothecary, but is best known for his collection of prophecies. And, although it is known that he was born in the month of December, historians are not certain on which day.*

```
xsd
<xs:element name="leap_day"
  type="xs:gMonthDay"/>
```

```
xml
<leap_day>--02-29</leap_day>
```

Figure 10.13 *February 29th is Leap Day. It occurs every four years (with the exception of century years not divisible by 400, such as 1800) to resync our calendar with the revolution of the Earth around the sun.*

```
xsd
<xs:element name="ides"
  type="xs:gDay"/>
```

```
xml
<ides>---15</ides>
```

Figure 10.14 *The word* ides *comes from the Latin word "idus," meaning "half division." It is often thought to mean the 15th day of the month because of Julius Caesar's assassination on the Ides of March, March 15th. Actually, in ancient Roman times,* ides *referred to the 15th day of March, May, July, and October, but the 13th day of the other months.*

- Use **xs:gYear** to require that an element's content be a year **(Figure 10.11)**. It should be formatted **YYYY**.
- Use **xs:gYearMonth** to require that an element's content be a year and month. It should be formatted **YYYY-MM**.
- Use **xs:gMonth** to require that an element's content be a month **(Figure 10.12)**. It should be formatted **--MM**. (That's two initial dashes: One to represent the "missing" year, and one to act as a separator). For example, April would be written: --04.
- Use **xs:gMonthDay** to require that an element's content be the day of a month **(Figure 10.13)**. It should be formatted **--MM-DD**. (That's two initial dashes: One to represent the "missing" year, and one to act as a separator.) For example, September 14th would be written as --09-14.
- Use **xs:gDay** to require that an element's content be a day of the month **(Figure 10.14)**. It should be formatted **---DD**. (Three initial dashes here: One for each "missing" piece, and one as a separator.) For example, the 7th day of the month would be written as ---07.

✔ Tips

- All time types can also end with an optional time zone indicator. You would type **Z** for UTC or one of **-hh:mm** or **+hh:mm** to indicate an offset from UTC. UTC (Coordinated Universal Time) is the same time as Greenwich Mean Time.
- Time types can also include fractional seconds in the format **hh:mm:ss.sss**. You can include as many digits as you'd like.
- The *g* in the simple types on this page stands for Gregorian. This refers to the Gregorian calendar, which is the most commonly used calendar today.

Using Number Types

XML Schema also has several more refined simple types for numbers **(Figure 10.15)**. To define the acceptable content for an XML element using one of these types, replace Step 4 on page 120 with one of the types below.

To use number types:

- Use **xs:decimal** when you want the content to be either positive or negative numbers that have a finite number of digits on either side of the optional decimal point, such as 4.26, –100, or 0.
- Use **xs:integer** when you want the content to be positive or negative whole numbers; that is, those that have no fractional part, like 542 or –7.
- Use **xs:positiveInteger** (1, 2, etc.), **xs:negativeInteger** (–1, –2, etc.), **xs:nonPositiveInteger** (0, –1, –2, etc.), or **xs:nonNegativeInteger** (0, 1, 2, etc.) when you want the content to one be those kinds of numbers.
- Use **xs:int** when you want the content to be a signed 32-bit integer, often used for database ID fields.
- Use **xs:float** when you want the content to be single precision, 32-bit floating point numbers like 43e–2. This includes positive and negative zero (0 and –0), positive and negative infinity (INF and –INF), and "not a number" (NaN).

✔ Tips

- You can find more number types explained at: *www.w3.org/TR/xmlschema-2/*, such as `short`, `byte`, and the unsigned versions of some I've already listed here.
- You can also use these types (as well as the ones listed on the previous pages) as the foundation on which to define your own data types *(see page 126)*.

```
xsd
<xs:element name="years_standing"
  type="xs:positiveInteger"/>

<xs:element name="height"
  type="xs:decimal"/>
```

Figure 10.15 *It's more precise to require a positive integer for* years_standing. *(An integer, or even a non-negative integer, would not be appropriate, allowing either a negative value, or even zero). The* height *element could well use the precision of a decimal number.*

```
xml
<years_standing>
  1602</years_standing>

<height>384.25</height>
```

Figure 10.16 *Based on the XML Schema definition in Figure 10.15, as long as the* years_standing *is an integer greater than 0, the element is valid. The* height *may have both a fractional and a whole part.*

```
xml
<years_standing>
  1602.5</years_standing>

<height>384</height>
```

Figure 10.17 *The* years_standing *element in this excerpt is invalid. Since it was defined to be an integer, it cannot have a decimal part. The* height *element is valid, however, since a decimal number may have a fractional portion, but it is not required to.*

```
xsd
<xs:element name="how_destroyed"
 type="xs:string" fixed="fire"/>
```

Figure 10.18 *Defining the* how_destroyed *element with a fixed value means as long as it appears in the XML, it must be the string "fire" (or be empty, in which case it's considered to have the string "fire").*

```
xml
<how_destroyed>fire</how_destroyed>
```

```
xml
<how_destroyed></how_destroyed>
```

```
xml
<how_destroyed>
  earthquake</how_destroyed>
```

Figure 10.19 *The first XML excerpt is valid because the* how_destroyed *element matches the fixed value from the XML Schema excerpt in Figure 10.18. The second XML excerpt is valid because the element is empty, so it's set to the fixed value. The third isn't valid because it doesn't match the fixed value.*

```
xsd
<xs:element name="how_destroyed"
 type="xs:string" default="fire"/>
```

Figure 10.20 *Defining the* how_destroyed *element with a default value means that value will be set as the initial content whether or not the* how_destroyed *element appears in the XML document.*

```
xml
<how_destroyed>fire</how_destroyed>
```

```
xml
<how_destroyed></how_destroyed>
```

```
xml
<how_destroyed>
  earthquake</how_destroyed>
```

Figure 10.21 *All these XML examples are valid based on the XML Schema excerpt in Figure 10.20. The default attribute only sets an initial value, and any other value is also acceptable.*

Predefining an Element's Content

There are two ways to use an XML Schema to predefine what an element's content should be. You can either set the element's value using a *fixed* value **(Figure 10.18)**. Or, you can set the element's value if it's empty or omitted using a *default* value **(Figure 10.20)**.

To set an element's value:

1. Within the element tag, type **fixed=**.
2. Then, type **"value"**, where *value* is what the element must be equal to, in order to be considered valid (unless the element is omitted from the XML document, which is also valid).

To set an element's default value:

1. Within the element tag, type **default=**.
2. Then, type **"value"**, where *value* is what the element will be equal to, if the element is empty or omitted.

✔ Tips

- The `fixed` attribute only sets the content if the element actually appears empty in the XML **(Figure 10.19)**. If it is omitted, then no content is set.
- If the element has a value that is different from the fixed value, then the XML document is not valid.
- The `default` attribute sets the content if the element appears empty in the XML or if it is omitted **(Figure 10.21)**.
- If the element has a value that is different from the default value, the XML document is valid, and the element's value is the one specified in the XML document.
- You cannot set both a `default` and a `fixed` attribute at the same time. Since they contradict each other, an XML Schema processor will not allow this.

Deriving Custom Simple Types

The XML Schema language contains many built-in simple types. Using these types as a foundation, the language allows you to derive your own custom simple types.

To derive a custom simple type:

1. First, identify the name of the XML element that you are using XML Schema to define. To do so, type **<xs:element name="label">**, where *label* is the name of the XML element **(Figure 10.22)**.
2. Type **<xs:simpleType>** to start deriving your custom simple type.
3. Type **<xs:restriction base="foundation">**, where *foundation* is any one of the built-in simple types upon which you'd like to base your custom type.
4. Specify as many restrictions (or *facets*) as necessary to define your new custom type. Facets, which are the way that you can customize built-in simple types, are discussed in detail on pages 128–134.
5. Type **</xs:restriction>**.
6. Type **</xs:simpleType>** to complete your new custom simple type.
7. Finally, type **</xs:element>** to complete the definition of the element.

✔ Tips

- This custom simple type is called an *anonymous custom type*. There is also such a thing as a *named custom type (see page 127)*. The difference between these two is that a named type can be used more than once (by setting the simple type's `type` attribute to the custom name), but the anonymous type (which has no name) can only be used for the element in which it is contained.
- You can also create list simple types. For more information, consult *Deriving a List Type* on page 135.

```
xsd
<xs:element name="story">
 <xs:simpleType>
  <xs:restriction base="xs:string">
   <xs:length value="1024"/>
  </xs:restriction>
 </xs:simpleType>
</xs:element>
```

Figure 10.22 *Here, I've derived a custom type for the* story *element. I started with a base foundation of the* xs:string *simple type. I then extended this by adding a restriction that limits the content's length to be a maximum of 1024 characters.*

```
xsd
<xs:simpleType name="story_type">
 <xs:restriction base="xs:string">
  <xs:length value="1024"/>
 </xs:restriction>
</xs:simpleType>
```

Figure 10.23 *Compare this custom type definition with the element definition using a custom type in Figure 10.22 on the previous page. The definition of the* story *element in both examples is identical. The principle difference is that the custom type shown above can be reused for any other element in your XML Schema. Notice how the* xs:simpleType *element's* name *attribute is set to* story_type. *This is the name that can be used to reference the custom type.*

```
xsd
<xs:element name="story"
  type="story_type"/>

<xs:element name="summary"
  type="story_type"/>

<xs:element name="another_story"
  type="story_type"/>
```

Figure 10.24 *I can now use the new* storyType *custom type in as many element definitions as I'd like.*

Deriving Named Custom Types

If you are going to use a custom type to define more than one element in your XML Schema, you can name it **(Figure 10.23)**. Then, each time you want to use it, you can include a cross-reference between the XML element and your new custom type.

To derive a named custom type:

1. Type **<xs:simpleType** to start your custom simple type.
2. Then, type **name="custom_type_name">**, where *custom_type_name* identifies your new custom simple type.
3. Type **<xs:restriction base="foundation">**, where *foundation* is the simple type upon which you are building your custom type.
4. Specify as many restrictions (or *facets*) as you would like to define your new custom type *(see pages 128–134)*.
5. Type **</xs:restriction>**.
6. Finally, type **</xs:simpleType>** to complete your custom simple type definition.
7. Then, to use your new custom type, for the definition of the element, you would type **<xs:element name="label" type="custom_type_name">**, using the *custom_type_name* you gave you new custom type in Step 2 above **(Figure 10.24)**.

✔ Tips

- Once you've defined your named custom type, you can use it instead of the simple types described in Step 4 on page 120.
- Notice that you refer to your new custom type as `custom_type_name`, instead of `xs:custom_type_name`. This is because the `"xs:"` prefix refers to the XML Schema namespace, and your new custom type is not part of that namespace. See Part 5 of the book for more details on namespaces.

Specifying a Range of Acceptable Values

In XML Schema, in addition to defining an XML element's type, you can also place restrictions on what would be considered valid content. These restrictions are called *facets*. By using facets, you can create custom simple types, as discussed on pages 126 and 127.

One of the most common facets used is to specify the highest or lowest value (or both) that an XML element can have to be considered valid.

To specify the highest possible value:

1. Within a custom type definition (that is, for Step 4 on either page 126 or 127), type **<xs:maxInclusive**. (Notice the capital *I* that begins the word *Inclusive*).
2. Then, type **value="n"**, where the element's content must be less than or equal to *n* in order to be valid.
3. Finally, type **/>** to complete the `xs:maxInclusive` facet **(Figure 10.25)**.

Another way to specify the highest possible value:

1. Within a custom type definition (that is, for Step 4 on either page 126 and 127), type **<xs:maxExclusive**. (Notice the capital *E* that begins the word *Exclusive*).
2. Then, type **value="n"**, where the element's content must be less than (but not equal to) *n* in order to be valid.
3. Finally, type **/>** to complete the `xs:maxExclusive` facet **(Figure 10.27)**.

xsd
```
<xs:element name="total_bases">
 <xs:simpleType>
  <xs:restriction base="xs:integer">
   <xs:maxInclusive value="6856"/>
  </xs:restriction>
 </xs:simpleType>
</xs:element>
```

Figure 10.25 *The* xs:maxInclusive *facet specifies the highest possible value for an element. In this case, the maximum value is Hank Aaron's All-Time Total Bases record in Major League Baseball of 6,856 total bases.*

xml
```
<total_bases>6855</total_bases>
```

xml
```
<total_bases>6856</total_bases>
```

Figure 10.26 *These* total_bases *elements are both valid based on the XML Schema in Figure 10.25, since the first is less than, and the second is equal to, the* xs:maxInclusive *value.*

xsd
```
<xs:element name="total_bases">
 <xs:simpleType>
  <xs:restriction base="xs:integer">
   <xs:maxExclusive value="6856"/>
  </xs:restriction>
 </xs:simpleType>
</xs:element>
```

Figure 10.27 *This XML Schema custom type uses the* xs:maxExclusive *facet to specify that the highest acceptable value is one less than the maximum. That is, the* total_bases *element's content must be lower than (and not equal to) the* xs:maxExclusive *value, Hank Aaron's record.*

xml
```
<total_bases>6855</total_bases>
```

xml
```
<total_bases>6856</total_bases>
```

Figure 10.28 *With the changed XML Schema from Figure 10.27, the first* total_bases *element is still valid, while the second is invalid. (And, nobody yet has tied or broken Hank Aaron's total bases record!)*

```
xsd
<xs:element name="game_day">
 <xs:simpleType>
  <xs:restriction base="xs:date">
   <xs:minInclusive
     value="1954-04-13"/>
  </xs:restriction>
 </xs:simpleType>
</xs:element>
```

Figure 10.29 *Here, the* xs:minInclusive *facet is specifying the lowest (or earliest)* game_day: *Hank Aaron's Major League debut game on April 13, 1954.*

```
xml
<game_day>1954-04-13</game_day>
```

```
xml
<game_day>1954-04-14</game_day>
```

Figure 10.30 *These excerpts are both valid, based on the XML Schema defined in Figure 10.29 above.*

```
xsd
<xs:element name="game_day">
 <xs:simpleType>
  <xs:restriction base="xs:date">
   <xs:minInclusive
     value="1954-04-13"/>
   <xs:maxInclusive
     value="1976-10-03"/>
  </xs:restriction>
 </xs:simpleType>
</xs:element>
```

Figure 10.31 *This XML Schema custom type uses both the* xs:minInclusive *and* xs:maxInclusive *facets to specify that valid elements contain dates that are equal to, or fall in-between, April 13, 1954 and October 3, 1976, Hank Aaron's Major League career.*

```
xml
<game_day>1976-07-20</game_day>
```

Figure 10.32 *This is valid (Aaron's 755th home run game), given the XML Schema in Figure 10.31.*

```
xml
<game_day>2008-07-04</game_day>
```

Figure 10.33 *This* game_day *element is not valid.*

To specify the lowest possible value:

1. Within a custom type definition (that is, for Step 4 on either page 126 or 127), type **<xs:minInclusive**. (Notice the capital *I* that begins the word *Inclusive*).
2. Then, type **value="n"**, where the element's content must be greater than or equal to *n* in order to be valid.
3. Finally, type **/>** to complete the `xs:minInclusive` facet **(Figure 10.29)**.

Another way to specify the lowest possible value:

1. Within a custom type definition (that is, for Step 4 on either page 126 or 127), type **<xs:minExclusive**. (Notice the capital *E* that begins the word *Exclusive*).
2. Then, type **value="n"**, where the element's content must be greater than (but not equal to) *n* in order to be valid.
3. Finally, type **/>** to complete the `xs:minExclusive` facet.

✔ Tips

- While you can't use the two min limits (or the two max limits) simultaneously for the same type (it wouldn't make sense), you can mix and match the mins and maxes as needed **(Figure 10.31)**. Of course, you can also use just one.
- You can use these min and max facets with date, time, and numeric simple types.
- What it means for a number to be greater or less than another is pretty obvious. For a date or time to be greater, it must represent a later date or time. For a date or time to be less, it should represent an earlier date or time.

Specifying a Set of Acceptable Values

With the facets described on the previous two pages, you can set minimums, maximums, and value ranges for valid XML elements. In some cases, however, there may be a specific set of acceptable values that you want to define as valid. In these cases, you would use an *enumeration* facet **(Figure 10.34)**.

To specify a set of acceptable values:

1. Within a custom type definition (that is, for Step 4 on either page 126 or 127), type **<xs:enumeration**.
2. Then, type **value="choice"**, to identify one acceptable *choice* for the content of the element or attribute.
3. Finally, type **/>** to complete the `xs:enumeration` element.
4. Repeat Steps 1–3 for each additional value choice that the element can have.

✔ Tips

- Each enumeration value must be unique.
- Enumeration values may contain white space.
- You can use the `xs:enumeration` facet with all simple types, except `boolean`.

```
xsd
<xs:element name="wonder_name">
 <xs:simpleType>
  <xs:restriction base="xs:string">
   <xs:enumeration value=
      "Colossus of Rhodes"/>
   <xs:enumeration value=
     "Great Pyramid of Giza"/>
   <xs:enumeration value=
     "Hanging Gardens of Babylon"/>
   <xs:enumeration value=
     "Statue of Zeus at Olympia"/>
   <xs:enumeration value=
     "Temple of Artemis at Ephesus"/>
   <xs:enumeration value=
     "Mausoleum at Halicarnassus"/>
   <xs:enumeration value=
     "Lighthouse of Alexandria"/>
  </xs:restriction>
 </xs:simpleType>
</xs:element>
```

Figure 10.34 *The* wonder_name *element can and must now contain one of these values.*

```
xml
<wonder_name>
  Great Pyramid of Giza</wonder_name>
```

Figure 10.35 *This* wonder_name *element is perfectly valid, since it matches one of the enumerated choices from the XML Schema in Figure 10.34.*

```
xml
<wonder_name>
  Great Pyramid</wonder_name>
```

```
xml
<wonder_name>
  Lighthouse of Alexandria
  Hanging Gardens of Babylon
</wonder_name>
```

Figure 10.36 *Neither of these* wonder_name *elements is valid. The first one contains only a part of a choice. (While it's often referred to as the "Great Pyramid", that doesn't match any of the enumeration choices, and thus is not valid.) The second one contains two choices, but only one is allowed with enumerations. Defining an element that allows multiple selections from a set of values is an advanced topic not covered in this book.*

```
xsd
<xs:element name="wonder_code">
 <xs:simpleType>
  <xs:restriction base="xs:string">
   <xs:length value="5"/>
  </xs:restriction>
 </xs:simpleType>
</xs:element>
```

Figure 10.37 *You can create a custom type that specifies the length of a valid element's string value.*

```
xml
<wonder_code>w_285</wonder_code>
```

Figure 10.38 *This* wonder_code *element is valid since it contains 5 characters as specified by the custom type in Figure 10.37. If* wonder_code *elements are consistently one character, an underscore, and then three digits, I could use a pattern facet to more precisely define the element* (see page 132).

```
xsd
<xs:element name="brief_description">
 <xs:simpleType>
  <xs:restriction base="xs:string">
   <xs:maxLength value="256"/>
  </xs:restriction>
 </xs:simpleType>
</xs:element>
```

Figure 10.39 *You can limit the length of an element's string value to keep it from getting too large, or to match specific length constraints, such as those required of a database.*

```
xml
<brief_description>In 294 BC, a huge
  statue was built honoring the god
  Helios. This Colossus of Rhodes,
  often depicted straddling the
  harbor, likely stood by it. The
  statue was toppled by earthquake,
  and wasn't rebuilt. Even broken,
  many still traveled to see it.
</brief_description>
```

Figure 10.40 *This* brief_description *element is valid because its value is comprised of 243 characters, which is less than the 256-character maximum limit defined by the custom type in Figure 10.39.*

Limiting the Length of an Element

One of the ways you can further restrict an XML element with a custom type is to use a facet that specifies or limits its length.

To specify the exact length of an element:

◆ Within a custom type definition (that is, for Step 4 on either page 126 or 127), type **<xs:length value="g"/>**, where *g* is the number of characters that the element must have **(Figure 10.37)**.

To specify the minimum length of an element:

◆ Within a custom type definition (that is, for Step 4 on either page 126 or 127), type **<xs:minLength value="n"/>**, where *n* is the minimum length in characters of the element.

To specify the maximum length of an element:

◆ Within a custom type definition (that is, for Step 4 on either page 126 or 127), type **<xs:maxLength value="x"/>**, where *x* is the maximum length in characters of the element **(Figure 10.39)**.

✔ Tips

- You can use the `length` facet with `string`, and other string-based XML Schema simple types such as `anyURI` or `hexBinary`.
- The values for `xs:length`, `xs:minLength`, and `xs:maxLength` must all be non-negative integers.
- If the element is based on a binary type, such as `hexBinary`, the `length` facet limits the number of octets of binary data. If the element is derived by list *(see page 135)*, the `length` facet limits the number of list items.

Specifying a Pattern for an Element

In XML Schema, you can also restrict what a valid XML element can contain using a pattern facet **(Figures 10.41 and 10.42)**. To construct a pattern, you use a regular expression (*regex*) language. This enables you to define a pattern that the XML element's content must match in order to be considered valid.

The regex language in XML Schema is based on Perl's regex language, and could fill a chapter of its own. I'll give you a brief taste here.

To specify a pattern for an element:

1. Within a custom type definition (that is, for Step 4 on either page 126 or 127), type **<xs:pattern**.
2. Then, type **value="regex"**, where *regex* is the regular expression that the XML element's content must match.

   Regular expressions are made up of letters, numbers, and special symbols; in the order which those letters, numbers, and symbols should appear in the content. Symbols include:

   . (a period) for any character at all.

   \d for any digit; **\D** for any non-digit.

   \s for any white space (including space, tab, newline, and return); **\S** for any character that is not white space.

   x* to have *zero or more x's*; **(xy)*** to have zero or more *xy's*.

   x? to have *zero or one x*; **(xy)?** to have zero or one *xy*.

   x+ to have *one or more x's*; **(xy)+** to have one or more *xy's*.

   [abc] to include one of a group of values (*a*, *b*, or *c*).

   [0–9] to include the *range of values* from 0 to 9.

xsd
```
<xs:element name="wonder_code">
 <xs:simpleType>
  <xs:restriction base="xs:string">
   <xs:pattern value="w_\d{3}"/>
  </xs:restriction>
 </xs:simpleType>
</xs:element>
```

Figure 10.41 *This pattern limits the content of the* wonder_code *element to strings that begin with the letter* w, *an underscore, and then three digits. Any character that appears in the element must appear in that same position in the regex for the element to be considered valid.*

xml
```
<wonder_code>w_285</wonder_code>
```

xml
```
<wonder_code>285_w</wonder_code>
```

Figure 10.42 *The first XML excerpt shows a valid instance of the* wonder_code *element, based on the bit of XML Schema shown in Figure 10.41. The second element shown is not valid because the order of the content does not match the regex pattern.*

```
xsd
<xs:element name="race_time">
 <xs:simpleType>
  <xs:restriction base="xs:duration">
   <xs:pattern value=
     "PT\d+H\d+M\d+S"/>
  </xs:restriction>
 </xs:simpleType>
</xs:element>
```

Figure 10.43 *You can also use patterns to control the contents of elements based on other types besides* string. *For example, if you want the* race_time *element to contain an* xs:duration *value only containing hours, minutes, and seconds, you might set the pattern as shown here. Note that this pattern doesn't "understand" what the duration type needs. It simply requires that the content include a capital letter P, a capital letter T, followed by one or more digits, a capital letter H, one or more digits, a capital letter M, one or more digits, and finally, a capital letter S.*

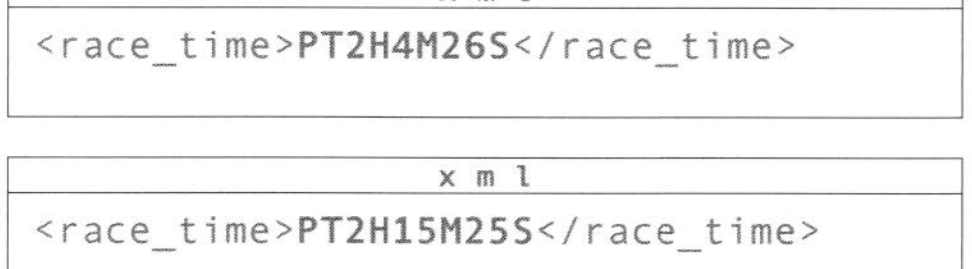

```
xml
<race_time>PT2H4M26S</race_time>
```

```
xml
<race_time>PT2H15M25S</race_time>
```

Figure 10.44 *Here are two valid examples of the* race_time *element defined in Figure 10.43. The first represents the current men's world record for a marathon race run by Haile Gebrselassie from Ethiopia. The second represents the current women's world record for a marathon race run by Paula Radcliffe from the United Kingdom.*

this | that to have *this* or *that* in the content. Separate additional choices with additional vertical bars.

x{5} to have *exactly 5 x's* (in a row).

x{5,} to have *at least 5 x's* (in a row).

x{5,8} to have *at least 5* and *at most 8 x's* (in a row).

(xyz){2} to have *exactly two xyz's* (in a row).

Note: Parentheses control what the curly brackets and other modifiers, such as ?, +, and *, affect.

3. Finally, type **/>** to complete the `xs:pattern` element.

✔ Tips

- It's a little beyond the scope of this book to cover regular expressions in more detail. Instead, let me refer you to another book: *Perl and CGI for the World Wide Web: Visual QuickStart Guide*, by Elizabeth Castro, published by Peachpit Press. It has many more examples and background information. You can also find more specific information about XML Schema regular expressions at *www.w3.org/TR/2004/REC-xmlschema-2-20041028/datatypes.html#regexs*.
- The regular expressions used in XML Schema are very similar to those used in Perl. However, one important technical difference is that in XML Schema regex, the comparison is always made between the regular expression and the entire contents of the element. There are no ^ or $ characters to limit a match to the beginning or end of a line (as there are in Perl).
- You can use the pattern facet with any of the simple types.

Limiting a Number's Digits

You saw how to limit the value of numeric elements with the min and max facets on pages 128 and 129. In XML Schema, you can also limit the total number of digits, as well as the number of digits after the decimal point of numeric elements **(Figure 10.45)**.

To specify the total number of digits in a number:

1. Within a custom type definition (that is, for Step 4 on either page 126 or 127), type **<xs:totalDigits**.
2. Then, type **value="n"**, where *n* is the maximum number of digits that can appear in the number.
3. Finally, type **/>** to complete the `xs:totalDigits` facet.

To specify the number of digits after the decimal point:

1. Within a custom type definition (that is, for Step 4 on either page 126 or 127), type **<xs:fractionDigits**.
2. Then, type **value="n"**, where *n* is the maximum number of digits that can appear after the decimal in the number.
3. Finally, type **/>** to complete the `xs:fractionDigits` facet.

✔ Tips

- You may use either of these facets with any numerical type.
- The `xs:totalDigits` facet must be a positive number, and it may not be less than the `xs:fractionDigits` value.
- The `xs:fractionDigits` facet must be a non-negative integer (0, 1, 2, or higher).
- Both facets specify the maximum values allowed. The number is still considered valid if fewer digits are present.

```
xsd
<xs:element name="atomic_weight">
 <xs:simpleType>
  <xs:restriction base="xs:decimal">
   <xs:totalDigits value="6"/>
   <xs:fractionDigits value="4"/>
  </xs:restriction>
 </xs:simpleType>
</xs:element>
```

Figure 10.45 *The* totalDigits *value determines the total number of digits, and the* fractionDigits *value specifies how many digits must appear in the fractional part of the number, after the decimal point.*

```
xml
<atomic_weight>
  12.0107</atomic_weight>
```

```
xml
<atomic_weight>
  55.845</atomic_weight>
```

Figure 10.46 *Both of these elements are valid, based on the XML Schema excerpt in Figure 10.45, since they contain a maximum of six digits (and sometimes less), and a maximum of four fractional digits (and sometimes less). John Dalton and Jöns Jakob Berzelius are credited with being the first scientists to determine atomic weights. These two XML elements represent the atomic weights for carbon and iron, respectively.*

```
xml
<atomic_weight>
  196.9665</atomic_weight>
```

```
xml
<atomic_weight>
  1.00794</atomic_weight>
```

Figure 10.47 *These two* atomic_weight *elements are invalid, the first because there are too many total digits (7 instead of 6), the second because while there are the proper number of total digits, there are too many fractional digits (5 instead of 4). Although not valid for the given XML Schema, these XML elements accurately represent the atomic weights of gold and hydrogen respectively.*

```
xsd
<xs:element name="recent_eclipses">
 <xs:simpleType>
  <xs:list itemType="xs:dateTime"/>
 </xs:simpleType>
</xs:element>
```

Figure 10.48 *A list must be based on an existing built-in or custom simple type. This list type for the* recent_eclipses *element is based on the* xs:dateTime *type.*

```
xml
<recent_eclipses>
  2008-02-21T03:26:00Z
  2007-08-28T10:37:00Z
</recent_eclipses>
```

Figure 10.49 *According to the XML Schema in Figure 10.48, a valid* recent_eclipses *element must contain a list of zero or more* xs:dateTime *units. These units are separated by white space, as shown in this valid example of the last two total lunar eclipses.*

```
xsd
<xs:simpleType name="dateTime_list">
 <xs:list itemType="xs:dateTime"/>
</xs:simpleType>
...
<xs:element name="recent_eclipses"
  type="dateTime_list"/>
```

Figure 10.50 *Compare this XML Schema excerpt to the one in Figure 10.48. In that excerpt, I used an anonymous list type to define the* recent_eclipses *element. In this excerpt, I define the* recent_eclipses *element with a named list type* dateTime_list. *In both cases, the element is considered valid if it contains a white-space-separated list of* xs:dateTime *types.*

```
xml
<recent_eclipses>
  2010-12-21T08:17:00Z
  2011-06-15T20:13:00Z
  2011-12-10T14:32:00Z
</recent_eclipses>
```

Figure 10.51 *The* recent_eclipses *element in this excerpt is valid, according to the XML Schema in Figure 10.50; it lists the next three total lunar eclipses.*

Deriving a List Type

So far, your elements can only contain one unit each. If you define an element as a date, it can contain just one date. But if you need an element to contain an entire list of dates, then you could derive a list type from the date type to accommodate the situation **(Figure 10.48)**.

To derive a list type:

1. First, identify the name of the XML element that you are using XML Schema to define. To do so, type **<xs:element name="label">**, where *label* is the name of the XML element.
2. Type **<xs:simpleType>** to start deriving your custom simple type.
3. Type **<xs:list itemType="list_element"/>**, where *list_element* is the simple type (built-in or custom) that defines each individual unit in your list.
4. Type **</xs:simpleType>** to complete your new custom simple type.
5. Finally, type **</xs:element>** to complete the definition of the element.

✔ Tips

- Lists should not be confused with enumerations *(see page 130)*. Enumerations provide a set of optional values for an element. Lists are sequences of values within the element itself.
- In a list, spaces separate one item from the next. Therefore, a list of strings will be misinterpreted if any item in the list has a space itself. For example, the list "Colossus of Rhodes Lighthouse of Alexandria" would represent six items, not two.
- As with derived simple types *(see pages 126 and 127)*, if you aren't going to reuse the list, create an anonymous list type, as shown in the steps above (Figure 10.48). If you are going to reuse the list, then create a named list type **(Figure 10.50)**.

Deriving a Union Type

In the same way I can define an XML element to be one of a number of different values, sometimes I might need to define an XML element to be defined as one of a number of different simple types **(Figure 10.52)**.

To define an XML element to be one of two (or more) different simple types, you can derive a new type as the combination of these other simple types. This newly derived simple type is called a *union*, and is made from a group of other simple types **(Figure 10.53)**.

To derive a union:

1. First, identify the name of the XML element that you are using XML Schema to define. To do so, type **<xs:element name="label">**, where *label* is the name of the XML element.
2. Type **<xs:simpleType>** to start your custom simple type.
3. Type **<xs:union memberTypes="union_ elements"/>**, where *union_elements* is a white-space-separated group of simple types (built-in or custom) that define the valid simple types for this element.
4. Type **</xs:simpleType>** to complete your new custom simple type.
5. Finally, type **</xs:element>** to complete the definition of the element.

✔ Tip

- As with derived simple types *(see pages 126 and 127)*, if you aren't going to reuse the union, create an anonymous union type as shown in the steps above. If you are going to reuse the union, then you would create a named union type.

```
xsd
<xs:simpleType name="isbn10">
 <xs:restriction base="xs:string">
  <xs:pattern value="\d{9}[\d|X]"/>
 </xs:restriction>
</xs:simpleType>

<xs:simpleType name="isbn13">
 <xs:restriction base="xs:string">
  <xs:pattern value="\d{3}-\d{10}"/>
 </xs:restriction>
</xs:simpleType>
```

Figure 10.52 *In this XML Schema excerpt, I have defined two named custom simple types,* isbn10 *and* isbn13. *Each custom type is a string restricted to meet the format of its respective ISBN standard.*

```
xsd
<xs:element name="book">
 <xs:simpleType>
  <xs:union
    memberTypes="isbn10 isbn13"/>
 </xs:simpleType>
</xs:element>
```

Figure 10.53 *Here, the* book *element is defined to be a* union *of the custom types defined in Figure 10.52. This means that the* book *element can be either an* isbn10 *custom type or an* isbn13 *custom type.*

```
xml
<!-- The Fountainhead,
  by Ayn Rand -->
<book>0452286751</book>
```

```
xml
<!-- The Kill a Mockingbird,
  by Harper Lee-->
<book>044508376X</book>
```

```
xml
<!-- XML: Visual QuickStart Guide
      (2nd Edition),
  by Kevin Howard Goldberg -->
<book>978-0321559678</book>
```

Figure 10.54 *All three XML excerpts of the* book *element are valid, based on the XML Schema in Figure 10.53. The first two use the* isbn10 *custom type and the last one uses the* isbn13 *custom type.*

11

Defining Complex Types

In the previous chapter, I discussed that simple type XML elements can only contain a value and not child elements or attributes. In this chapter, I will discuss *complex type* elements. A complex type element is one that can contain child elements, attributes, or some combination of the two.

There has been some discussion in the XML community about the intricacies of complex types, specifically, how difficult they are to understand. Even still, since you'll want your XML document to contain more than just a root element, you'll at least need one complex type element to allow the root element to have a child element of its own. Another important reason to use complex types in your XML Schema is to allow elements to have attributes.

While you certainly can, and will, get the basic gist of how to write complex types, I will endeavor to give you the foundation of why they are constructed the way they are. I go into this foundational detail in *Complex Type Basics* on page 138. And, I will continue with step-by-step examples thereafter.

Complex Type Basics

In XML Schema, all XML elements are defined using either simple or complex types. Complex type elements can have child elements and/or attributes, whereas simple type elements cannot.

Complex type elements are further subdivided into those with *simple content*, and those with *complex content*. Both can have attributes, but simple content only allows string content, whereas complex content allows child elements.

The Four Complex Types

The first is called "text only" and is a complex type element with simple content *(allows text and attributes)* **(Figure 11.1)**.

The second is called "element only" and is a complex type element with complex content *(allows children and attributes)* **(Figure 11.2)**.

The third is the "empty element" and is also a complex type element with complex content **(Figure 11.3)**. It's a complex type element because it may contain attributes. It's considered complex content because simple content allows text, and, since I am defining an empty element, it cannot allow text content.

Finally, the fourth complex type XML element is called "mixed content." This is because it is a complex type element with both complex content and simple content *(allows text, child elements, and attributes)* **(Figure 11.4)**.

XML Schema Type Hierarchy

An important building block of the XML Schema language is that all element types are hierarchically derived from a single root type. In fact, the built-in simple types are all derived from this root type as well. This single root type branches into the two types I have discussed: Simple types and complex types. Then, complex types branch again into simple content and complex content. This root type is named *anyType*, and it is used to define an XML element that contains any content of any type.

xml
```
<year_built era="BC">
  282</year_built>
```

Figure 11.1 *The* year_built *element is a complex type element that only contains text (and an attribute), and is thus considered "text only."*

xml
```
<ancient_wonders>
 <wonder>
...
 </wonder>
</ancient_wonders>
```

Figure 11.2 *The* ancient_wonders *element is a complex type element that contains a child element,* wonder, *but no text. This element is considered "element only." Although this particular element has no attributes, as an "element only" complex type, it could.*

xml
```
<source sectionid="101"
  newspaperid="21"/>
```

Figure 11.3 *The* source *element is a complex type element and is considered an "empty" element; it has no content. This particular empty element has attributes (but not all do).*

xml
```
<story>In 294 BC, the people of the
  island of Rhodes began building a
  colossal statue of the sun god
  Helios. They believed that it was
  because of his blessings that they
  were able to withstand a long siege
  on the island and emerge victorious.
  <para/>
  The Colossus was built with bronze,
  reinforced with iron, ...
</story>
```

Figure 11.4 *This* story *element is a complex type element that contains text and a child element called* para. *It is considered as having "mixed" content. Note that this is not a very common structure for XML elements, especially those in database type applications.*

```
xsd
<xs:element name="year_built">
 <xs:complexType>
  <xs:simpleContent>
   <xs:extension
     base="xs:positiveInteger">
    <xs:attribute name="era"
      type="xs:string"/>
   </xs:extension>
  </xs:simpleContent>
 </xs:complexType>
</xs:element>
```

Figure 11.5 *This XML Schema defines the XML element in Figure 11.1. This complex type is derived from an extension of simple content with an attribute.*

```
xsd
<xs:element name="ancient_wonders">
<xs:complexType>
 <xs:complexContent>
  <xs:restriction base="xs:anyType">
   <xs:sequence>
    <xs:element name="wonder"
      type="wonderType"/>
   </xs:sequence>
  </xs:restriction>
 </xs:complexContent>
</xs:complexType>
</xs:element>
```

Figure 11.6 *This XML Schema defines the XML element in Figure 11.2. It shows the complex type is derived from* complexContent *that restricts* anyType.

```
xsd
<xs:element name="ancient_wonders">
<xs:complexType>
 <xs:sequence>
  <xs:element name="wonder"
    type="wonderType"/>
 </xs:sequence>
</xs:complexType>
</xs:element>
```

Figure 11.7 *This XML Schema also defines the XML element in Figure 11.2. Notice that I have removed the default condition for complex types: Deriving from complex content with a restriction on the base* anyType. *Not only does it take up less space, it is much easier to read!*

Deriving a Complex Type

In the last chapter, you saw how to derive custom simple types from the built-in simple types, *Deriving Custom Simple Types* on page 126. With complex types, there aren't any built-in types to use. To use a complex type, it must be derived.

To derive a "text only" content type (such as is seen in Figure 11.1), you can use the `<xs:simpleContent>` element **(Figure 11.5)**. Here, the `year_built` element is derived from simple content with a positive integer base. It also has a string value attribute called `era`. This is discussed more in *Defining Elements to Contain Only Text* on page 146.

To derive an "element only" complex type (such as is seen in Figure 11.2), you can use the `<xs:complexContent>` element **(Figure 11.6).** Here, the `ancient_wonders` element is derived from complex content that restricts the root type `anyType`. It uses an `<xs:sequence>` restriction, allowing the `ancient_wonders` element to have children. This is discussed in *Defining Complex Types That Contain Child Elements* on page 142.

The Default Condition

Probably the most important thing to know about working with complex types is that the default derivation for complex types is:

complex content that restricts anyType

With this default condition, you can and should always omit the `<xs:complexContent>` and `<xs:restriction base="anyType">` elements from your XML Schema definitions of complex types **(Figure 11.7)**.

This default is often overlooked when discussing complex types in XML Schema, and it will be reiterated often throughout the chapter.

Deriving Anonymous Complex Types

As with simple types, you can derive a complex type anonymously, or you can name it (and reuse it throughout the XML Schema). If you don't need to reuse a complex type, it's faster to create it anonymously within the element definition itself **(Figure 11.8)**.

To derive an anonymous complex type:

1. Begin the definition of the element by typing **<xs:element name="label">**, where *label* is the name of the XML element that you are defining. In other words, you're writing the XML Schema to define the <label> element in your XML document.
2. Then, type **<xs:complexType>** to begin the anonymous complex type.
3. Within the `xs:complexType` element:

   Declare the *content type* to be either simple content or complex content *(see page 138)*.

   Create the guts of the element (which the bulk of this chapter is devoted to explaining).

   Define the attributes *(see page 154)* that should appear, if any.
4. Next, type **</xs:complexType>** to complete the anonymous complex type definition.
5. Finally, type **</xs:element>** to complete the definition of the complex type element.

✔ Tip

- The only difference between an anonymous type and a named type is that a named type can be used more than once, and can be used as the base for new complex types. An anonymous type can only be used for the element in which it is contained.

xsd
```
<xs:element name="year_built">
 <xs:complexType>
  <xs:simpleContent>
   <xs:extension
     base="xs:positiveInteger">
    <xs:attribute name="era"
      type="xs:string"/>
   </xs:extension>
  </xs:simpleContent>
 </xs:complexType>
</xs:element>
```

Figure 11.8 *This XML Schema excerpt is an anonymous complex type definition. It is defining the* year_built *element as a "text only" element requiring a positive integer for its text value. It also defines that* year_built *will have an attribute, called* era, *which has a string value.*

xml
```
<year_built era="BC">
  282</year_built>
```

Figure 11.9 *Here is a valid XML element, based on the XML Schema in Figure 11.8.*

```
xsd
<xs:complexType name="yearType">

 <xs:simpleContent>

  <xs:extension
    base="xs:positiveInteger">

  <xs:attribute name="era"
   type="xs:string"/>

  </xs:extension>

</xs:simpleContent>

</xs:complexType>
```

Figure 11.10 *When compared with the anonymous definition in Figure 11.8 on the previous page, you can see that the "guts" of the definitions are identical. The principle difference is that a named complex type can be reused for any other element in the XML Schema. Notice how the* xs:complexType *element has defined its* name *attribute to be "yearType". This is the name other elements will use when referring to this complex type.*

```
xsd
<xs:complexType name="historyType">

 <xs:sequence>

  <xs:element name="year_built"
    type="yearType"/>

  <xs:element name="year_destroyed"
    type="yearType"/>
```

Figure 11.11 *I can now use the new* yearType *in as many element definitions as I'd like.*

```
xml
<year_built era="BC">
  282</year_built>
<year_destroyed era="BC">
  226</year_destroyed>
```

Figure 11.12 *Here is a valid XML instance based on the Schema in Figure 11.10. Notice that I am able to use the one named complex type* yearType *for both the* year_built *and* year_destroyed *elements.*

Deriving Named Complex Types

If you are going to use a complex type to define more than one element in your XML Schema, you can create a named complex type **(Figure 11.10)**. Then, each time you want to use it, you can include a reference between the XML element and your new custom type.

To derive a named complex type element:

1. Type **<xs:complexType** to begin the named complex type.
2. Then, type **name="complex_type_name">**, where *complex_type_name* identifies your new complex type.
3. Within the `xs:complexType` element:

   Declare the *content type* to be either simple content or complex content *(see page 138)*.

   Create the guts of the element (which the bulk of this chapter is devoted to explaining).

   Define the attributes *(see page 154)* that should appear, if any.
4. Finally, type **</xs:complexType>** to complete the named complex type definition.
5. Then, to use the named complex type for the definition of the XML element, you'll type **<xs:element name="label" type="complex_type_name">**, where *complex_type_name* is the name you gave the new complex type in Step 2 above **(Figure 11.11)**.

✔ Tip

- Notice that you refer to your new complex type as `complex_type_name`, instead of `xs:complex_type_name`. This is because the `"xs:"` prefix refers to the XML Schema namespace, not custom types. See Part 5 for more details.

Defining Complex Types That Contain Child Elements

One of the most common complex types is one that contains child elements. This complex type can also contain attributes, but it cannot contain a value of its own. It's described (even with attributes) as "element only."

To define an "element only" complex type:

1. Type **<xs:complexType**.
2. Then, type **name="complex_type_name">**, where *complex_type_name* identifies your new complex type.
3. Next, you'll define the structure and order of the child elements of this parent element. You'll declare a sequence, an unordered list, or a choice; each of which is discussed on the next three pages.
4. Then, declare the attributes *(see page 154)* that should appear in this complex type element, if any.
5. Finally, type **</xs:complexType>** to complete the "element only" complex type definition **(Figure 11.13)**.

✔ Tips

- As discussed on page 139, the default condition for complex types is that they derive from `xs:complexContent` that restricts `xs:anyType`. Because of this, you can omit these XML Schema element declarations **(Figure 11.14)**.
- The child elements of a complex type are referred to as its *content model*.
- The content model of a complex type must either be a sequence, an unordered list, or a choice. These are called *model groups*, and they indicate the structure and order of child elements within their parent.

```
xsd
<xs:element name="ancient_wonders">

 <xs:complexType>

  <xs:complexContent>

   <xs:restriction base="xs:anyType">

    <xs:sequence>

     <xs:element name="wonder"
       type="wonderType"/>

    </xs:sequence>

   </xs:restriction>

  </xs:complexContent>

 </xs:complexType>

</xs:element>
```

Figure 11.13 *Here is an anonymous complex type definition that contains a sequence of one child element called* wonder, *defined to be of the type* wonderType. *(Notice that this complex type element is derived from complex content that restricts* anyType *which is the default condition for complex types.)*

```
xsd
<xs:element name="ancient_wonders">
 <xs:complexType>
  <xs:sequence>
   <xs:element name="wonder"
     type="wonderType"/>
  </xs:sequence>
 </xs:complexType>
</xs:element>
```

Figure 11.14 *Here is another complex type definition for the* ancient_wonders *element. I have omitted the default condition elements:* <xs:complexContent> *and* <xs:restriction base="xs:anyType">. *Because these are default conditions, this XML Schema excerpt defines the* exact same *XML element as shown in Figure 11.13, and is the way complex type elements will almost always be written.*

```
xsd
<xs:complexType name="wonderType">

 <xs:sequence>

  <xs:element name="name"
    type="nameType"/>

  <xs:element name="location"
    type="xs:string"/>

  <xs:element name="height"
    type="heightType"/>

  <xs:element name="history"
    type="historyType"/>

  <xs:element name="main_image"
    type="imageType"/>

  <xs:element name="source"
    type="sourceType"/>

 </xs:sequence>

</xs:complexType>
```

Figure 11.15 *This XML Schema excerpt defines a complex type named* wonderType. *Now, any XML element defined with the type* wonderType *will have to contain the child elements* name, location, height, history, main_image, *and* source, *in order. In fact, in Figure 11.14, the* wonder *element is defined with the* wonderType *complex type. It is not at all uncommon for one complex type to have child elements that are also complex type elements.*

Requiring Child Elements to Appear in Sequence

If you want a complex type element to contain child elements, *in order*, you have to define a sequence of those elements **(Figure 11.15)**.

To require child elements to appear in sequence:

1. Type **<xs:sequence**.
2. If desired, specify how many times the sequence of elements itself can appear by setting the `minOccurs` and `maxOccurs` attributes, as described on page 151.
3. Then, type **>** to complete the opening tag.
4. Declare the simple type elements and/or complex type elements you want in the sequence, in the order in which they should appear.
5. Finally, type **</xs:sequence>** to complete the model group.

✔ Tips

- A sequence defines the order in which its child elements must appear in an XML document.
- Since an XML element may only have one child, it's perfectly legitimate for a sequence to contain only one element.
- A sequence can also contain other sequences, choices *(see page 145)*, or references to named groups *(see page 152)*.
- A sequence may be contained in a complex type definition, other sequences, a set of choices *(see page 145)*, or in named group definitions *(see page 152)*.
- The `<xs:sequence>` element is basically equivalent to the comma (,) in DTDs.

Allowing Child Elements to Appear in Any Order

If you want a complex type element to contain child elements in any order, you can list those children with an `all` element **(Figure 11.16)**.

To allow child elements to appear in any order:

1. Type **<xs:all** to begin the unordered list of elements.
2. Optionally, you can specify how many times the unordered list itself can appear by setting the `minOccurs` and `maxOccurs` attributes, as described on page 151.
3. Then, type **>** to complete the opening tag.
4. Declare the simple type elements and/or complex type elements that you want in the unordered list.
5. Finally, type **</xs:all>** to complete the model group.

✔ Tips

- The members of an `xs:all` element (despite its name) may appear once or not at all (depending on their individual `minOccurs` and `maxOccurs` attributes), in any order.
- The `minOccurs` attribute may only be set to 0 or 1. The `maxOccurs` attribute may only be set to 1 *(see page 151)*.
- An `xs:all` element can only contain individual element declarations or references, not other groups. In addition, no element may appear more than once.
- An `xs:all` element can only be contained in, and must be the sole child of, an element only complex type definition *(see page 142)*.

xsd
```
<xs:complexType name="historyType">

 <xs:all>

  <xs:element name="year_built"
    type="yearType"/>

  <xs:element name="year_destroyed"
    type="yearType"/>

  <xs:element name="how_destroyed"
    type="destrType"/>

  <xs:element name="story"
    type="storyType"/>

 </xs:all>

</xs:complexType>
```

Figure 11.16 *Here, I am defining the complex type* historyType *using* xs:all. *This means that any XML element defined using the* historyType *will be valid if it contains the* year_built, year_destroyed, how_destroyed, *and* story *elements in any order.*

xml
```
<history>
 <year_built era="BC">
   282</year_built>
 <story>In 294 BC, the people of the
   island of Rhodes began building a
   colossal statue ...</story>
 <year_destroyed era="BC">
   226</year_destroyed>
 <how_destroyed>
   earthquake</how_destroyed>
</history>
```

xml
```
<history>
<story>In 294 BC, the people of the
   island of Rhodes began building a
   colossal statue ...</story>
 <year_built era="BC">
   282</year_built>
<how_destroyed>
   earthquake</how_destroyed>
 <year_destroyed era="BC">
   226</year_destroyed>
</history>
```

Figure 11.17 *In these XML excerpts, both* history *elements are valid based on the XML Schema in Figure 11.16, since the order of its child elements is unimportant.*

```
xsd
<xs:complexType name="wonderType">
 <xs:sequence>
  <xs:element name="name"
    type="nameType"/>
  <xs:choice>
   <xs:element name="location"
     type="xs:string"/>

   <xs:sequence>
    <xs:element name="city"
      type="xs:string"/>
    <xs:element name="country"
      type="xs:string"/>
   </xs:sequence>

  </xs:choice>
 ...
 </xs:sequence>
</xs:complexType>
```

Figure 11.18 *If the information for the ancient wonders came from different sources, each having a different structure, I could use a set of choices to support this. In this XML Schema excerpt, I replace the* location *element with a choice model group, allowing a single* location *element, or a set of two elements,* city *and* country.

```
xml
<wonder>
 <name language="English">
   Colossus of Rhodes</name>
  <location>Rhodes, Greece</location>
...
</wonder>
```

```
xml
<wonder>
 <name language="English">
   Colossus of Rhodes</name>
  <city>Rhodes</city>
  <country>Greece</country>
...
</wonder>
```

Figure 11.19 *Based on the XML Schema excerpt in Figure 11.18, both of these* wonder *elements are valid. In the top XML excerpt, the* location *field is present. In the bottom excerpt, instead of a* location *field, there is a sequence consisting of a* city *and* country *element.*

Creating a Set of Choices

It's sometimes useful to declare a complex type element so that it can contain one child element (or a group of child elements) or another. You do that by creating a choice model group **(Figure 11.18)**.

To offer a choice of child elements:

1. Type **<xs:choice**.
2. Optionally, you can specify how many times the set of choices itself can appear by setting the `minOccurs` and `maxOccurs` attributes, as described on page 151.
3. Then, type **>** to complete the opening tag.
4. Declare the simple type elements and/or complex type elements that you want to make up the set of choices.
5. Finally, type **</xs:choice>** to complete the model group.

✔ Tips

- The default `minOccurs` and `maxOccurs` attribute values are both 1. With these defaults, only one of the elements in a set of choices can appear in a valid XML document. If the value of the `maxOccurs` attribute is greater than 1, that value determines how many of the choices may appear. Using `maxOccurs="unbounded"` is equivalent to adding an asterisk (*) to a set of choices in a DTD *(see Chapter 5)*.
- A set of choices can also contain sequences *(see page 143)*, additional choice sets, or references to named groups *(see page 152)*.
- A set of choices may be contained in a complex type definition, in sequences *(see page 143)*, in other sets of choices, or in named group definitions *(see page 152)*.
- The `<xs:choice>` element is basically equivalent to the vertical bars in DTDs.

Defining Elements to Contain Only Text

Another common complex type element is called "text only." It contains a text value and no child elements. This complex type name is a little misleading, however, in that it can (and often will), also have one or more attributes.

To define a "text only" complex type:

1. Type **<xs:complexType**.
2. Then, type **name="complex_type_name">**, where *complex_type_name* identifies your new complex type.
3. Type **<xs:simpleContent>**.
4. Next, type **<xs:extension** to use a simple type for the text value of the element.

   Or type **<xs:restriction** to limit the base simple type with additional facets.
5. Then, type **base="foundation">**, where *foundation* indicates the simple type on which you're basing the new complex type element.
6. If you chose `xs:restriction` in Step 4, declare the additional facets *(see Chapter 10)* that should limit the simple content in this complex type definition.
7. Next, declare the attributes *(see page 154)* that should appear in this complex type element, if any.
8. Then, type **</xs:extension>** or **</xs:restriction>** to match Step 4.
9. Type **</xs:simpleContent>**.
10. Finally, type **</xs:complexType>** to complete the complex type definition **(Figure 11.20)**.

xsd
```
<xs:complexType name="yearType">

 <xs:simpleContent>

  <xs:extension base=
    "xs:positiveInteger">

  <xs:attribute name="era"
type="xs:string"/>

  </xs:extension>

 </xs:simpleContent>

</xs:complexType>
```

Figure 11.20 *This is a "text only" complex type definition. This indicates that any XML elements defined using the* yearType *type must contain a positive integer, but no child elements. They will also have an attribute named* era *which contains a string value. For more details on attributes, see page 154.*

xml
```
<year_built era="BC">
  282</year_built>
```

Figure 11.21 *This* year_built *element is valid, based on the complex type definition in Figure 11.20, because it contains an integer and has an* era *attribute.*

xml
```
<year_built era="BC">
  long ago</year_built>
```

Figure 11.22 *This* year_built *element, however, is invalid, because "long ago" is not an integer. The* yearType *complex type requires that the element's value be an* xs:positiveInteger, *specified by the base simple type from which the complex type was extended.*

```
xsd
<xs:complexType name="sourceType">

 <xs:attribute name="sectionid"
   type="xs:positiveInteger"/>

 <xs:attribute name="newspaperid"
   type="xs:positiveInteger"/>

</xs:complexType>
```

Figure 11.23 *This complex type definition defines the* sourceType *complex type. It is an* empty element *that contains two attributes,* sectionid *and* newspaperid.

```
xsd
<xs:complexType name="sourceType">

 <xs:complexContent>

  <xs:restriction base="xs:anyType">

   <xs:attribute name="sectionid"
     type="xs:positiveInteger"/>

   <xs:attribute name="newspaperid"
     type="xs:positiveInteger"/>

  </xs:restriction>

 </xs:complexContent>

</xs:complexType>
```

Figure 11.24 *Here is another complex type definition for the* sourceType *complex type. In this excerpt, I have added back in the default condition elements (derived from complex content that restricts* anyType*). While it defines the* exact same *complex type as shown in Figure 11.23, it is much more cumbersome and is not written this way in practice.*

```
xml
<source sectionid="101"
  newspaperid="21"/>
```

Figure 11.25 *This* source *element is valid based on the XML Schema shown in either Figure 11.23 or Figure 11.24.*

Defining Empty Elements

Elements that can contain attributes, but have no content between the opening and closing tags are called "empty elements." Since these are complex type elements, they can (and often do), have one or more attributes.

To define an "empty element" complex type:

1. Type **<xs:complexType**.
2. Then, type **name="complex_type_name">**, where *complex_type_name* identifies your new complex type.
3. Next, declare the attributes *(see page 154)* that should appear in this complex type element, if any.
4. Finally, type **</xs:complexType>** to complete the complex type definition **(Figure 11.23)**.

✔ Tip

- As discussed on page 139, the default condition for complex types is that they derive from `xs:complexContent` that restricts `xs:anyType`. Because of this, you can omit these XML Schema element declarations **(Figure 11.24)**.

Defining Elements with Mixed Content

While pure database-driven content rarely has elements that contain both child elements and text, more text-centered documents wouldn't find it strange at all. A complex type that supports this is called "mixed content." When creating this complex type, you must declare that the content will be *mixed* **(Figure 11.26)**.

To create a "mixed content" complex type:

1. Type **<xs:complexType**.
2. Then, type **name="complex_type_name"**, where *complex_type_name* identifies your new complex type.
3. Next, type **mixed="true">** to indicate that the element can contain elements and text, (and may even contain attributes as well).
4. Declare a sequence *(see page 143)*, an unordered list *(see page 144)*, or a choice *(see page 145)* to specify the child elements and structure within the complex type.
5. Then, declare the attributes *(see page 154)* that should appear in this complex type element, if any.
6. Finally, type **</xs:complexType>** to complete the complex type definition.

✔ Tips

- Mixed content elements are ideal for descriptive, text-based chunks of information. They are not very common in database-type applications.
- As discussed on page 139, the default condition for complex types is that they derive from `xs:complexContent` that restricts `xs:anyType`. Because of this, I have omitted these XML Schema elements.

xsd
```
<xs:complexType name="story"
  mixed="true">

 <xs:sequence>

  <xs:element name="para"
    maxOccurs="unbounded">
   <xs:complexType/>
  </xs:element>

 </xs:sequence>

</xs:complexType>
```

Figure 11.26 *By setting the* mixed *attribute to* true, *the* story *element can contain both text and child elements. Notice that the* para *element is an empty complex type element with no attributes (see page 147). The XML Schema attribute* maxOccurs="unbounded" *means that there can be an unlimited number of* para *elements within the* story *element.*

xml
```
<story>
  In 294 BC, the people of the island
  of Rhodes began building a colossal
  statue of the sun god Helios. They
  believed that it was because of his
  blessings that they were able to
  withstand a long siege on the
  island and emerge victorious.
  <para/>
  The Colossus was built with bronze,
  reinforced with iron, and weighted
  with stones. While it is often
  depicted straddling Mandrákion
  harbor, this is now considered
  technically impossible; and
  therefore, it likely stood beside
  the harbor.
  <para/>
  The statue was toppled by an
  earthquake in 226 BC. ...
</story>
```

Figure 11.27 *This valid XML* story *element contains both loose text and* para *elements (bolded).*

Deriving Complex Types from Existing Complex Types

You can also create new complex types based on existing complex types. The new complex type begins with all the information from the existing type **(Figure 11.28)**, and then adds or removes features.

To derive a new complex type from an existing type:

1. Type **<xs:complexType**.
2. Then, type **name="complex_type_name"**, where *complex_type_name* identifies your new complex type.
3. Type **<xs:complexContent>**.
4. Next, type **<xs:extension** to indicate that features will be *added* to the existing complex type **(Figure 11.29)**.

   Or type **<xs:restriction** to indicate that features will be *removed* from the existing complex type **(Figure 11.30)**.
5. Then, type **base="existing_type">**, where *existing_type* identifies the name of the existing type from which the new complex type will be derived.
6. Declare the attributes *(see page 154)* that should be part of the new complex type.
7. Type a matching closing tag for Step 4.
8. Type **</xs:complexContent>**.
9. Finally, type **</xs:complexType>** to complete the complex type definition.

✔ Tips

- New complex types derived using restrictions must be valid subsets of the existing complex type. Some acceptable restrictions include setting default or fixed values (Figure 11.30).
- As this is an advanced topic, I have only identified the basics here.

xsd

```
<xs:complexType name="historyType">
 <xs:sequence>
  <xs:element name="year_built"
    type="yearType"/>
  <xs:element name="year_destroyed"
    type="yearType" minOccurs="0"/>
  <xs:element name="how_destroyed"
    type="destrType" minOccurs="0"/>
  <xs:element name="story"
    type="storyType"/>
 </xs:sequence>
</xs:complexType>
```

Figure 11.28 *This* historyType *is the base complex type that I'll be using for the two examples below.*

xsd

```
<xs:complexType name="newHistoryType">
 <xs:complexContent>
  <xs:extension base="historyType">
   <xs:sequence>
    <xs:element name="who_built"
      type="xs:string"/>
   </xs:sequence>
  </xs:extension>
 </xs:complexContent>
</xs:complexType>
```

Figure 11.29 *Here, I have derived a new complex type called* newHistoryType *as an* extension *of the* historyType *shown in Figure 11.28. This new type adds a* who_built *element to the end of the sequence from the existing base complex type.*

xsd

```
<xs:complexType name="newHistoryType">
 <xs:complexContent>
  <xs:restriction base="historyType">
   <xs:sequence>
    <xs:element name="year_built"
      type="yearType"/>
    <xs:element name="year_destroyed"
      type="yearType"/>
    <xs:element name="how_destroyed"
      type="destrType" fixed="fire"/>
    <xs:element name="story"
      type="storyType"/>
   </xs:sequence>
  </xs:restriction>
 </xs:complexContent>
</xs:complexType>
```

Figure 11.30 *When deriving a new complex type using* restriction, *you duplicate the base type and then refine it. Here, I have set a fixed value of "fire" for the* how_destroyed *element.*

Deriving Complex Types from Existing Complex Types

Referencing Globally Defined Elements

In an XML Schema document, elements defined as children of the `xs:schema` root element are said to be defined *globally*. Named complex types are an example of an element that is globally defined.

You can also globally define an individual element **(Figure 11.31)**. Once defined, in order for this element to be used in the XML Schema document, it must be called or *referenced*.

To reference a globally defined element:

1. In the sequence *(see page 143)*, unordered list *(see page 144)*, or set of choices *(see page 145)* in which the element should appear, type **<xs:element**.
2. Then, type **ref="label"**, where *label* is the name of the globally defined element.
3. If desired, specify how many times the element can appear at this point using `minOccurs` or `maxOccurs` *(see page 151)*.
4. Finally, type **/>** to complete the global element reference **(Figure 11.32)**.

✔ Tips

- You can reference a globally declared element in your XML Schema as many times as you like. As well, each reference may contain its own distinct values for `minOccurs` and `maxOccurs`.
- *Locally declared* elements are automatically referenced by the parent definition in which they appear. They cannot be referenced anywhere else.
- For more information about local and global declarations, consult *Local and Global Definitions* on page 159.

xsd
```
<xs:schema xmlns:xs="http://
  www.w3.org/2001/XMLSchema">

 <xs:element name="name">
  <xs:complexType>
   <xs:simpleContent>
    <xs:extension base="xs:string">
     <xs:attribute name="language"
       type="xs:string"/>
    </xs:extension>
   </xs:simpleContent>
  </xs:complexType>
 </xs:element>
```

Figure 11.31 *This* name *element, which is a child of the* xs:schema *element, is considered globally defined. As such, it can be referenced within any complex type definition, as shown below.*

xsd
```
<xs:complexType name="wonderType">
 <xs:sequence>
  <xs:element ref="name"/>
  <xs:element name="location"
    type="xs:string"/>
  <xs:element name="height"
    type="heightType"/>
...
```

Figure 11.32 *In this complex type definition for the* wonderType, *I reference the globally defined* name *element shown in Figure 11.31.*

xml
```
<wonder>
 <name language="English">
   Colossus of Rhodes</name>
 <location>Rhodes, Greece</location>
 <height units="feet">107</height>
...
```

Figure 11.33 *This is a valid XML excerpt, based on the XML Schema in Figures 11.31 and 11.32. It shows a* wonder *element with a valid* name *element.*

```
xsd
<xs:complexType name="wonderType">
 <xs:sequence>
...
  <xs:element name="contributor">
   <xs:complexType>
    <xs:sequence>
     <xs:element ref="name"
       minOccurs="0"
       maxOccurs="unbounded"/>
    </xs:sequence>
   </xs:complexType>
  </xs:element>
```

Figure 11.34 *I added a new* contributor *element to* wonderType. *It has one child element called* name, *defined using a reference to the globally defined* name *element shown in Figure 11.31. In a valid XML document, the* contributor *element can have from zero to an infinite number of* name *child elements.*

```
xsd
<xs:element name="contributor">
 <xs:complexType>
  <xs:choice minOccurs="1"
    maxOccurs="4">
   <xs:element ref="name"/>
   <xs:element name="organization"
     type="xs:string"/>
  </xs:choice>
 </xs:complexType>
</xs:element>
```

Figure 11.35 *The* minOccurs *and* maxOccurs *attributes can also be applied to sequences, unordered lists, or sets of choices. In this excerpt, between 1 and 4 elements of this set of choices are allowed. That is, there can only be between one and four* contributor *child elements, made up of any number of* name *and/or* organization *elements.*

Controlling How Many

Using XML Schema, you can control how many times a given element, sequence, unordered list, or set of choices can appear in a valid XML document **(Figures 11.34 and 11.35)**.

To specify the minimum number of occurrences:

◆ In the opening tag, type **minOccurs="n"**, where *n* indicates the fewest number of times the element, sequence, unordered list, or set of choices may occur for the XML document to be considered valid.

To specify the maximum number of occurrences:

◆ In the opening tag, type **maxOccurs="n"**, where *n* indicates the maximum number of times the element, sequence, unordered list, or set of choices may occur for the XML document to be considered valid.

✔ Tips

- The default value for both `minOccurs` and `maxOccurs` is 1. In other words, unless specified by either of these occurrence attributes, an element must appear exactly one time in a valid XML document.
- The `minOccurs` attribute must be a non-negative integer (0, 1, 2, 3, or higher).
- The `maxOccurs` attribute can be any non-negative integer, or the word `unbounded` to indicate that the element can appear any number of times.
- The `minOccurs` and `maxOccurs` attributes *cannot* be used when defining an element globally. They only make sense with local references to global elements, or locally defined elements.
- When using the `xs:all` element *(see page 144)*, you can only set `minOccurs` to 0 or 1, and `maxOccurs` can only be set to 1.

Defining Named Model Groups

If a collection of elements appears together in several places in your XML document, you can group the elements together to make it easier to refer to them all at once.

In other words, in the same way that you can create a globally defined element and refer to it throughout your XML Schema, you can name a model group (sequence, unordered list, or choice), and refer to the group throughout your XML Schema.

To define a named model group:

1. Type **<xs:group**.
2. Then, type **name="model_group_name"**, where *model_group_name* identifies your group of elements.
3. Next, type **>** to complete the opening group tag.
4. Declare sequences *(see page 143)*, unordered lists *(see page 144)*, and/or sets of choices *(see page 145)* that will make up the named model group.
5. Finally, type **</xs:group>** to complete the definition of the group **(Figure 11.36)**.

✔ Tips

- Like globally defined elements, a named model group may only be defined at the top-level of a schema (a child element of `xs:schema`). And, like globally defined elements, it may be referenced as many times as you would like *(see page 153)*.
- A named model group is analogous to a parameter entity in DTDs *(see Chapter 7)*.

xsd

```
<xs:group name="image_element">
 <xs:sequence>

  <xs:element name="image">
   <xs:complexType>
    <xs:attribute name="file"
      type="xs:anyURI"/>
    <xs:attribute name="w"
      type="xs:positiveInteger"/>
    <xs:attribute name="h"
      type="xs:positiveInteger"/>
   </xs:complexType>
  </xs:element>

  <xs:element name="source"
    type="xs:string"/>

 </xs:sequence>
</xs:group>
```

Figure 11.36 *This named model group* image_element *has an* image *element, which is an empty complex type with attributes, and another child element called* source, *which takes a string value.*

```
xsd
<xs:element name="main_image">
 <xs:complexType>
  <xs:sequence>
   <xs:group ref="image_element" />
   <xs:element name="caption"
     type="xs:string"/>
  </xs:sequence>
 </xs:complexType>
</xs:element>

<xs:element name="thumbnail_image">
 <xs:complexType>
  <xs:sequence>
   <xs:group ref="image_element" />
   <xs:element name="frame_border"
     type="xs:string"/>
  </xs:sequence>
 </xs:complexType>
</xs:element>
```

Figure 11.37 *Both the* main_image *and the* thumbnail_image *elements are now defined by the* image_element *named model group defined in Figure 11.36. They each can also have additional, individual elements,* caption *and* frame_border, *respectively.*

```
xml
<main_image>
 <image file="colossus.jpg"
   w="528" h="349" />
 <source>
   Greek Historical Archives</source>
 <caption>Part of a series of the
   Seven Wonders of the World,
   engraved by Marten Heemskerk.
 </caption>
</main_image>

<thumbnail_image>
 <image file="colossus_tn.jpg"
   w="80" h="120" />
 <source>
   Greek Historical Archives</source>
 <frame_border>Blue</frame_border>
</thumbnail_image>
```

Figure 11.38 *In this valid XML excerpt, based on the XML Schema in Figures 11.36 and 11.37,* main_image *and* thumbnail_image *have the elements defined in the named model group. As well, each also has its own individual elements.*

Referencing a Named Model Group

Once you've created a named model group, you can reference it in as many complex type definitions as you'd like (**Figure 11.37**). You can even reference it in other groups.

To reference a named model group:

1. In the part of your schema where you want the elements in the group to appear, type **<xs:group**.
2. Then, type **ref="model_group_name"**, where *model_group_name* identifies the group you created in Step 2 on the preceding page.
3. Finally, type **/>** to complete the reference.

✔ Tip

- You can reference a group in a complex type definition *(see page 142)*, a sequence *(see page 143)*, an unordered list *(see page 144)*, a set of choices *(see page 145)*, or in other named groups *(see page 152)*.

Defining Attributes

Attributes are simple type elements since they contain neither child elements nor attributes. However, since they always appear within complex type elements, they are discussed in this chapter rather than in the previous.

To define an attribute:

1. Within the definition of the complex type, type **<xs:attribute**.
2. Then, type **name="attribute_name"**, where *attribute_name* is the name of the XML attribute that you are defining.

Then, starting with Step 3, follow one of the three tasks below.

To use a base or named simple type:

3. Type **type="simple_type"/>**, where *simple_type* is the named or base type of the attribute that you are defining **(Figure 11.39)**.

To use an anonymous simple type:

3. Type **>** to complete the opening tag.
4. Then, type **<xs:simpleType>.**
5. Add any restrictions (or *facets*) you like.
6. Next, type **</xs:simpleType>** to close the simple type element.
7. Finally, type **</xs:attribute>** to close the opening tag, see Figure 11.39.

To use a globally defined attribute:

3. Type **ref="label"/>**, where *label* identifies an attribute definition that you've already globally defined.

✔ Tip

- Attributes *must* be defined at the very end of the complex type to which they belong; that is, after all the elements in the complex type have been defined.

xsd

```
<xs:complexType name="sourceType">

 <xs:attribute name="sectionid"
   type="xs:positiveInteger"/>

 <xs:attribute name="newspaperid">
  <xs:simpleType>
   <xs:restriction
     base="xs:positiveInteger">
    <xs:pattern value="\d{4}"/>
   </xs:restriction>
  </xs:simpleType>
 </xs:attribute>

</xs:complexType>
```

Figure 11.39 *In this excerpt, the* sectionid *element is declared with the base simple type* xs:positiveInteger. *The* newspaperid *element is declared with an anonymous simple type definition using pattern facet restriction allowing exactly 4 digits.*

xml

```
<source sectionid="101"
  newspaperid="21"/>
```

Figure 11.40 *Based on the XML Schema in Figure 11.39, this XML excerpt is invalid. While* sectionid *and* newspaperid *are both positive integers,* newspaperid *is now required to be exactly 4 digits.*

```
x s d
<xs:complexType name="sourceType">

 <xs:attribute name="sectionid"
   type="xs:positiveInteger"
   use="required"/>

 <xs:attribute name="newspaperid">
  <xs:simpleType>
   <xs:restriction
     base="xs:positiveInteger">
    <xs:pattern value="\d{4}"/>
   </xs:restriction>
  </xs:simpleType>
 </xs:attribute>

</xs:complexType>
```

Figure 11.41 *Since the default condition is for an attribute to be optional, you must specifically indicate that it be required.*

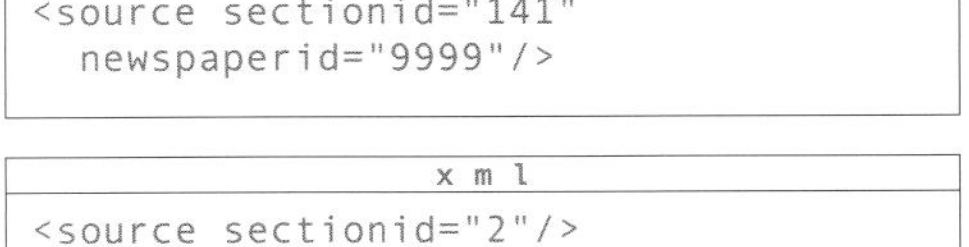

```
x m l
<source sectionid="141"
  newspaperid="9999"/>
```

```
x m l
<source sectionid="2"/>
```

Figure 11.42 *Both of these* source *elements are valid since only* sectionid *is required according to the XML Schema in Figure 11.41. If an attribute is not explicitly required, it is considered optional.*

Requiring an Attribute

Unless you specify otherwise, an attribute is always optional. In other words, it may appear or be absent from a valid XML document. However, if you'd prefer, you can insist that an attribute be present (or not), when determining if the XML document is valid.

To require that an attribute be present:

1. Within an attribute definition, type **use="required"** to indicate that the attribute must appear for an XML document to be considered valid **(Figure 11.41)**.
2. You may also add **value="must_be"**, where *must_be* is the only acceptable value for the attribute.

To require that an attribute *not* be present:

◆ Within an attribute definition, type **use="prohibited"** so that the XML document will only be considered valid if the attribute is not present.

✔ Tip

■ You could also type **use="optional"** within an attribute definition, but since that's the default condition, it's unnecessary.

Predefining an Attribute's Content

There are two ways to use XML Schema to predefine what an attribute's content should be. You can either dictate the attribute's content, or set an initial value for the attribute regardless of whether it appears or not. The former is called a *fixed* value; the latter is called a *default* value.

To dictate an attribute's content:

- Within an attribute definition, type **fixed="content"**, where *content* determines what the value of the attribute should be for the document to be considered valid **(Figure 11.43)**. (This only applies if the attribute appears in the XML document.)

To set an attribute's initial value:

- Within an attribute definition, type **default="content"**, where *content* determines the value the that attribute should be set to if it is omitted from the XML document **(Figure 11.45)**.

✔ Tips

- The `fixed` attribute only sets a value if the attribute actually appears in the XML. If the attribute is omitted, then no content is set.
- If the `default` attribute is set and the attribute is omitted from the XML document, then the attribute's value is set to the default value.
- If you set the `default` attribute, the only `use` attribute value you can have is `optional`, see *Requiring an Attribute* on page 155
- You may not have values for both `default` and `fixed` in the same attribute definition.

```
xsd
<xs:attribute name="sectionid"
  type="xs:positiveInteger"/>
<xs:attribute name="newspaperid"
  type="xs:positiveInteger"
  fixed="21"/>
```

Figure 11.43 *The* newspaperid *attribute, as long as it appears in the XML document, must contain the value "21." The attribute may, however, be omitted.*

```
xml
<source sectionid="101"
  newspaperid="21"/>
```

```
xml
<source sectionid="101"</source>
```

```
xml
<source newspaperid="64"/>
```

Figure 11.44 *The first two XML excerpts are valid. In the first,* newspaperid *is equal to the fixed value. In the second,* newspaperid *is omitted (and will remain excluded). In the third,* newspaperid *is not equal to the fixed value, and is therefore invalid.*

```
xsd
<xs:attribute name="sectionid"
  type="xs:positiveInteger"/>
<xs:attribute name="newspaperid"
  type="xs:positiveInteger"
  default="21"/>
```

Figure 11.45 *The* newspaperid *attribute now has a default value. This will be the initial value, whether or not the attribute is in the XML document.*

```
xml
<source sectionid="101"
  newspaperid="21"/>
```

```
xml
<source sectionid="101"/>
```

```
xml
<source newspaperid="64"/>
```

Figure 11.46 *Here, all three XML excerpts are valid. In the second, the* newspaperid *attribute will be created automatically and set to the default value.*

```
xsd
<xs:attributeGroup name="imageAttrs">

 <xs:attribute name="file"
   type="xs:anyURI" use="required"/>

 <xs:attribute name="w"
   type="xs:positiveInteger"
   use="required"/>

<xs:attribute name="h"
   type="xs:positiveInteger"
   use="required"/>

</xs:attributeGroup>
```

Figure 11.47 *By defining a group of attributes, it is easy to reuse those attributes in multiple XML Schema element definitions (see Referencing Attribute Groups on page 158).*

Defining Attribute Groups

If you need to use the same set of attributes in several places in your XML document, it's more efficient to define an attribute group and then refer to the attributes all at once.

This is the same concept you have seen used with globally defined elements and named model groups.

To define an attribute group:

1. Type **<xs:attributeGroup**.
2. Then, type **name="attribute_group_name">**, where *attribute_group_name* identifies your attribute group.
3. Define or reference each attribute that belongs to the group *(see page 154)*.
4. Finally, type **</xs:attributeGroup>** to complete the attribute group definition **(Figure 11.47)**.

✔ Tips

- Like all other globally defined elements, an attribute group may only be defined at the top-level of a schema (a child element of `xs:schema`). And, like all other globally defined elements, it may be referenced as many times as you like *(see page 158)*.
- In Step 2 above, you can only reference attributes that are globally defined; that is, those that were declared at the top level of the schema. For more details, see *Local and Global Definitions* on page 159.
- An attribute group can contain references to other attribute groups.

Referencing Attribute Groups

Once you've defined an attribute group, you can reference it wherever those attributes are needed; whether in complex type definitions or even in other attribute groups **(Figure 11.48)**.

To reference an attribute group:

1. Within a complex type definition, after declaring any elements that should be contained, type **<xs:attributeGroup**.
2. Then, type **ref="attribute_group_name"/>**, to identify the attribute group that you created in Step 2 on page 157.

✔ Tips

- Attributes and attribute groups *must* be defined at the very end of the complex type to which they belong, after all other elements have been defined.
- Attribute groups are analogous to parameter entities in DTDs *(see Chapter 7)*. However, they are limited to representing only collections of attributes.

```
xsd
<xs:complexType name="imageType">
 <xs:attributeGroup ref="imageAttrs"/>
</xs:complexType>

<xs:complexType name="videoType">
 <xs:attributeGroup ref="imageAttrs"/>
 <xs:attribute name="format"
   type="xs:string"/>
</xs:complexType>
```

Figure 11.48 *Using the* imageAttrs *attribute group defined in Figure 11.47 on the previous page, I've created two named complex types,* imageType *and* videoType. *The* imageType *will be used for the* main_image *element. The* videoType *will be used to create a* main_video *element. Note that it has an additional* format *attribute declared after the attribute group.*

```
xml
<main_image file="colossus.jpg"
  w="528" h="349"/>

<main_video file="colossus.mov"
  w="320" h="240"
  format="quicktime"/>
```

Figure 11.49 *Both the* main_image *and* main_video *elements share the* file*, as well as the* w *and* h *attributes. The benefit of the attribute group is that all three attributes were only defined once, but have been used in more than one complex type definition.*

```
xsd
<xs:element name="name">
 <xs:complexType>
  <xs:simpleContent>
   <xs:extension base="xs:string">
    <xs:attribute name="language"
      type="xs:string"
      use="required"/>
   </xs:extension>
  </xs:simpleContent>
 </xs:complexType>
</xs:element>
```

Figure 11.50 *The example shown in Figure 11.34 on page 151 works, in part, because the globally defined* name *element does not require the* language *attribute. However, if it did require the* language *attribute, as shown here, all* name *elements that were children of* contributor *would be invalid.*

```
xsd
<xs:complexType name="wonderType">
 <xs:sequence>
   <xs:element name="name">
    <xs:complexType>
     <xs:simpleContent>
      <xs:extension base="xs:string">
       <xs:attribute name="language"
       type="xs:string"
       use="required"/>
      </xs:extension>
     </xs:simpleContent>
    </xs:complexType>
   </xs:element>
...
  <xs:element name="contributor">
   <xs:complexType>
    <xs:sequence>
     <xs:element name="name"
       type="xs:string" minOccurs="0"
       maxOccurs="unbounded"/>
    </xs:sequence>
   </xs:complexType>
  </xs:element>
...
</complexType>
```

Figure 11.51 *Considering the dilemma described in Figure 11.50, it would be better to have each of the* name *elements defined locally; one for the* wonder *element and one for the* contributor *element.*

Local and Global Definitions

In XML Schema, elements can be defined either locally or globally. A *globally* defined element is defined as a child of the `xs:schema` element. Since it is defined at the top-most level of the schema, it's scope (meaning where it can be used) is anywhere in the entire schema.

Conversely, a *locally* defined element is defined as the child of some other element. Since it is defined as a child element, its scope is within its parent element only.

Globally defined elements, like named custom types, do not automatically become part of an XML Schema. The definition only determines what that element will look like. Global elements must be explicitly *referenced* in order to actually appear in a valid XML document.

Locally defined elements, however, like anonymous custom types, automatically become part of an XML document. Where they are defined determines where in the XML document the element must appear.

I have already shown the benefits of reusing globally defined elements (see *Referencing Globally Defined Elements* on page 150, *Referencing a Named Model Group* on page 153, and *Referencing Attribute Groups* on page 158).

On the flip side, one of the benefits of using locally defined elements is that the element's scope is isolated. An isolated scope means that the element's name and definition cannot conflict with other elements in the same XML Schema using the same name. Which one to choose is dependent on your need for reusability, versus your need to isolate an element and its definition **(Figures 11.50 and 11.51)**.

✔ Tip

- In a DTD, every element is declared globally; there is no such thing as a locally defined element.

Part 5: Namespaces

12

XML Namespaces

You've learned how to create XML documents, transform, and display them, as well as define the set of elements and attributes that they can contain. Now, imagine that you want to combine some of your XML documents with someone else's. In doing so, you find out that they have used some of the same names for elements that you have. For example, the *Wonders of the World* document uses the `name` element to contain the name of each specific wonder, while the other person uses the `name` element to contain the name of an ancient civilization. If I combine these XML documents, the source element data will become unclear and effectively meaningless.

The solution to this problem is to group the element names from each XML document into its own space. Then, when referring to a particular element, it would be identified with the space in which it resides. This format would provide a way to distinguish elements in one group of XML documents from the other. For example, I could call my space "Kevin," and identify the elements in my XML documents with that name. Now, the `Kevin:name` element can't be confused with the other `name` element.

This group of element names, is actually called a *namespace* (one word), and the identifier I used is called a *namespace name*. And, while it's fun to use "Kevin" as my namespace name, the required format of a namespace name is a bit more structured, as you'll see in this chapter.

Designing a Namespace Name

Since the whole point of namespaces is to distinguish elements with the same name from each other, a namespace must have an absolutely unique and permanent name. In XML, namespace names are written in the form of a URI (*Uniform Resource Identifier*).

To design a namespace name:

1. Start with your domain name.
2. Add descriptive information (as if it were a path in a URI) to create a unique name for your namespace **(Figure 12.1)**.

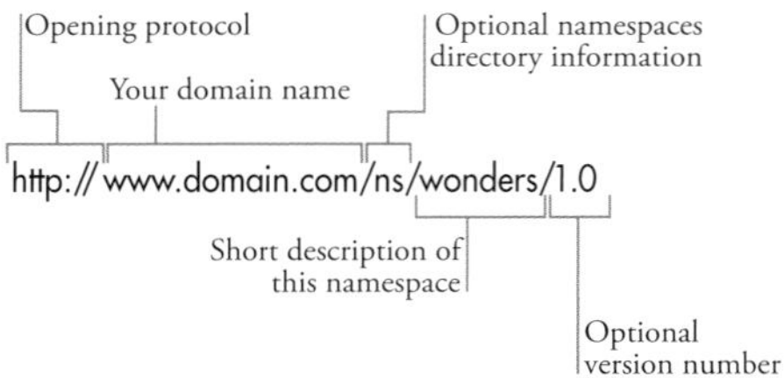

Figure 12.1 *A namespace name should be in the form of a URI. I recommend using a URL format. The URL does not have to (and typically will not), point to an actual file!*

✔ Tips

- A URI is a string of characters that identifies a resource. A URL (*Uniform Resource Locator*) is the most common form of URI, and I recommend using it for designing a namespace name.
- Using your own domain as the foundation for your namespace name gives you the ability to ensure that the name is unique. No one else can use your domain name.
- The only requirements for the URI are that it be *unique*, and that it be *persistent* (practically permanent). I'd also recommend it being *consistent* if you're going to create numerous namespaces.
- You can also add version information to your namespace, if desired.
- There is a lot of confusion over what is pointed to by the namespace name. In fact, while the namespace name *may* point to a DTD or XML Schema, this is not common, nor is it required in the W3C's XML Namespaces Recommendation. Furthermore, even if the URI does point to a file, XML software does not even look at it.

```
xml
<ancient_wonders
  xmlns="http://
  www.kehogo.com/ns/wonders/1.0">

 <wonder>

  <name language="English">
    Colossus of Rhodes</name>

  <name language="Greek">
    Κολοσσός της Ρόδου</name>

  <location>Rhodes, Greece</location>

  <height units="feet">107</height>
```

Figure 12.2 *With this default namespace declaration, all the document's elements are part of the* http://www.kehogo.com/ns/wonders/1.0 *namespace.*

```
xml
<ancient_wonders
  xmlns="http://
  www.kehogo.com/ns/wonders/1.0">

 <wonder>
  <name language="English">
    Colossus of Rhodes</name>
  <name language="Greek">
    Κολοσσός της Ρόδου</name>
  <location>Rhodes, Greece</location>

  <civilization
    xmlns="http://www.kehogo.com/ns
    /ancient_civ/2.3">
   <name>Greece</name>
   <locale>Mediterranean Sea</locale>
   <period>750 BC - 146 BC</period>
  </civilization>

  <height units="feet">107</height>
```

Figure 12.3 *In this example, I have added a new* civilization *element, which is declared to be part of the* http://www.kehogo.com/ns/ancient_civ/2.3 *namespace. Consequently,* civilization, name, historical_data *and all other children of* civilization *are part of its default namespace (the one for ancient civilizations). By declaring this default namespace for the* civilization *element, I have avoided the element conflict between the "wonders of the world"* name *element, and the "ancient civilization"* name *element.*

Declaring a Default Namespace

Once you've designed a namespace name, you can declare it as the default namespace for your XML document (**Figure 12.2**).

To declare a default namespace for your XML document:

1. Within the opening tag of the root element, type **xmlns=**. (This is the attribute for declaring an xml namespace.)
2. Then, type **"URI"**, where *URI* identifies the name of your namespace *(see page 164)*.

✔ Tips

- Declaring a default namespace for the root element means that all the elements in the document are considered to be from that namespace.
- You can declare a default namespace for any element in your document, not just the root element. To do so, you would follow the steps above replacing the root element with the element for which you want to declare a default namespace. This will override the default namespace declared by any ancestor element (**Figure 12.3**).
- Labeling any element with a default namespace affects not only that particular element, but all of its children as well.
- You can override a default namespace by specifying a prefixed namespace for an individual element, as described on pages 166–167. In this case, the child elements are not affected.
- In the case where a default namespace is not declared for a particular element, nor has it inherited a namespace from one of its ancestors, it is considered "in no namespace." Elements in no namespace can be assigned default namespaces, thereby overriding the no namespace state.

Declaring a Namespace Name Prefix

Declaring a default namespace for an element applies to all that element's children. You can also choose to label specific individual elements in your document with a namespace, and not affect those elements' children. To do so, you can declare a special nickname, or *prefix*, for the namespace, and then use that prefix to label the individual elements specifically.

To declare a prefix for a namespace name:

1. In the document's root element, type **xmlns:prefix**, where *prefix* will be the nickname for this namespace.
2. Then, type **="URI"**, where *URI* identifies the name of the namespace to which the prefix will refer **(Figure 12.4)**.

✔ Tips

- Prefixes may not begin with the letters *xml*, in any combination of upper or lowercase.
- You may use a prefix in any element contained wherein you declared the prefix, including the containing element itself. That is, if you declare a prefix in the root element, you can use the prefix in any element in the document, including in the root element itself. If you declare the prefix in an element other than the root element, it can only be used in that element and/or in that element's descendants **(Figure 12.5)**.
- You can declare as many namespace prefixes as necessary in any element.

```
xml
<ancient_wonders
  xmlns="http://
  www.kehogo.com/ns/wonders/1.0"

  xmlns:anc_civ="http://
  www.kehogo.com/ns/ancient_civ/2.3">

 <wonder>
  <name language="English">
    Colossus of Rhodes</name>
  <name language="Greek">
    Κολοσσός της Ρόδου</name>
  <location>Rhodes, Greece</location>
  <anc_civ:civilization>
   <anc_civ:name>
     Greece</anc_civ:name>
   <anc_civ:locale>Mediterranean
     Sea</anc_civ:locale>
   <anc_civ:period>
     750 BC - 146 BC</anc_civ:period>
  </anc_civ:civilization>
 <height units="feet">107</height>
```

Figure 12.4 *Here, I am declaring the ancient civilization namespace in the document's root element, and assigning it a prefix of* anc_civ. *I can then use that namespace prefix throughout the document to indicate individual elements that belong to that namespace.*

```
xml
<ancient_wonders
  xmlns="http://www.kehogo.com/ns
  /wonders/1.0">

 <wonder>
  <name language="English">
    Colossus of Rhodes</name>
  <name language="Greek">
    Κολοσσός της Ρόδου</name>
  <location>Rhodes, Greece</location>

  <anc_civ:civilization
    xmlns:anc_civ="
    http://www.kehogo.com/ns
    /ancient_civ/2.3">

   <anc_civ:name>Greece ...
```

Figure 12.5 *In this example, the* anc_civ *namespace prefix is not declared in the root element, but rather in the* anc_civ:civilization *element. Consequently, it can only be used for that element and its children.*

```
xml
<ancient_wonders
  xmlns="http://www.kehogo.com/ns
  /wonders/1.0"

  xmlns:anc_civ="
  http://www.kehogo.com/ns
  /ancient_civ/2.3">

 <wonder>
  <name language="English">
    Colossus of Rhodes</name>
  <name language="Greek">
    Κολοσσός της Ρόδου</name>
  <location>Rhodes, Greece</location>
  <anc_civ:locale>
    Mediterranean Sea</anc_civ:locale>
  <anc_civ:period>
    750 BC - 146 BC</anc_civ:period>
  <height units="feet">107</height>
  <history>
   <year_built era="BC">
     282</year_built>
   <year_destroyed era="BC">
     226</year_destroyed>
   <how_destroyed>earthquake
     </how_destroyed>
       <anc_civ:gods>
        <anc_civ:god>
          Helios</anc_civ:god>
        <anc_civ:domain>
          Sun</anc_civ:domain>
       </anc_civ:gods>
   <story>
     In 294 BC, the people of the
     island of Rhodes began building
     a colossal statue of the sun god
     Helios. They believed that it
     was because of his blessings ...
```

Figure 12.6 *Each element in the ancient civilization namespace is preceded by its prefix* anc_civ:, *to show that it belongs to that namespace. While typing* anc_civ: *a bunch of times is a little cumbersome, typing* http://www.kehogo.com/ns/ancient_civ/2.3 *would be even worse.*

Labeling Elements with a Namespace Prefix

Once you've declared a prefix for a namespace name, you can use that prefix to label individual elements. In this way, you can assign these elements to different namespaces in your XML, without affecting the siblings or children of those elements **(Figure 12.6)**.

To label individual elements with different namespaces:

1. Type **<** to begin the element.
2. Then, type **prefix:**, where *prefix* indicates the namespace to which this element belongs, as declared on the previous page.
3. Next, type **element**, where *element* is the name of the element you wish to use.
4. Finally, complete the element as usual. (See Chapter 1, *Writing XML,* for details.)

✔ Tips

- Only those elements whose names are preceded with a prefix are identified with the namespace declared with that prefix. This is different than default namespaces, where the element *and all of its children* are identified with the namespace.
- The XML processor considers unprefixed elements to belong to the default namespace *(see page 165)*, if there is one, or to no namespace, if there's not.
- An XML processor considers the prefix part of the element's name. Therefore, the closing tag must match the opening tag. So, if you've typed **<anc_civ:locale>** as an element's opening tag, you would use **</anc_civ:locale>** for its closing tag.
- If you're using a lot of elements from a given namespace in one section, it's easier to declare a default namespace for that section *(see page 165)*.

How Namespaces Affect Attributes

While you *could* associate an attribute with a specific namespace by prefixing it with the appropriate prefix, it's almost never necessary. Attributes are already made unique by the element that contains them.

For example, when you see the `sectionid` attribute within the `source` element, you know that it belongs to the `source` element, and therefore, its namespace. There is no confusion. If there were another `sectionid` attribute, say, in a `map` element, you'd recognize that `sectionid` attribute as belonging to the `map` element, without any other necessary clues. This is simply because it is physically contained within the `map` element **(Figure 12.7)**.

If an attribute has no prefix, which they rarely do, then it is considered to be "in no namespace" (because default namespaces do not apply to attributes). So, in this case, the attribute is locally *scoped*, which is a fancy way of saying that it is identified by the namespace of the element that contains it.

Although quite uncommon, there are cases where you would need to associate an attribute with a specific namespace, by prepending it with the appropriate prefix. Imagine that you need to combine two elements from different namespaces into a single element, and both have an attribute with the same name. In this case, you would need to differentiate each attribute, since a single element cannot have multiple attributes with the same name. By prefixing each attribute with the their respective namespace prefix, you would be creating unique attributes, because an XML processor considers the prefix part of an attribute's name **(Figure 12.8)**.

```xml
<source sectionid="101"
  newspaperid="21"/>

<map sectionid="a942"/>
```

Figure 12.7 *Even though* source *and* map *both have* sectionid *attributes, they don't overlap in the same way that identically named elements do.*

```xml
<main_image file="colossus.jpg"
  w="528" h="349"/>
```

```xml
<main_image file="local"/>
```

```xml
<main_image anc_civ:file="local"
  wow:file="colossus.jpg"
  w="528" h="349"/>
```

Figure 12.8 *In this example, the first two elements are* main_image *elements each containing a* file *attribute. The first is from the* wow: *namespace and the second is from the* anc_civ: *namespace. In the third XML file excerpt, I combined these two* main_image *elements into a single element by creating unique* file *attributes using their respective namespace prefixes.*

13

Using XML Namespaces

As you saw in the previous chapter, a namespace is a collection of related elements and attributes, identified by a namespace name. This namespace name must be unique, and is often referred to by its abbreviated name or prefix.

Namespaces are most often used to distinguish identically named elements from one another. Specifically, namespaces help to distinguish global elements that are identically named, since local elements and attributes are generally made unique by their context.

This combination of namespace name plus an element name is called an *expanded name*. Because a namespace name must be unique, the expanded name will also be unique. (Note: This combination is also referred to as a universal name, qualified name, or QName.)

Up until this part of the book, all the XML, XSL, DTD, and XML Schema documents have been "in no namespace." Now, with the introduction of namespaces in the XML documents, the relationship between the XML documents and these companion technologies will change.

In this chapter, I'll discuss some of the important details about how to use XML documents and XML namespaces with these languages.

Populating an XML Namespace

You saw in Part 4 of the book that XML Schemas specify the elements and attributes of which valid XML documents are composed. As it turns out, XML Schemas can also specify the elements and attributes contained in an XML namespace.

You don't have to do anything special in the way element and attributes are defined; you can simply follow the instructions in Chapters 10 and 11. You do, however, have to specify the *target namespace* to which the elements and attributes will belong. This process of specifying the elements and attributes for a target namespace is called *populating the namespace*.

To populate a namespace:

- In the root element of your XML Schema, type **targetNamespace="URI"**, where *URI* is the namespace name being populated **(Figure 13.1)**.

✔ Tips

- When populating a namespace, only the globally defined (top-level) elements and attributes are associated with the namespace. Remember, a globally defined element or attribute is a child of the `xs:schema` element, and could actually be an element, an attribute, a complex or simple type definition, a named model group, or a named attribute group.
- This does not mean that you cannot use or validate locally defined elements, such as the `wonder`, `name` or `location` elements in Figure 13.1. When you validate an XML document against the XML Schema shown in the figure, it will make sure that all the locally defined elements are not associated with a namespace.

xsd

```
<?xml version="1.0"?>

<xs:schema xmlns:xs=
  "http://www.w3.org/2001/XMLSchema"

  targetNamespace=
  "http://www.kehogo.com/ns/wow/1.0">

 <xs:element name="ancient_wonders">
  <xs:complexType>
   <xs:sequence>
    <xs:element name="wonder"
      type="wonderType"
      maxOccurs="unbounded"/>
   </xs:sequence>
  </xs:complexType>
 </xs:element>

 <xs:complexType name="wonderType">
  <xs:sequence>
   <xs:element name="name"
     type="nameType"
     maxOccurs="unbounded"/>
   <xs:element name="location"
     type="xs:string"/>
   <xs:element name="height"
     type="heightType"/>
   <xs:element name="history"
     type="historyType"/>
   <xs:element name="main_image"
     type="imageType"/>
   <xs:element name="source"
     type="sourceType" minOccurs="0"
     maxOccurs="unbounded"/>
  </xs:sequence>
 </xs:complexType>
```

Figure 13.1 *In this example, the* ancient_wonders *element and the* wonderType *complex type are now identified with the* http://www.kehogo.com/ns/wow/1.0 *namespace. The* wonder, name, location, height, history, main_image, *and* source *elements are not identified with the namespace since they are not globally defined elements.*

```
xml
<?xml version="1.0"?>

<ancient_wonders
  xmlns="http://
    www.kehogo.com/ns/wow/1.0"

  xmlns:xsi="http://
    www.w3.org/2001/
    XMLSchema-instance"

  xsi:schemaLocation="http://
    www.kehogo.com/ns/wow/1.0

    13-01.xsd">

 <wonder>
  <name language="English">
    Colossus of Rhodes</name>
  <name language="Greek">
    Κολοσσὸς της Ῥόδου</name>
  <location>Rhodes, Greece</location>
  <height units="feet">107</height>
  <history> ...
```

Figure 13.2 *The first highlighted line declares the namespace for the XML document. The second declares the namespace for the* xsi-*prefixed items. The third indicates the namespace, and then the actual file with which that namespace was populated.*

> **Why Is This Not Yet Valid?**
>
> Although the examples on these two pages have followed the outlined steps, the XML document is not yet valid. This is because the `wonder_type` complex type definition (and others) is part of the namespace populated by the XML Schema, but the reference to this complex type, as seen in Figure 13.1, does not use the namespace itself. Referencing a complex type using a namespace is discussed on page 172.

XML Schemas, XML Documents, and Namespaces

Now that your XML Schema has populated a namespace, you need to adjust the relationship between the XML Schema and your XML document. You've already seen how to indicate an XML Schema's location in an XML document when there is no namespace involved *(see page 117)*. Specifying the location of an XML Schema that has populated a namespace is pretty similar **(Figure 13.2)**.

To indicate the location of an XML Schema and the namespace it populated:

1. In the root element of the XML document, after the declaration of the XML Schema-populated namespace, type **xmlns:xsi="http://www.w3.org/2001/XMLSchema-instance"**. This declaration allows you to define the location of your XML Schema in the next three steps.
2. Then, type **xsi:schemaLocation="URI**, where *URI* is the namespace name just populated by your XML Schema document. (Notice, in this step, there's no closing double quotation mark.)
3. Next, type a space (or a return, if you prefer), to separate the namespace name and the XML Schema's location.
4. Finally, type **schema.uri">**, where *schema.uri* is the location of your XML Schema document. (Notice, in this step, there's no opening double quotation mark.)

✔ Tips

- If you need multiple namespaces and XML Schema documents, you can repeat Steps 2–4 as many times as needed.
- As an aside, in Step 1 above you are defining another namespace for your XML document. It has a prefix of `xsi:`, and defines the attribute being set in Steps 2–4.

Referencing XML Schema Components in Namespaces

In XML Schema, *components* are either named simple or complex types, elements, attributes, named model groups, or named attribute groups. Once you have associated XML Schema components with a namespace *(see page 170)*, you can refer to them within that (or any other) XML Schema. However, since they are now associated with a namespace, you *must specify the namespace* when you refer to them.

To declare a default namespace for XML Schema components:

- In the root element of your XML Schema document, type **xmlns="URI"**, where *URI* is the namespace with which the referenced components are associated **(Figure 13.3)**.

To declare a namespace with a prefix for XML Schema components:

- In the root element of your XML Schema document, type **xmlns:prefix="URI"**, where *prefix* is how you will identify the components in this XML Schema that belong to the namespace indicated by the *URI*.

To then reference those components in the XML Schema:

- If you have declared a prefix for your namespace, type **prefix:component_name**, where you prepend the *component_name* with the defined namespace *prefix*. If you have declared a default namespace, simply type the component name as usual, see Figure 13.3.

✔ Tip

- A namespace declaration allows you to identify components in your document that are part of that namespace. A target namespace allows you to populate that namespace with components.

xsd

```
<?xml version="1.0"?>

<xs:schema xmlns:xs=
  "http://www.w3.org/2001/XMLSchema"

  xmlns=
  "http://www.kehogo.com/ns/wow/1.0"

  targetNamespace=
  "http://www.kehogo.com/ns/wow/1.0">

 <xs:element name="ancient_wonders">
  <xs:complexType>
   <xs:sequence>
    <xs:element name="wonder"
      type="wonderType"
      maxOccurs="unbounded"/>
   </xs:sequence>
  </xs:complexType>
 </xs:element>

 <xs:complexType name="wonderType">
  <xs:sequence>
   <xs:element name="name"
     type="nameType"
     maxOccurs="unbounded"/>
   <xs:element name="location"
     type="xs:string"/>
   <xs:element name="height"
     type="heightType"/>
   <xs:element name="history"
     type="historyType"/>
   <xs:element name="main_image"
     type="imageType"/>
   <xs:element name="source"
     type="sourceType" minOccurs="0"
     maxOccurs="unbounded"/>
  </xs:sequence>
 </xs:complexType>
```

Figure 13.3 *In the root element of the XML Schema, I've declared the default namespace as* http://www.kehogo.com/ns/wow/1.0. *This means that the definitions of the unprefixed global types* (wonderType *being the only one shown in the excerpt) can be found in the XML Schema that corresponds to the default namespace. (The definitions of the prefixed types,* xs:complexType, xs:string, *etc., are found in the XML Schema that corresponds to the* http://www.w3.org/2001/XMLSchema *namespace.)*

```
xml
<?xml version="1.0"?>

<wow:ancient_wonders

  xmlns:wow=
  "http://www.kehogo.com/ns/wow/1.0"

  xmlns:xsi=
  "http://www.w3.org/2001/XMLSchema-
   instance"
  xsi:schemaLocation=
  "http://www.kehogo.com/ns/wow/1.0
   13-03.xsd">

 <wonder>
  <name language="English">
    Colossus of Rhodes</name>
  <name language="Greek">
    Κολοσσός της Ρόδου</name>
  <location>Rhodes, Greece</location>
  <height units="feet">107</height>
  <history> ...
```

Figure 13.4 *In the XML Schema in Figure 13.3, the* ancient_wonders *element was associated with the namespace* http://www.kehogo.com/ns/wow/1.0. *So, for this XML document to be valid, I qualify the* ancient_wonders *element accordingly. Because* wonder *and the other elements were not associated with the target namespace (they were not global elements in the schema), they don't need to be qualified.*

It's All Good

The XML document is finally valid, as is the XML Schema document on the preceding page, both of which are now part of the same namespace.

Namespaces and Validating XML

You have populated an XML namespace and associated it with an XML document. In the XML Schema that populated the namespace, you have declared the namespace as the default namespace. Now, you're ready to validate an XML document against the XML Schema, both of which reference the same namespace.

When validating XML documents in Chapters 10 and 11, you didn't have to worry about namespaces, because none of the elements were *qualified* (associated with a target namespace). Now that all or some of your elements belong to a namespace, when validating your XML documents, you'll have to specify that namespace for those elements.

To write XML documents with qualified elements:

1. You must indicate the namespace of the desired elements by declaring a namespace with a prefix. Within the root element, type **xmlns:prefix="URI"**, where *prefix* will identify the elements in this XML document that belong to the namespace indicated by the *URI* **(Figure 13.4)**.
2. Finally, prefix those elements with the namespace prefix from Step 1 *(see Figure 13.4)*. Consult Chapter 12 for details.

✔ Tips

- You can also indicate the namespace of the desired elements in your XML document using a default namespace (**xmlns="URI"**), and using no prefix with the elements. This however, is not very common. Namespaces are only populated with the global elements by default; consequently most XML Schemas will end up containing a mixture of qualified and unqualified components.
- Remember to qualify only those elements that are actually associated with their corresponding namespace.

Adding All Locally Defined Elements

When populating a namespace with an XML Schema, only the globally defined (top-level) components are associated with the target namespace by default. As such, only the global components must be *qualified*, or identified with a namespace name, in a valid XML document.

You can also require that locally defined components (e.g., those that are one or more levels down from the root element) be added to the target namespace. In this case, these elements must be qualified for an XML document to be considered valid.

If you want to add locally defined components, you can add all the elements and/or attribute declarations at once, both of which are shown below. You can also add elements and/or attributes individually, as shown on page 175.

To add all locally defined elements to the target namespace:

- In the xs:schema element, type **elementFormDefault="qualified"**. **(Figure 13.5)**.

To add all locally defined attributes to the target namespace:

- In the xs:schema element, type **attributeFormDefault="qualified"**.

✔ Tips

- The default value for each of these attributes is *unqualified*, which means that only globally defined (top-level) components are associated with the target namespace, unless you specify otherwise.
- It is considered best practices to add all locally defined elements when populating a namespace, even though this overrides the default **(Figure 13.6)**.

```
xsd
<?xml version="1.0"?>

<xs:schema xmlns:xs=
  "http://www.w3.org/2001/XMLSchema"

  xmlns=
  "http://www.kehogo.com/ns/wow/1.0"

  targetNamespace=
  "http://www.kehogo.com/ns/wow/1.0"

  elementFormDefault="qualified">

 <xs:element name="ancient_wonders">

...
```

Figure 13.5 *Because the* elementFormDefault *attribute is set to* qualified, *the locally declared elements will be associated with the target namespace. As such, they must be written using a qualified name for an XML document to be considered valid.*

```
xml
<wow:ancient_wonders
  xmlns:wow="http://
  www.kehogo.com/ns/wow/1.0"

  xmlns:xsi="http://www.w3.org
  /2001/XMLSchema-instance"

  xsi:schemaLocation="http://
  www.kehogo.com/ns/wow/1.0
  13-05.xsd">

 <wow:wonder>
  <wow:name language="English">
    Colossus of Rhodes</wow:name>
  <wow:name language="Greek">
    Κολοσσός της Ρόδου</wow:name>
  <wow:location>
    Rhodes, Greece</wow:location>
  <wow:height units="feet">
    107</wow:height>
  <wow:history>
   <wow:year_built era="BC">
     282</wow:year_built>

...
```

Figure 13.6 *In this valid XML document, all locally defined elements in the XML Schema are now qualified with the* wow: *prefix.*

```
xsd
<?xml version="1.0"?>

<xs:schema xmlns:xs=
  "http://www.w3.org/2001/XMLSchema"

  xmlns=
  "http://www.kehogo.com/ns/wow/1.0"

  targetNamespace=
  "http://www.kehogo.com/ns/wow/1.0"

  elementFormDefault="qualified">

 <xs:element name="ancient_wonders">
  <xs:complexType>
   <xs:sequence>
    <xs:element name="wonder"
      type="wonderType"
      maxOccurs="unbounded"/>
   </xs:sequence>
  </xs:complexType>
 </xs:element>

 <xs:complexType name="wonderType">
  <xs:sequence>
   <xs:element name="name"
     type="nameType"
     maxOccurs="unbounded"/>
   <xs:element name="location"
     type="xs:string"/>
   <xs:element name="height"
     type="heightType"/>
   <xs:element name="history"
     type="historyType"/>
   <xs:element name="main_image"
     type="imageType"
     form="unqualified"/>
   <xs:element name="source"
     type="sourceType" minOccurs="0"
     maxOccurs="unbounded"/>
  </xs:sequence>
 </xs:complexType>
```

Figure 13.7 *Despite the* elementFormDefault *setting in the* xs:schema *element, the* main_image *element will not be associated with the target namespace, because its form attribute overrides the* elementFormDefault *value.*

Adding Particular Locally Defined Elements

The form attribute is useful for specifying whether a particular locally defined element should be associated with the target namespace, regardless of the default *(see page 174)*.

To add a particular locally defined element to the target namespace:

- In the element's definition, type **form="qualified"**. Regardless of where that element is defined, it will be associated with the target namespace.

Conversely, if you've decided to set the elementFormDefault attribute to qualified in the xs:schema element, you can use the form attribute to prevent a particular locally defined element from being associated with the target namespace (**Figure 13.7**).

To keep a particular locally defined element from being associated with a target namespace (despite the default):

- In the element's definition, type **form="unqualified"**. Regardless of where that element is defined, it will not be associated with the target namespace.

✓ Tip

- Like elements, XML Schema attributes can use the same form attribute to identify whether they should be associated with the target namespace (or not), regardless of the default.

XML Schemas in Multiple Files

You can divide an XML Schema's components into various individual files in order to reuse them in several different XML Schemas, or simply to make it easier to handle large XML Schemas.

To include XML Schema components:

1. Divide the XML Schema components among files. Each file should be text-only and be saved with the `.xsd` extension **(Figure 13.8)**.
2. Finally, reference the XML Schema document in which you wish to include these components. Directly after the `xs:schema` element, type **<xs:include schemaLocation="includedfile.uri"/>**, where *includedfile.uri* is the URI of the XML Schema document that contains the components you wish to include **(Figure 13.9)**.

✔ Tips

- The `targetNamespace` attribute of the included XML Schema document must be the same as the `targetNamespace` attribute of the XML Schema document receiving the components. To add XML Schema components with different target namespaces, consult *XML Schemas with Multiple Namespaces* on page 177.
- If the included XML Schema has no target namespace specified, it is assumed that its target namespace is the same as the one for the XML Schema document in which it is being included.

xsd

```
<?xml version="1.0"?>

<xs:schema xmlns:xs="
  http://www.w3.org/2001/XMLSchema"

  targetNamespace="
   http://www.kehogo.com/ns/wow/1.0">

 <xs:complexType name="civType">
  <xs:sequence>
   <xs:element name="name"
     type="xs:string"/>
   <xs:element name="locale"
     type="xs:string"/>
   <xs:element name="period"
     type="xs:string"/>
  </xs:sequence>
 </xs:complexType>

</xs:schema>
```

Figure 13.8 *First, I create a new XML Schema shown here with the* civType *complex type definition. Then, I can use this definition in other XML Schemas.*

xsd

```
<?xml version="1.0"?>

<xs:schema xmlns:xs=
  "http://www.w3.org/2001/XMLSchema"

  xmlns=
  "http://www.kehogo.com/ns/wow/1.0"

  targetNamespace=
  "http://www.kehogo.com/ns/wow/1.0">

 <xs:include schemaLocation=
   "13-08.xsd"/>
...
 <xs:complexType name="wonderType">
  <xs:sequence>
   <xs:element name="name"
     type="nameType"
     maxOccurs="unbounded"/>
   <xs:element name="location"
     type="xs:string"/>
   <xs:element name="civilization"
     type="civType"/>
...
```

Figure 13.9 *Here, I am including and referencing the* civType *complex type defined in the XML Schema shown in Figure 13.8.*

```
xsd
<?xml version="1.0"?>

<xs:schema xmlns:xs=
  "http://www.w3.org/2001/XMLSchema"
  xmlns=
  "http://www.kehogo.com/ns/wow/1.0"
  targetNamespace=
  "http://www.kehogo.com/ns/wow/1.0"
  xmlns:anc_civ=
  "http://www.kehogo.com/ns
   /ancient_civ/2.3">

 <xs:import namespace=
   "http://www.kehogo.com/ns
    /ancient_civ/2.3"

   schemaLocation=
    "13-10-anc_civ.xsd"/>
...
 <xs:complexType name="wonderType">
  <xs:sequence>
   <xs:element name="name"
     type="nameType"
     maxOccurs="unbounded"/>
   <xs:element name="location"
     type="xs:string"/>
   <xs:element name="civilization"
     type="anc_civ:civType"/>
...
```

Figure 13.10 *Importing one XML Schema into another makes the components from the first available for defining components in the second.*

XML Schemas with Multiple Namespaces

If you want to use XML Schema components from other XML Schemas with *different* target namespaces, you would use the `xs:import` element. This enables you to validate XML documents whose elements are associated with more than one namespace.

To import components from XML Schemas with different target namespaces:

1. Directly after the `xs:schema` element in the XML Schema document into which you're importing the XML Schema components, type **<xs:import**.
2. Then, type **namespace="URI"**, where *URI* indicates the namespace name of the XML Schema components to be imported.
3. Next, type **schemaLocation="schema.uri"**, where *schema.uri* specifies the location of the file that contains the XML Schema defining the namespace in Step 2.
4. Finally, type **/>** to complete the `xs:import` element **(Figure 13.10)**.
5. Additionally, you will need to declare a prefix for the imported namespace in the `xs:schema` element *(see page 172)* so that you can refer to the imported components in your XML Schema *(see Figure 13.10)*.

✔ Tip

- You'll use `xs:import` when you need XML Schema definitions from different XML namespaces, since a single XML Schema file cannot contain components from more than one namespace. You'll use `xs:include` *(see previous page)* to break up a large XML Schema file into various modular files, and then include the ones you need for a particular XML Schema.

The Schema of Schemas as the Default

In Chapter 9, *XML Schema Basics*, you learned how to start a basic XML Schema. The first line of an XML Schema is an XML declaration. This means that an XML Schema document is, in fact, an XML document itself.

The second line of an XML Schema document is the `xs:schema` element, which is the root element. And, as you may have already realized, `xs:` is a prefix for a namespace, the W3C's XML Schema namespace. Often called "the Schema of Schemas," this namespace contains definitions for components that you have come to know, such as `xs:element` `xs:complexType`, and `xs:attribute`.

But, the XML Schema specification doesn't require using the `xs:` prefix for this namespace. I could just as easily use `zorch:`, `fondo:`, or practically anything else.

So, if your XML Schema is mostly composed of built-in types, it may be easier and quicker to declare the Schema of Schemas as the default namespace. Then, you wouldn't have to use a prefix for the elements from this namespace at all **(Figure 13.11)**.

To declare the Schema of Schemas as the default namespace:

1. To begin defining the XML Schema root element, after the XML declaration, type **<schema** (notice that it's not *xs:schema*).
2. Then, type **xmlns="http://www.w3.org/2001/XMLSchema"** to declare the Schema of Schemas as the default namespace.
3. Continue as you normally would, identifying target namespaces, and XML namespaces as you wish.
4. Finally, type **>** to complete the `schema` tag.

xsd

```
<?xml version="1.0"?>

<schema xmlns=
  "http://www.w3.org/2001/XMLSchema"

  xmlns:wow=
  "http://www.kehogo.com/ns/wow/1.0"
  targetNamespace=
  "http://www.kehogo.com/ns/wow/1.0">

 <element name="ancient_wonders">
  <complexType>
   <sequence>
    <element name="wonder"
      type="wow:wonderType"
      maxOccurs="unbounded"/>
   </sequence>
  </complexType>
 </element>

 <complexType name="wonderType">
  <sequence>
   <element name="name"
     type="wow:nameType"
     maxOccurs="unbounded"/>
   <element name="location"
     type="string"/>
   <element name="height"
     type="wow:heightType"/>
   <element name="history"
     type="wow:historyType"/>
   <element name="main_image"
     type="wow:imageType"/>
   <element name="source"
     type="wow:sourceType"
     minOccurs="0"
     maxOccurs="unbounded"/>
  </sequence>
 </complexType>
```

Figure 13.11 *This document is equivalent to the one shown in Figure 13.3. The only difference is one of notation. Because the Schema of Schemas is the default namespace, I don't prefix XML Schema element names (*schema, element, complexType, *etc.), or built-in types (*string, positiveInteger*) with* xs:.

On the other hand, an XML Schema document cannot have two default namespaces. Consequently, I need to give the http://www.kehogo.com/ns/wow/1.0 *namespace a prefix (*wow:*), and prefix the components from the* wow: *namespace, such as* wow:wonderType, wow:nameType, *and* wow:heightType.

Namespaces and DTDs

One of the largest and most consistent complaints about DTDs is that they don't support XML namespace declarations.

Interestingly enough, you can, in fact, use a `prefix:element` structure in your DTD names. The problem is that there is no way for the parser to know which XML namespace that prefix refers to. In actuality, the parser doesn't consider the characters before the colon a prefix at all. You may have the element `wow:height`, but this has no more meaning than any other element. For example, it does not mean the height element in the `wow:` namespace, it just means the `wow:height` element.

If you think this is kind of a pain, you're not alone. The lack of direct support for XML namespaces is one of the main reasons that DTDs are being supplanted by XML Schema.

For more information on DTDs, see Part 3.

XSLT and Namespaces

In Chapter 2, *XSLT*, you learned how to start a basic XSLT Style Sheet. As with XML Schemas, the first line of an XSLT Style Sheet is an XML declaration. Therefore, an XSLT Style Sheet is an XML document itself.

Consequently, if you are working with XML elements that belong to a namespace, you will need to declare the namespace and prefix each of these elements in your XSLT Style Sheet **(Figure 13.12)**.

To use an XML namespace in an XSLT Style Sheet:

1. Within the opening tag of the root element `xsl:stylesheet`, type **xmlns:prefix**, where *prefix* will identify the XML namespace in this XSLT Style Sheet.
2. Then, type **="URI"**, where *URI* identifies the name of the XML namespace to which the prefix in Step 1 will refer.
3. Finally, label individual elements as necessary by typing **<prefix:element>**, where *prefix* is the namespace prefix defined in Step 1 and indicates the namespace to which this *element* belongs.

✔ Tip

- Unlike XML Schema documents, the default namespace in an XSLT Style Sheet is *not* used for unprefixed names. In other words, you can't remove the `xsl:` prefix from a style sheet's elements by setting the W3C's XSLT namespace as the default namespace.

xslt

```
<?xml version="1.0"?>

<xsl:stylesheet

  xmlns:xsl="http://www.w3.org/1999
   /XSL/Transform" version="1.0"

  xmlns:wow="
   http://www.kehogo.com/ns/wow/1.0">

<xsl:template match="/">
 <html><head><title>Wonders of the
   World</title></head>
 <body>
  <h1 align="center">Seven Wonders
     of the Ancient World</h1>
...
  <p>These ancient wonders are

  <xsl:for-each
    select="wow:ancient_wonders/
    wonder/name[@language='English']">

  <xsl:value-of select="."/>
...
```

Figure 13.12 *This XSLT excerpt shows the declaration of the* http://www.kehogo.com/ns/wow/1.0 *namespace and its prefix (*wow:*). The* ancient_wonders *element is the only qualified element from the namespace, and it is written as* wow:ancient_wonders *in the XSLT Style Sheet.*

Part 6: Recent W3C Recommendations

14

XSLT 2.0

XSL, the eXtensible Stylesheet Language, is used to transform XML documents into other documents, such as HTML *(see Part 2)*. It is a family of three languages: XPath for selecting nodes from source documents; XSLT, for transforming those selected nodes; and XSL-FO, a language often used to generate PDFs.

On January 23, 2007, the W3C published eight new XML-centric Recommendations. These Recommendations defined new versions of both XSLT and XPath, as well as a new XML language called XQuery.

Like XSLT, XQuery gives users the ability to query XML data, based on the logical structure of an XML document. In fact, you can do most of the same things with XQuery 1.0 that you can with XSLT 2.0. However, XQuery differs from XSLT 2.0 in its ability to also directly query databases as opposed to only querying text-based documents.

Both XSLT and XQuery rely on the XPath language to select content from XML source information. This selection process uses the XML source's logical structure, which is known as the *data model*. This XML Data Model (XDM) is the exact same for all three languages, XQuery 1.0, XPath 2.0, and XSLT 2.0. It is, in essence, the glue that binds them all.

You can read more about these languages at: *www.w3.org/2007/01/qt-pressrelease.*

Extending XSLT

XSLT is an XML language whose purpose is to transform a given XML source document into something else, such as an HTML document or a new XML document.

XSLT 1.0 became an official W3C Recommendation in 1999, and was rapidly adopted by the XML community. With that, came feedback, critique, and ultimately the formation of a new W3C Working Group to revise and improve XSLT.

Some of the primary goals of this effort were to:

- Improve ease of use.
- Support multiple output documents.
- Enable the creation of user-defined functions.
- Support the use of XML Schema.
- Simplify content grouping.
- Retain backward compatibility.

This last goal, being backward compatible, was an important goal to make it easier for users to adopt this new Recommendation. By retaining backward compatibility, you can use an XSLT 2.0 processor with your existing XSLT 1.0 style sheets, with little to no modification. Then, you can begin using XSLT 2.0 features and functions at your convenience **(Figure 14.1)**.

Although the XSLT 2.0 Recommendation hasn't changed much since the Working Draft was published in 2003, version 1.0 is still more widely used and supported. In fact, none of the major browsers support version 2.0 yet. Therefore, in order to view the XSLT examples in this chapter, you'll need to use an XSLT processor that supports version 2.0. If you don't have one already, see Appendix A.

xslt

```
<?xml version="1.0"?>

<xsl:stylesheet xmlns:xsl="http://
  www.w3.org/1999/XSL/Transform"
  version="2.0">

 <xsl:output method="html"/>

 <xsl:template match="/">

  <html>

   <head><title>Wonders of the World
     </title></head>

   <body>

    <p>The famous Greek historian
Herodotus wrote of seven great
architectural achievements. And
although his writings did not survive,
he planted seeds for what has become
the list of <strong>Seven Wonders
of the Ancient World</strong>.</p>

    <p>These ancient wonders are

     <xsl:for-each select="
       ancient_wonders/wonder/name
       [@language='English']">

      <xsl:value-of select="."/>

...

     </xsl:for-each>

    </p>

   </body>

  </html>

 </xsl:template>

</xsl:stylesheet>
```

Figure 14.1 *This XSLT style sheet will be processed using the XSLT 2.0 specification, because the* version *attribute of the* xsl:stylesheet *element is set to* "2.0." Note*: This is a shortened version of the master XSLT 1.0 style sheet used throughout the earlier chapters of the book. Notice that nothing has changed in the style sheet, except the value of the* version *attribute.*

```
xslt
<?xml version="1.0"?>

<html xmlns:xsl="http://
  www.w3.org/1999/XSL/Transform"
  xsl:version="2.0">

  <head><title>Wonders of the World
   </title></head>

  <body>

  <p>The famous Greek historian
Herodotus wrote of seven great
architectural achievements. And
although his writings did not survive,
he planted seeds for what has become
the list of the <strong>Seven Wonders
of the Ancient World</strong>.</p>

  <p>These ancient wonders are

   <xsl:for-each select="
     ancient_wonders/wonder/name
     [@language='English']">

   <xsl:value-of select="."/>

...

   </xsl:for-each>

  </p>

 </body>

</html>
```

Figure 14.2 *This is a simplified style sheet based on the style sheet in Figure 14.1.*

Creating a Simplified Style Sheet

One goal of XSLT 2.0 was to improve its ease of use over XSLT 1.0. An example of this is seen with style sheets that only have a template rule for the root node (`<xsl:template match="/">`), and no other template rules, such as in Figure 14.1.

In these cases, you can simplify your XSLT style sheet by combining the content from the `xsl:stylesheet` and `xsl:template` elements into your opening `<html>` tag, and removing the `xsl:stylesheet`, `xsl:output`, and `xsl:template` elements completely.

To create a simplified style sheet:

1. Type **<?xml version="1.0"?>** to indicate that the XSLT style sheet is an XML document.
2. Type **<html** .
3. Next, type **xmlns:xsl="http://www.w3.org/1999/XSL/Transform"** which is the standard declaration for the XSLT namespace and its prefix.
4. Then, type **xsl:version="2.0">** to identify that this document will use version 2.0 of the XSLT namespace.
5. Enter the instructions for your style sheet.
6. Finally, type the end tag **</html>** to complete the `html` element from Step 2 above, as well as to complete the simplified style sheet **(Figure 14.2)**.

✔ Tips

- The `version` attribute in the opening `html` tag is different than the standard version attribute. In a simplified style sheet, the `version` attribute must be prefixed with `xsl:` to indicate that it belongs to the XSLT namespace.
- There cannot be `xsl:apply-template` elements in your simplified style sheet.

Generating XHTML Output Documents

XHTML is a more structured form of HTML; essentially a marriage of HTML and XML. It became a W3C Recommendation in January 2000, and has been widely adopted in the creation of Web pages.

In XSLT 1.0, there is no direct support for generating XHTML-compliant output documents. This feature has been added to XSLT 2.0.

To generate XHTML-compliant output documents:

1. Within the `xsl:stylesheet` declaration, type **xmlns="http://www.w3.org/1999/xhtml"** to declare the XHTML namespace.
2. Immediately after the `xsl:stylesheet` declaration, type **<xsl:output** .
3. Finally, type **method="xhtml"/>** to identify the output method as XHTML and close the output instruction **(Figure 14.3)**.

Another way to generate XHTML-compliant output documents:

1. Within the `xsl:stylesheet` declaration, type **xmlns="http://www.w3.org/1999/xhtml"** to declare the XHTML namespace.
2. Immediately after the template for the root node (`<xsl:template match="/">`), type **<xsl:result-document**.
3. Then, type **method="xhtml">** to identify the output method as XHTML.
4. Finally, immediately *before the closing tag* of the root node template, type **<xsl:result-document/>** to close the output instruction **(Figure 14.4)**.

✔ Tip

- There are other attributes for both these output instructions, including control for character encoding, indentation, and more.

```
xslt
<?xml version="1.0"?>

<xsl:stylesheet xmlns:xsl="http://
  www.w3.org/1999/XSL/Transform"
  version="2.0" xmlns=
  "http://www.w3.org/1999/xhtml">

 <xsl:output method="xhtml"/>

 <xsl:template match="/">
```

Figure 14.3 *In this example, I've used the* xsl:output *instruction to tell the XSLT processor to generate XHTML-compliant output.*

```
xslt
<?xml version="1.0"?>

<xsl:stylesheet xmlns:xsl="http://
  www.w3.org/1999/XSL/Transform"
  version="2.0" xmlns=
  "http://www.w3.org/1999/xhtml">

 <xsl:template match="/">

  <xsl:result-document method="xhtml">

  <html><head><title>Wonders of the
    World</title></head><body>

...

   <h2>History</h2>

   <xsl:apply-templates select="
     ancient_wonders/wonder/history">

    <xsl:sort select="year_built"
      order="descending"
      data-type="number" />

   </xsl:apply-templates>

  </body></html>

  </xsl:result-document>

</xsl:template>
```

Figure 14.4 *In this example, I've used the* xsl:result-document *instruction to tell the XSLT processor to generate XHTML-compliant output. Notice how the* xsl:result-document *instruction encloses the output and instructions within the root template.*

```
xslt
...
<xsl:result-document
  href="history.html" method="xhtml">

 <html><body><head><title>Wonders of
   the World</title></head>
  <h2>History</h2>

  <xsl:apply-templates select="
    ancient_wonders/wonder/history">

   <xsl:sort select="year_built"
     order="descending"
     data-type="number" />

  </xsl:apply-templates>

 </body></html>

</xsl:result-document>
```

Figure 14.5 *This excerpt of an XSLT style sheet will generate an output document for the History section of the wonders output named* history.html. *A second output document is created automatically and contains all the remaining XSLT output, including a list of all the wonders, each of which must link to its place in the new history output document* (see Figure 14.6).

```
xslt
...
<a>
 <xsl:attribute name="href">
   history.html#<xsl:value-of select=
   "name[@language='English']"/>
 </xsl:attribute>

 <strong><xsl:value-of select="name
   [@language='English']"/></strong>
</a>
```

Figure 14.6 *Further down in the XSLT document excerpted in Figure 14.5, I adjust the anchor tags that link to the history section for each of the wonders. Each anchor tag now links to its proper place in the new* history.html *document.*

Generating Multiple Output Documents

In XSLT 1.0, when an XSLT style sheet is processed, only one output document is produced. If you want to create a multiple documents from your XML content, you have to run the XSLT processor for each document you want.

With XSLT 2.0, however, you can produce multiple output documents from a single run of the processor. As well, you can include instructions for how to create each of the output documents in a single XSLT document.

To generate multiple output documents:

1. For each output document, identify the XSLT instructions that will generate the output you wish.
2. Before the first XSLT instruction identified in Step 1, type **<xsl:result-document** to begin the output declaration.
3. Then, type **href="output.uri"**>, where *output.uri* identifies the location of the document where the output from these XSLT instructions will be saved.
4. Finally, after the last XSLT instruction identified in Step 1, type **</xsl:result-document>** to complete the output instruction (**Figure 14.5**).

✔ Tips

- You may use as many `xsl:result-document` instructions in your XSLT style sheet as you wish.
- You can choose to have your output be XHTML-compliant using the `method` attribute as described on page 186.
- The output of an XSLT transformation is called a *final result tree*. For any XSLT instructions not enclosed by an `xsl:result-document` element, a final result tree is created automatically.

Creating User Defined Functions

User Defined Functions (UDFs) in XSLT 2.0 act just like functions in other programming languages. You declare the UDF's name, input, what it does with the input, and its output.

To create a User Defined Function:

1. As a top-level element (a child of the root element `xsl:stylesheet`), type **<xsl:function** to begin your UDF.
2. Type **name="UDF_name">**, where *UDF_name* is the name of your function.
3. Optionally (to begin identifying any UDF input parameters), type **<xsl:param name="param_name"/>**, where *param_name* is the name you will use to refer to this parameter within your UDF.
4. Repeat Step 3 for as many input parameters you wish to declare. You may also choose to not have any input parameters, and skip Step 3 altogether.
5. Type the XSLT 2.0 and XPath 2.0 instructions for your function that will generate the return value of the UDF.
6. Finally, type **</xsl:function>** to finish creating the UDF **(Figure 14.7)**.

To create the namespace for your User Defined Functions:

1. Within the opening tag of the root element, type **xmlns:prefix**, where *prefix* is the namespace prefix for your UDF.
2. Then, type **="URI"**, where *URI* is the namespace to which the prefix will refer.

✔ Tips

- Your UDF must part of its own namespace to eliminate potential naming conflicts with functions in the default namespace.
- Optionally, use `exclude-result-prefixes` so your UDF's namespace won't be part of the output document *(see Figure 14.7)*.

xslt

```
<?xml version="1.0"?>

<xsl:stylesheet xmlns:xsl="http://
  www.w3.org/1999/XSL/Transform"
  version="2.0" xmlns:khg="http://
  www.kehogo.com/ns/khg"
  exclude-result-prefixes="khg">

 <xsl:template match="/">
  <html><head><title>Hello World
    </title></head><body>
   <xsl:value-of select="
     khg:helloWorld()"/>
  </body></html>
 </xsl:template>

 <xsl:function name="khg:helloWorld">

  Hello World on
  <xsl:value-of select="
   format-dateTime(current-dateTime(),
  '[M01]/[D01]/[Y0001] at
   [H01]:[m01]:[s01]')"/>

 </xsl:function>

</xsl:stylesheet>
```

Figure 14.7 *The style sheet in this example declares a UDF called* helloWorld *which is part of the* khg: *namespace. It returns the literal string "Hello World on ", followed by today's date and time. Notice the use of the* exclude-result-prefixes *attribute in the root element; it excludes the* khg *namespace from the output document.*

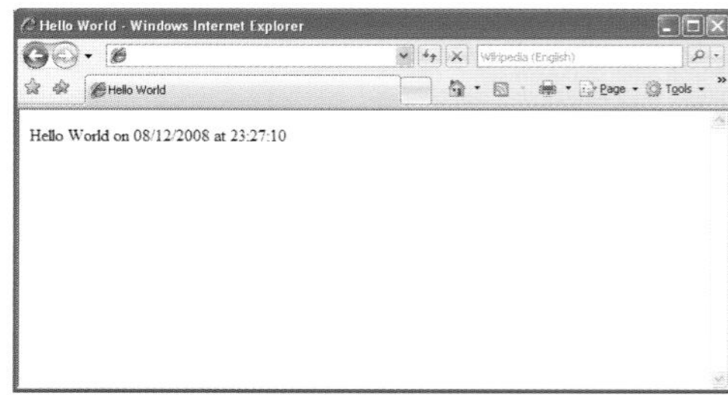

Figure 14.8 *The execution of the XSLT 2.0 style sheet in Figure 14.7, as seen in a browser.*

```
xslt
<?xml version="1.0"?>

<xsl:stylesheet xmlns:xsl="http://
  www.w3.org/1999/XSL/Transform"
  version="2.0" xmlns="http://
  www.w3.org/1999/xhtml"
  xmlns:khg="http://
  www.kehogo.com/ns/khg"
  exclude-result-prefixes="khg">

...

<xsl:function name="khg:third">

 <xsl:param name="dimension"/>
 <xsl:value-of select="
   (ceiling($dimension div 3))"/>

</xsl:function>
```

Figure 14.9 *This UDF, named* khg:third, *takes a single input parameter,* dimension. *It divides the value of* dimension *by 3, and uses the ceiling function to round up to the nearest integer. Then, the UDF returns this final value to the calling statement.*

```
xslt
<xsl:template match="main_image">
 <img>
  <xsl:attribute name="src">
    <xsl:value-of select="./@file"/>
  </xsl:attribute>

  <xsl:attribute name="width">
   <xsl:value-of select="
     khg:third(./@w)"/>
  </xsl:attribute>

  <xsl:attribute name="height">
   <xsl:value-of select="
     khg:third(./@h)"/>
   </xsl:attribute>

 </img>
</xsl:template>
```

Figure 14.10 *Here are the two places where the* khg:third() *function is called. I am using this UDF to divide the* w *and* h *attributes of the* main_image *element by 3, effectively shrinking the display size of the images by a third.*

Calling User Defined Functions

Of course, creating a UDF doesn't do anything itself **(Figure 14.9)**; you need to call the UDF from within the style sheet. To use the functionality created by your UDF, you call it from anywhere an XPath expression is expected.

To call a User Defined Function:

1. Anywhere an XPath expression is expected, type **prefix:**, where *prefix* matches the one you used in Step 1 at the bottom of page 188. (This is the namespace prefix that you defined for your UDF.)
2. Then, type **UDF_name(**, where *UDF_name* matches the one you used in Step 2 at the top of page 188 (which is the name you gave your function).
3. Next, type the value(s) of any input parameters defined in Step 3 at the top of page 188, separated by a comma. If there are no input parameters declared, you will skip this step.
4. Finally, type **)** to finish calling your UDF **(Figure 14.10)**.

✔ Tips

- An `xsl:function` declaration can appear anywhere in your XSLT style sheet, provided it is a top-level element.
- Unlike in many other procedural programming languages, optional input parameters are not allowed in UDFs.
- As in many other procedural programming languages, UDFs can call themselves, thereby creating recursive functions.
- In XSLT 1.0, advanced users created UDF-like functionality by tricking the processor into using named templates, or by writing functions in another language outside the style sheet itself.

Grouping Output Using Common Values

Grouping a set of elements based on common content (such as elements with the same name or attribute value) is extremely difficult in XSLT 1.0, and not something the average user can easily accomplish. Fortunately, in XSLT 2.0, grouping is much easier and is supported by a set of built-in functions.

To group by a common value:

1. Type **<xsl:for-each-group**.
2. Then, type **select="node_set"**, where *node_set* identifies the set of items to be grouped. This is also called the *population*.
3. Next, type **group-by="group_key">**, where *group_key* is an expression that is evaluated for each item in the population. The result of this evaluation is defined to be that item's *group value*. Each item in the population is then placed into a group with other items that have the same group value.
4. Specify what processing should take place.
5. Finally, type **</xsl:for-each-group>** to complete the grouping **(Figure 14.11)**.

✔ Tips

- Both the *node_set* in Step 2, and the *group_key* in Step 3 must be XPath expressions. In fact, they must be XPath 2.0 expressions, since the `xsl:for-each-group` is an XSLT 2.0 element. XPath 2.0 is discussed in Chapter 15.
- When the `xsl:for-each-group` instruction is being processed, you can use a function called `current-group()`. It is a collection of all the items from the population that are assigned to the group being processed *(see Figure 14.11)*.
- You can also use an `xsl:sort` instruction within the `xsl:for-each-group` instruction to sort the resulting content.

```
xslt
...

<table border="1">
 <tr><th>Newspaper ID</th>
   <th>Section ID</th></tr>

 <xsl:for-each-group
   select="//source"
   group-by="@newspaperid">

 <tr>

  <td><xsl:value-of select=
     "@newspaperid"/></td>

  <td><xsl:value-of select=
  "current-group()/@sectionid"/></td>

 </tr>

</xsl:for-each-group>

</table>
```

Figure 14.11 *To generate a listing of* source *elements grouped by their* newspaperids*, I have set the* select *attribute of the* xsl:for-each-group *to* //source, *and the* group-by *attribute to* newspaperid. *The* current-group() *component above returns all the* sectionid *values of each group. Without this, the output would only show the current* newspaperid*'s* sectionid, *not all the* sectionids *in the group.*

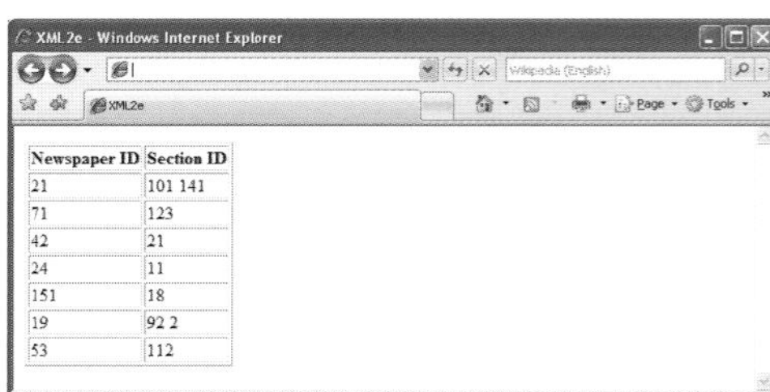

Newspaper ID	Section ID
21	101 141
71	123
42	21
24	11
151	18
19	92 2
53	112

Figure 14.12 *The XSLT in Figure 14.11 generates this listing above. Notice that* newspaperids *21 and 19 each have multiple* sectionids *listed. Without using the* current-group() *component, the output would only show the current* newspaperid*'s* sectionid *value, not all the values.*

```
xslt
<?xml version="1.0"?>
<xsl:stylesheet xmlns:xsl="http://
  www.w3.org/1999/XSL/Transform"
  version="2.0">
 <xsl:output method="xml"
   indent="yes"/>

 <xsl:import-schema
   schema-location="14-13.xsd"/>

 <xsl:template match="/">

  <sources xsl:validation="strict">

   <xsl:for-each-group select="
    //source" group-by="@newspaperid">
    <newspapers>
     <newspaperid>
      <xsl:value-of select="
        @newspaperid"/>
     </newspaperid>
     <sectionid>
      <xsl:value-of select="
        current-group()/@sectionid"/>
     </sectionid>
    </newspapers>
   </xsl:for-each-group>
  </sources>
 </xsl:template>
</xsl:stylesheet>
```

Figure 14.13 *Instead of having XSLT generate an HTML table of the* source *elements* (Figure 14.11), *here it is generating that information as an XML document. I am validating the XML document prior to it being output, using the imported schema,* 14-13.xsd.

```
xml
<?xml version="1.0" encoding="UTF-8"?>
<sources>
 <newspapers>
  <newspaperid>21</newspaperid>
  <sectionid>101 141</sectionid>
 </newspapers>
 <newspapers>
  <newspaperid>71</newspaperid>
  <sectionid>123</sectionid>
 </newspapers>
 ...
```

Figure 14.14 *This is an excerpt of the validated XML output document, generated by the XSLT style sheet in Figure 14.13.*

Validating XSLT Output

In addition to transforming XML documents into (X)HTML for display, XSLT is often used to transform XML documents into other XML documents. These new XML documents can then be used for different purposes than those of the original XML document.

XSLT 1.0 however, cannot validate its own output against an XML Schema. As a result, to ensure that XML documents generated from an XSLT transformation have the correct structure, they have to be validated in a separate step. This has been rectified in XSLT 2.0 by including the ability to validate the output of an XSLT transformation against an XML Schema, as part of the XSLT transformation.

To validate XSLT Output:

1. Anywhere at the top-level of the style sheet (outside the root template rule), type **<xsl:import-schema**.
2. Then, type **schema-location="schema.uri"/>**, where *schema.uri* identifies the location of the XML Schema you wish to use for your validation.
3. Additionally (in the XSLT style sheet), within the root element of the output you wish to validate, type **xsl:validation="strict"** **(Figure 14.13)**.

✔ Tips

- Using this same model, you can validate different parts of the XSLT output with different imported XML Schemas.
- Instead of identifying a schema location in the `xsl:import-schema` element, you can include the rules of your XML Schema in the XSLT style sheet itself. Having an inline schema means that you can't easily reuse it in another XSLT style sheet. It does, however, provide you with quick access to both the style sheet and the schema in a single file.

15

XPath 2.0

XPath (*XML Path Language*) is a language for selecting and processing parts of an XML document. XPath 2.0 is part of the eight W3C Recommendations published together in January 2007, and includes significant changes to the original version published in 1999.

One fundamental change is in the data model used by XPath. In version 1.0, the data model used is based on node sets *(see Chapter 3)*. In version 2.0, the data model is based on *sequences*. A sequence is a collection of *items* (nodes and/or values), whereas a node set is a collection of nodes only. This distinction, while subtle, is an important enhancement to XPath 2.0 that I'll discuss more in this chapter.

In addition to a new data model, XPath 2.0 has a larger set of functions; it supports conditional expressions (if-then-else statements), and it supports loops and variables (which were only available in XSLT previously).

By design, upgrading to XPath 2.0 should be relatively easy, because everything you know about XPath 1.0 applies to version 2.0 as well. Further, many of the changes in version 2.0 are based on well-known programming constructs that you may already be familiar with.

As with XPath 1.0, version 2.0 is not a stand-alone language; it was designed to be used within a "host language," such as XSLT 2.0. The examples in this chapter will use XSLT 2.0 to show the XPath 2.0 functionality. If you need to, review XSLT 1.0 and XPath 1.0 in Part 2 of the book, as well as Chapter 14, *XSLT 2.0*.

XPath 1.0 and XPath 2.0

XPath 2.0 is a superset of XPath 1.0. In other words, all you have learned about XPath 1.0 *(see Chapters 3 and 4)* also applies to XPath 2.0.

XPath Basics

There are two primary purposes that XPath serves. The first is finding and returning specific parts of an XML document. To do this, XPath converts an XML document into an *XML node tree*. An XML node tree is a hierarchical representation of an XML document. Then, based on the *location path* that you define, XPath uses the XML node tree to find and return the information you requested. A location path is a way to describe the position of the desired content in the XML document relative to some current context **(Figure 15.1)**.

XPath's second primary purpose is to perform operations on those selected parts. XPath has built-in functions to perform basic arithmetic operations on, or to alter the format of, data returned by a location path **(Figure 15.3)**.

XPath 2.0 Data Model

The new data model that supports version 2.0 of the XPath language is called XDM (*XQuery/XPath Data Model*). It is an extension of the XML Infoset, the data model for XPath 1.0. An important component of using XDM is that it includes support for XML Schema types *(see Part 4)*, making XPath 2.0 a *strongly typed* language. This means that the use of values is strictly dependent on each value's type. For example, trying to do math on the string "2008" will yield an error, which was not the case in XPath 1.0 *(see Figure 15.25 on page 203)*.

Having support for XML Schema also allows XSLT 2.0 style sheets (which only work with the XPath 2.0 language) to be connected to an XML document's schema. Then, when transforming the document, you would be alerted to misspellings, invalid paths, and type errors based on the schema. As well, you would be

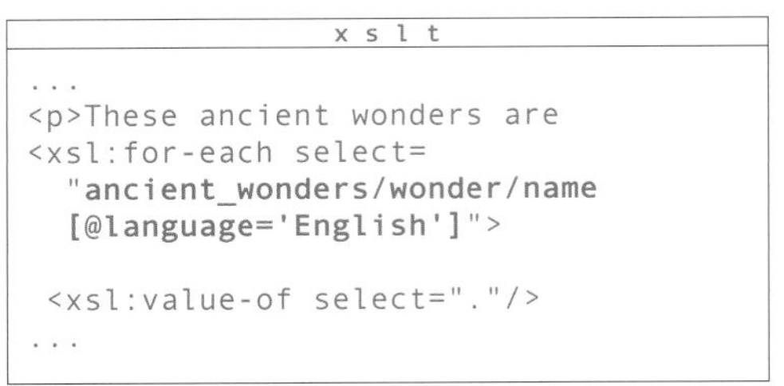

```
xslt
...
<p>These ancient wonders are
<xsl:for-each select=
  "ancient_wonders/wonder/name
  [@language='English']">

 <xsl:value-of select="."/>
...
```

Figure 15.1 *This location path is requesting the* name *nodes with a* language *attribute equal to 'English.' These nodes are children of* wonder *nodes, which are children of the* ancient_wonders *node.*

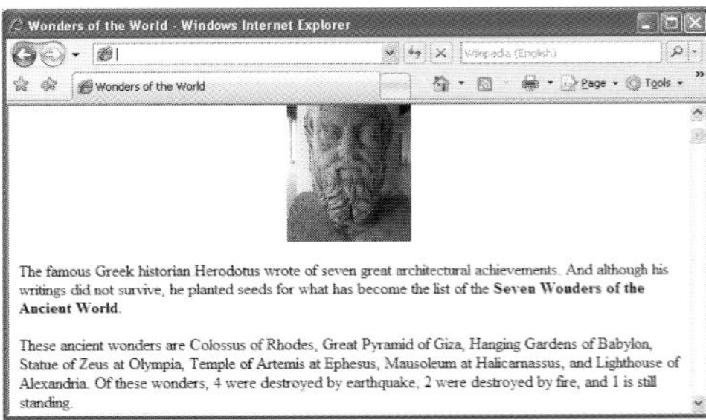

Figure 15.2 *The results of the location path in Figure 15.1 within the style sheet's HTML.*

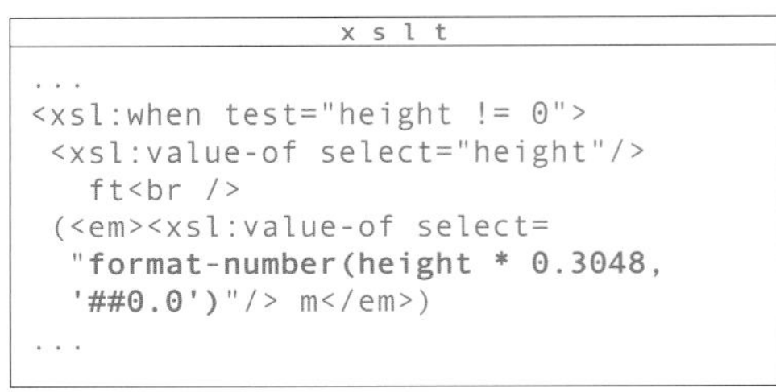

```
xslt
...
<xsl:when test="height != 0">
 <xsl:value-of select="height"/>
   ft<br />
 (<em><xsl:value-of select=
  "format-number(height * 0.3048,
  '##0.0')"/> m</em>)
...
```

Figure 15.3 *Using multiplication and the* format-number *function to convert the height into meters.*

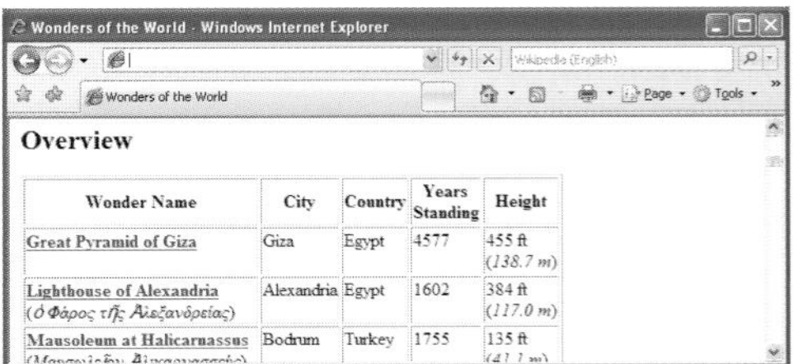

Figure 15.4 *Displaying each wonder's height, formatted as described in the XSLT in Figure 15.3.*

xslt
```
(8, 'Logan', 58.3)
```

Figure 15.5 *In XPath 2.0, everything is processed as a* sequence. *A sequence is an ordered list of mixed type items. To define a sequence, write the values you want in a set of parentheses, separated by a comma (the space after the comma is not required but makes for increased legibility).*

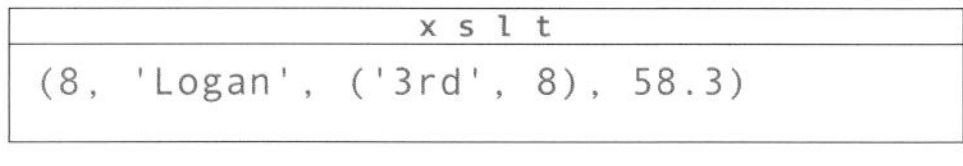

xslt
```
(8, 'Logan', ('3rd', 8), 58.3)
```

xslt
```
(8, 'Logan', '3rd', 8, 58.3)
```

Figure 15.6 *Sequences cannot be nested within other sequences. This means that the top example is automatically converted in the bottom one. Notice also that sequences allow duplication.*

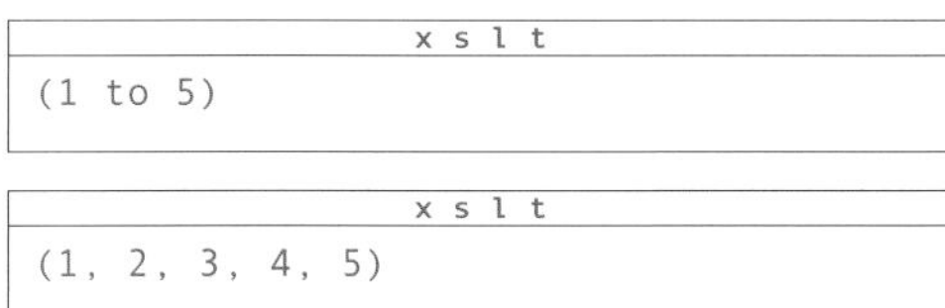

xslt
```
(1 to 5)
```

xslt
```
(1, 2, 3, 4, 5)
```

Figure 15.7 *Sequences can be constructed using the* to *operator which returns integers in consecutive order. The top example is automatically converted into the bottom example.*

xslt
```
reverse(1 to 10)
```

xslt
```
(10, 9, 8, 7, 6, 5, 4, 3, 2, 1)
```

Figure 15.8 *As I'll show in the rest of this chapter, functions can act on and return sequences. In this example, the* reverse *function takes each item in the top sequence and reverses the order to generate the bottom sequence.*

alerted to any changes required in your XSLT necessitated by changes in the XML Schema.

XPath 2.0 Sequences

XPath 1.0 is not a strongly typed language. Expressions in XPath 1.0 return only one of four different types: node sets, strings, numbers, and boolean values. On the other hand, XPath 2.0 is a strongly typed language, and expressions can return many more types.

To support this difference, the return value of expressions in XPath 2.0 is a *sequence* **(Figure 15.5)**. (And, as you'll see throughout the rest of this chapter, the additional functionality connected with sequences is significant.)

A sequence is comma-separated, ordered list of items, where an item is defined as either a node or an *atomic value*. An atomic value is basically any value; or, more specifically, it is a simple type or a custom type derived by restriction *(see Chapters 10 and 11)*.

Other characteristics of sequences include that they can have duplicate items (node sets in XPath 1.0 cannot). They are also flat structures; in other words, you cannot have a sequence within another sequence **(Figure 15.6)**. Just as with node sets in XPath 1.0, sequences can include operators **(Figure 15.7)**, be the object of functions **(Figure 15.8)**, and take predicates (which are the "filters" written in square backets `[` and `]`). Sequences can also be used in loops, in a way similar to the `xsl:for-each` element in XSLT (see *Looping Over Nodes* on page 28).

✔ Tip

- Since XPath 2.0 is a superset of version 1.0, everything you've learned about XPath 1.0 *(see Chapters 3 and 4)* applies to version 2.0. You can even use XPath 2.0 with your existing style sheets. The very few exceptions are noted at: *www.w3.org/TR/xpath20/#id-backwards-compatibility*.

Averaging Values in a Sequence

In XPath 1.0, there are functions for counting the number of nodes in a nodeset, and for totaling the values of the nodes in a nodeset **(Figure 15.9)**. XPath 2.0 has these same functions for sequences, and has added three new similar functions: `avg()`, `min()`, and `max()`.

One of these new functions is to average all the values in a sequence.

To average the values in a sequence:

1. Type **avg(**.
2. Then, type the sequence or the location path to the sequence whose items should be averaged.
3. Finally, type **)** to complete the function **(Figure 15.10)**.

✔ Tip

- The results from this function, as well as the other two new functions discussed on page 197, could be generated in XPath 1.0. However, especially in the case of `min()` and `max()`, it would take a lot more than a single line of XSLT and XPath.

```
xslt
...
<td valign="top">
 <xsl:value-of select="
  format-number(
   sum(ancient_wonders/wonder/height)
   div count(ancient_wonders/wonder/
   height[.!=0]), '##0.0')" />ft
</td>
```

Figure 15.9 *This XPath 1.0 excerpt calculates the* sum() *of all the ancient wonder's heights, and then divides that sum by the* count() *of the ancient wonders that have a non-zero height (remember that the height of the Hanging Gardens of Babylon is set to zero in our XML document).*

```
xslt
...
<td valign="top">
 <xsl:value-of select="
   format-number(
    avg(ancient_wonders/wonder/
    height[.!=0]),'##0.0')" /> ft
</td>
```

Figure 15.10 *Here, I am using the XPath 2.0 function* avg() *to do the same thing as in Figure 15.9. It produces the same result with fewer lines of code.*

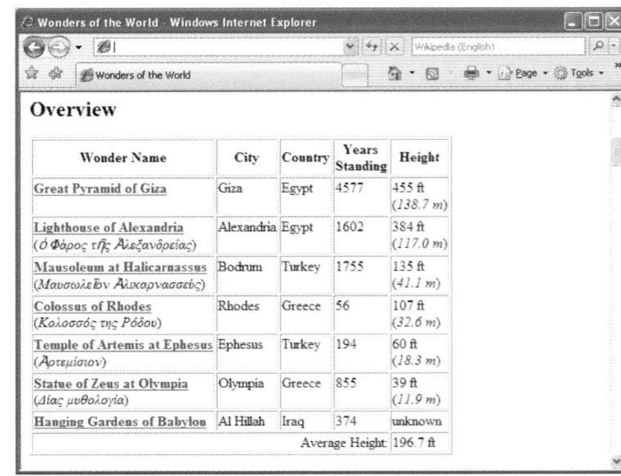

Figure 15.11 *The resulting HTML from the XSLT 2.0 / XPath 2.0 code in Figure 15.10, as seen in Internet Explorer 7. (The XSLT 1.0 / XPath 1.0 code in Figure 15.9 generates the exact same HTML.)*

Averaging Values in a Sequence

```
xslt
...
and they ranged in height from
<xsl:value-of select="
  min(ancient_wonders/wonder/
  height[.!=0])"/>
to
<xsl:value-of select="
  max(ancient_wonders/wonder/
  height[.!=0])"/>
feet.
```

Figure 15.12 *Using both the* min() *and* max() *functions, I have added a statement to the final output about the range of height of the ancient wonders. And although possible in XPath 1.0, the* min() *and* max() *functions require much less code to return their results.*

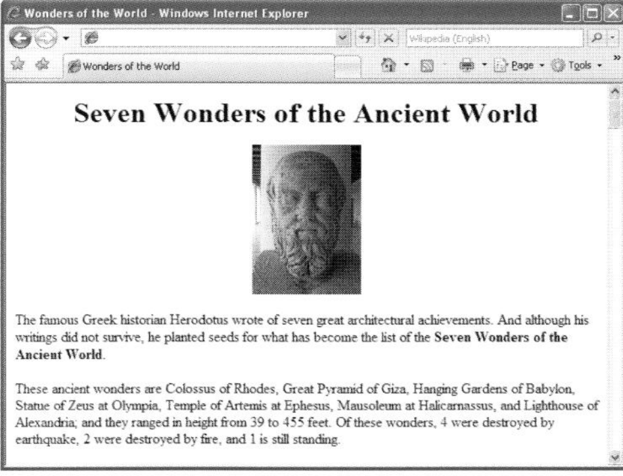

Figure 15.13 *The HTML result of the new instructions shown in Figure 15.12.*

Finding the Minimum or Maximum Value

In addition to averaging values in a sequence, XPath 2.0 also has functions to find the minimum and maximum values in a sequence (**Figure 15.12**).

To return the minimum value of the numbers in a sequence:

1. Type **min(**.
2. Then, type the sequence or the location path to the sequence whose smallest value should be returned.
3. Finally, type **)** to complete the function.

To return the maximum value of the numbers in a sequence:

1. Type **max(**.
2. Then, type the sequence or the location path to the sequence whose greatest value should be returned.
3. Finally, type **)** to complete the function.

✔ Tips

- These functions are called "aggregating functions" since they return a single value based on the values of a sequence. They are: `avg()`, `min()`, `max()`, `sum()`, and `count()`. The last two were available in XPath 1.0.
- For all aggregating functions, except for `count()`, the sequence must consist of similarly typed values. Either they must all be numeric, or they can be a single type (such as date types).

Formatting Strings

In XPath 2.0, there are a handful of new functions for formatting strings. Two such functions provide the ability to change a string to upper or lowercase. And, while you can convert string cases in XPath 1.0 **(Figure 15.14)**, it's quite a lot easier in XPath 2.0 **(Figure 15.15)**.

To convert a string to uppercase:

1. Type **upper-case(**.
2. Then, type the expression that contains the string to be converted to uppercase.
3. Finally, type **)** to complete the function.

To convert a string to lowercase:

1. Type **lower-case(**.
2. Then, type the expression that contains the string to be converted to lowercase.
3. Finally, type **)** to complete the function.

✔ Tips

- Numbers and punctuation are not affected by the case conversion.
- The `translate()` function that was used to do case conversions in XPath 1.0 still exists in XPath 2.0. It can be used for replacing specific characters in a string with other characters, or removing specific characters from a string altogether.

```
xslt
...
<strong>
<xsl:value-of select=
  "translate(../name
  [@language='English'],
  'abcdefghijklmnopqrstuvwxyz',
  'ABCDEFGHIJKLMNOPQRSTUVWXYZ')"/>
</strong>
```

Figure 15.14 *This XPath 1.0 excerpt uses the* translate() *function to convert each of the ancient wonder's English names to uppercase.*

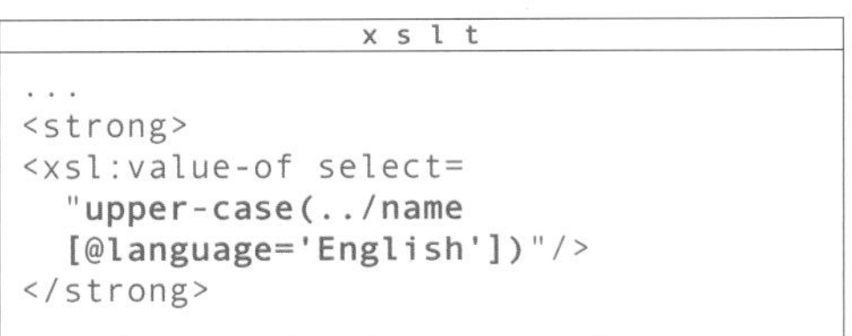

```
xslt
...
<strong>
<xsl:value-of select=
  "upper-case(../name
  [@language='English'])"/>
</strong>
```

Figure 15.15 *Here, I am using the XPath 2.0 function* upper-case() *to do the same thing as the code in Figure 15.14. Not only are there fewer lines of code in this example, but it's much easier to read and understand.*

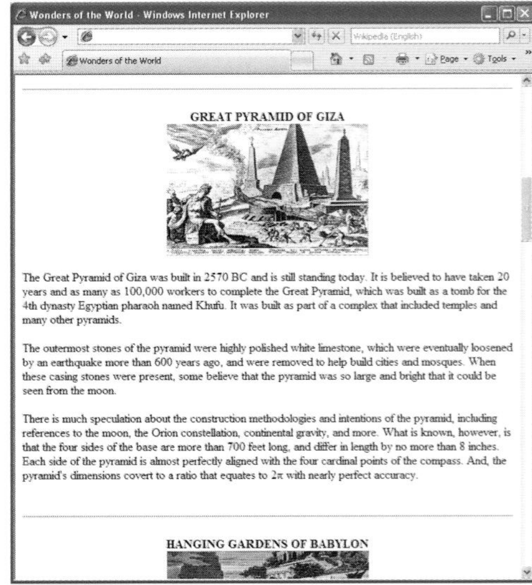

Figure 15.16 *With the new XPath 2.0 function, the HTML output remains the same as before; which was expected.*

```
xslt
...
<xsl:choose>
 <xsl:when test="
   history/year_destroyed != 0">
  <xsl:choose>
   <xsl:when test="history/
     year_destroyed/@era = 'BC'">
    <xsl:value-of select="
      history/year_built -
      history/year_destroyed"/>
   </xsl:when>
   <xsl:otherwise>
    <xsl:value-of select="
      history/year_built +
      history/year_destroyed - 1"/>
   </xsl:otherwise>
  </xsl:choose>
 </xsl:when>
 <xsl:otherwise>
  <xsl:value-of select="
    history/year_built + 2008 - 1"/>
 </xsl:otherwise>
</xsl:choose>
```

Figure 15.17 *This excerpt uses the XPath 1.0 conditional structure of "choose-when-otherwise." It calculates the number of years a wonder stood before being destroyed, accounting for the change in era from BC to AD, and for the Great Pyramid of Giza, which is still standing. It's a lot of code to write, and read!*

```
xslt
...
if (history/year_destroyed != 0)
 then (
  if (history/year_destroyed/@era =
    'BC')
   then (history/year_built -
     history/year_destroyed)
   else (history/year_built +
     history/year_destroyed - 1)
 )
 else (history/year_built + 2008 - 1)
```

Figure 15.18 *Written using XPath 2.0 conditional expressions, the code is a lot smaller, and a lot easier to read.*

Testing Conditions

In XPath 1.0, choosing which of two things to output, or whether to output anything at all, is done using either `xsl:if` or `xsl:choose` instructions **(Figure 15.17)**.

XPath 2.0 has the ability to test for conditions within an XPath expression itself. As well, the test condition can be any expression that evaluates to a boolean value (true or false), not only an expression using nodes.

To test a condition:

1. Anywhere you could have an XPath expression, type **if (**.
2. Specify the boolean expression that you wish to test.
3. Then, type **)** to end the *test expression*.
4. Next, type **then (**.
5. Specify the expression whose value will be returned if the boolean expression in Step 2 is true.
6. Then, type **)** to end the *then-expression*.
7. Next, type **else (**.
8. Specify the expression whose value will be returned if the boolean expression in Step 2 is false.
9. Finally, type **)** to end the *else-expression* and the conditional test **(Figure 15.18)**.

✔ Tips

- You may use an "if-then-else" expression as the expression in a "then" or "else" clause. Doing so creates what is called a nested "if-then-else" structure *(see Figure 15.18)*.
- The parentheses around the then-expression and the else-expression are optional. However, I recommend that you use them to make your XPath easier to read. The parentheses around the test expression, however, are not optional.

Quantifying a Condition

There may be times when you want to know if every one or some of the items in a sequence satisfy a certain condition. For example, were *every one* of Michael Phelps' medals in the 2008 Olympics gold? True. Or, did *some* of Misty May-Treanor and Kerri Walsh's matches in the 2008 Olympics result in a loss? False.

To test if every item in a sequence satisfies a condition:

1. Anywhere you could have an XPath expression (though usually as a test expression), type **every**.
2. Then, type **$var_name**, where *var_name* will refer to the value of the expression in Step 4 below.
3. Next, type **in (**.
4. Specify the expression which is the sequence of items to be tested by the expression in Step 7.
5. Then, type **)** to end the expression, sometimes called the *binding sequence*.
6. Next, type **satisfies (**.
7. Specify the test expression using *$var_name* from Step 2 to represent the items from the expression in Step 4.
8. Finally, type **)** to end the *test expression* and the conditional test **(Figure 15.19)**.

✔ Tips

- You can also test if *some* of the items in a sequence satisfy a condition. To do so, replace the word **every** in Step 1 with the word **some**.
- This construct is called a *quantified expression,* and its result is a boolean value.
- The parentheses around the binding sequence and the test expression are optional. However, I recommend that you use them to make your XPath easier to read.

```
xslt
...
Of these wonders,

<xsl:value-of select="

 if (every $wonder_history
  in (ancient_wonders/wonder/history)
  satisfies (exists
  ($wonder_history/how_destroyed)) )

 then ('all')

 else (

  if (some $wonder_history
   in (ancient_wonders/wonder/history)
   satisfies (exists
   ($wonder_history/how_destroyed)) )

  then ('some')

  else ('none')
 )
" />

have been destroyed.
```

Figure 15.19 *Here I am using both an* every *condition and a* some *condition to see if all, some, or none of the ancient wonders have been destroyed. Note the use of a nested if-then-else structure, as described on page 199. Also, notice the use of the XPath 2.0 function* exists()*, which returns a boolean value based on whether its argument exists or not.*

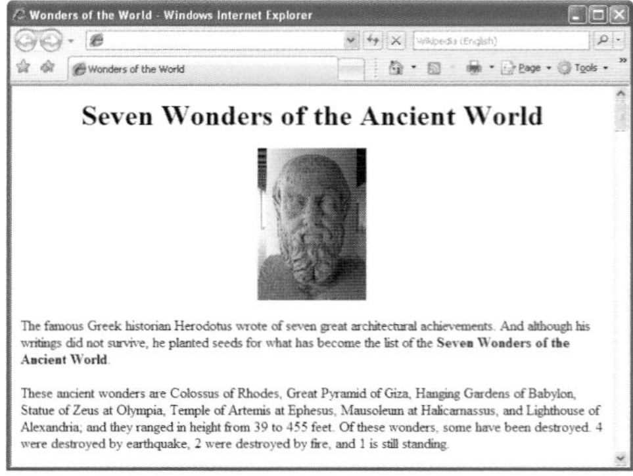

Figure 15.20 *As you probably already know, only* some *of the ancient wonders have been destroyed.*

```
xslt
...
They were built in

<xsl:for-each select=
  "distinct-values(ancient_wonders/
  wonder/substring-after
  (location, ','))">
 <xsl:sort select="."
   order="ascending"/>
  <xsl:value-of select="."/>
   <xsl:choose>
    <xsl:when test="position()=
      last()">;</xsl:when>
    <xsl:when test="position()=
      last()-1">, and </xsl:when>
    <xsl:otherwise>, </xsl:otherwise>
   </xsl:choose>
 </xsl:for-each>
```

Figure 15.21 *This XSLT 2.0 / XPath 2.0 example is using the* distinct-values() *function to remove the duplicate items from a sequence. The sequence is generated using the* substring-after() *function to return only the country name from the* location *element.*

```
html
<p>These ancient wonders are Colossus
  of Rhodes, Great Pyramid of Giza,
  Hanging Gardens of Babylon, Statue
  of Zeus at Olympia, Temple of
  Artemis at Ephesus, Mausoleum at
  Halicarnassus, and Lighthouse of
  Alexandria.

  They were built in Egypt, Greece,
  Iraq, and  Turkey; and they ranged
  in height from 39 to 455 feet.

  Of these wonders, some have been
  destroyed. 4 were destroyed by
  earthquake, 2 were destroyed by
  fire, and 1 is still standing.
</p>
```

Figure 15.22 *The code in Figure 15.21 returns a sequence of the countries in which the wonders were built. Notice that I also used* xsl:sort *to order the sequence alphabetically before displaying it.*

Removing Duplicate Items

One of the differences between node sets and sequences is that sequences can have duplicate items. This is an important upgrade of functionality from version 1.0 to version 2.0. However, there will be times when you want to have a sequence where each item is represented only once.

To remove duplicate items from a sequence:

1. Type **distinct-values(**.
2. Then, type the expression that contains the sequence to be processed.
3. Finally, type **)** to complete the function **(Figure 15.21)**.

✔ Tip

- The order of the items returned from the `distinct-values()` function may be different depending on your XSLT processor. If you need your sequence to be in a specific order, you can use the `xsl:sort` instruction to sort the resulting sequence in the way that you need **(Figure 15.22)**.

Removing Duplicate Items

Looping Over Sequences

One of the more powerful new features in XPath 2.0 is the ability to loop over a sequence. Though similar to the functionality of the XSLT 1.0 `xsl:for-each` instruction, the result of an XPath 2.0 loop is a sequence. And, this sequence can then be processed just as any other, enabling much more complex data transformations than were possible using XSLT 1.0 with XPath 1.0.

To loop over a sequence:

1. Anywhere you could have an XPath expression (though usually in an output capacity), type **for**.
2. Then, type **$range_var**, where *range_var* will be set to each of the items in the expression in Step 4 below. This is sometimes called the *range variable*.
3. Next, type **in (**.
4. Specify the expression which is the sequence of items used to set the range variable in Step 2 above.
5. Then, type **)** to end the expression, sometimes called the *binding sequence*.
6. Next, type **return (**.
7. Specify the return expression. This expression is evaluated once using *$range_var* from Step 2 to represent each of the items from the expression in Step 4.
8. Finally, type **)** to end the *return expression* **(Figure 15.23)**.

✔ Tips

- This XPath 2.0 construct is called a *for expression*. The return value of a for expression is a sequence.
- The parentheses around the binding sequence and the return expression are optional. However, I recommend that you use them to make your XPath easier to read.

```
xslt
...
and they stood from
<xsl:variable name="yrs_standing"
  select=
   "for $i in (ancient_wonders/wonder)
    return (

if ($i/history/year_destroyed != 0)
 then (
  if ($i/history/year_destroyed/@era
    ='BC')
   then ($i/history/year_built -
     $i/history/year_destroyed)
   else ($i/history/year_built +
     $i/history/year_destroyed - 1)
 )
 else ($i/history/year_built
   + 2008 - 1)

    ) "/>

<xsl:value-of
  select="min($yrs_standing)"/>
years to
<xsl:value-of
  select="max($yrs_standing)"/>
years.
```

Figure 15.23 *Here, I'm using the calculation shown in Figure 15.18 within a* for *expression. It returns a sequence of the years standing for all the wonders. The range variable* $i *refers to the current wonder in the* for *expression.*

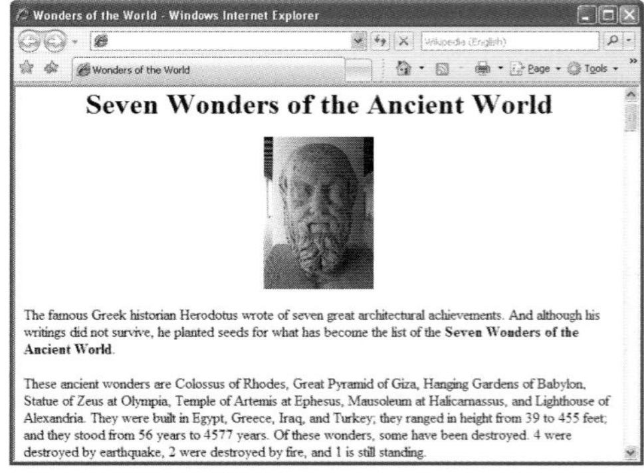

Figure 15.24 *The XPath 2.0* for *expression returns a sequence. This sequence can then be used elsewhere in the XSLT document. For example, at the bottom of the code in Figure 15.23, I used the* min() *and* max() *functions on the sequence. These functions were discussed on page 197.*

```
xslt
...
<xsl:variable name="cur_year"
  select="format-date
  (current-date(), '[Y0001]')"/>

and they stood from
<xsl:variable name="yrs_standing"
...
 else ($i/history/year_built
   + $cur_year - 1)
...
```

Figure 15.25 *In this excerpt, I am using the* format-date() *function to convert the value returned from the* current-date() *function to a four-digit year* ([Y0001]). *While this returns the current year (in this case, 2008), it does so as a string. Because XPath 2.0, is a strongly typed language, the math calculation of* year_built + $cur_year - 1 *generates an XSLT processing error (because you cannot perform math on a string).*

```
xslt
<?xml version="1.0"?>
<xsl:stylesheet xmlns:xsl="http://
www.w3.org/1999/XSL/Transform"
version="2.0" xmlns:xs="http://www.
w3.org/2001/XMLSchema">

...
<xsl:variable name="cur_year"
  select="format-date
  (current-date(), '[Y0001]')
  cast as xs:integer"/>

and they stood from
<xsl:variable name="yrs_standing"
...
 else ($i/history/year_built
   + $cur_year - 1)
...
```

Figure 15.26 *In order to fix the processing error in Figure 15.25, I have to change the string* '2008' *to be an integer* = 2008. *To do this, I declare the XML Schema namespace in the* xsl:stylesheet *element, and then use the* cast *operator to change* $cur_year *to an* xs:integer.

Using Today's Date and Time

XPath 2.0 has a significantly larger set of functions than XPath 1.0 has. I've discussed some of the aggregating functions on pages 196 and 197, as well as some string functions on page 198. In addition to these, there are three new functions in XPath 2.0 that return today's date and time.

To return today's date:

- Type **current-date() (Figure 15.25)**.

To return the current time:

- Type **current-time()**.

To return the current date and time:

- Type **current-dateTime()**.

✔ Tips

- Each of these new functions returns an XML Schema primitive type: `xs:date`, `xs:time`, and `xs:dateTime`, respectively.
- Each of these new functions can be formatted by a new XSLT 2.0 function: `format-date()`, `format-time()`, and `format-dateTime()`, respectively *(see Figure 15.25)*.
- To manipulate values that are `xs:date`, `xs:time`, `xs:dateTime`, or any other XML Schema data type, you must declare the namespace in the `xsl:stylesheet` element **(Figure 15.26)**.

Writing Comments

Being able to comment your XPath is extremely helpful. It allows you to explain what a particular instruction or set of instructions means. Surprisingly, this was not available in XPath 1.0 but is part of the XPath 2.0 specification.

To write comments:

1. Type **(:**.
2. Write your comment.
3. Finally, type **:)** to close the comment **(Figure 15.27)**.

✔ Tips

- XPath comments can only occur where an XPath expression is expected.
- XPath comments can span multiple lines, and can contain any characters, including spaces, text, elements, and line breaks. In fact, they can even contain a colon and a closing parenthesis (unless they are together, in which case you have closed your comment).
- Like XML comments, you can use XPath comments to hide a set of XPath instructions during development. This is called commenting out a section. Within a commented out section, the elements, along with any errors they may contain, will not be processed by the XPath processor.
- Unlike XML comments, however, you may nest XPath comments in other XPath comments. This enables you to comment out sets of XPath instructions that already contain comments of their own.

```
xslt
...
and they stood from
<xsl:variable name="yrs_standing"
  select="

(: This set of instructions
   calculates the total years
   standing of each wonder.

   If the wonder was destroyed in the
   BC era, the math is simple:
   subtract year_destroyed from
   year_built.

   If the wonder was destroyed in the
   AD era, the math is to add the
   year_built and the year_destroyed,
   but subtract 1 because there is no
   year zero.

   If the wonder has not been
   destroyed, the math is to add the
   year_built and the current year,
   but subtract 1 because there is no
   year zero. :)

   for $i in (ancient_wonders/wonder)
    return (

if ($i/history/year_destroyed != 0)
 then (
  if ($i/history/year_destroyed/@era
    ='BC')
   then ($i/history/year_built -
     $i/history/year_destroyed)
   else ($i/history/year_built +
     $i/history/year_destroyed - 1)
 )
 else ($i/history/year_built
   + $cur_year - 1)
...
```

Figure 15.27 *This calculation may make sense to me today. However, when returning to this code in one, six, or twelve months, it may be a little more difficult to follow without the XPath comment.*

Writing Comments

```
xslt
<?xml version="1.0"?>
<xsl:stylesheet xmlns:xsl="http://
  www.w3.org/1999/XSL/Transform"
  version="2.0" xmlns:xs="http://
  www.w3.org/2001/XMLSchema">
 <xsl:output method="html"/>

 <xsl:variable name="input_text"
   as="xs:string" select="
   unparsed-text(
     'julius_caesar-act-iii.txt')"/>

 <xsl:variable name="input_lines"
   as="xs:string" select="
   replace(
     $input_text, '\r?\n', ' ')"/>

 <xsl:variable name="no_speakers"
  as="xs:string*" select="
  tokenize(
    $input_lines, '\b[A-Z ]+\.')"/>
...
    <xsl:for-each select="
      $no_speakers">
     <xsl:analyze-string select="."
       regex=".*Caesar.*">
      <xsl:matching-substring>
       <p>
        <xsl:value-of select="."/>
       </p>
      </xsl:matching-substring>
     </xsl:analyze-string>
    </xsl:for-each>
...
```

Figure 15.28 *This example returns an HTML file with all the lines of dialogue from Act III of* Julius Caesar, *which contain the word 'Caesar.'*

The unparsed-text() *function sets* input_text *to be equal to the text from the file* julius_caesar-act-iii.txt.

The replace() *function changes all line breaks and carriage returns in* input_text *to spaces, and then saves the result in* input_lines.

The tokenize() *function breaks up* input_lines *into a sequence of strings, and saves it in the variable* no_speakers. *The breaking marker used is capital letter words followed by a period* (\b[A-Z]+\.). *These markers are the speakers' names in the text.*

The analyze-string() *function and its companion function* matching-substring() *function return the strings from* no_speakers, *which contain the word 'Caesar'. This could have been done using the* contains() *function as well.*

Processing Non-XML Input

Although it was technically possible to use non-XML input in XSLT 1.0 and XPath 1.0, it was not an easy task to process, and there were many constraints when trying to do so.

However, in XSLT 2.0 / XPath 2.0, there are a handful of new functions that make processing non-XML input much easier **(Figure 15.28)**. This is a rather advanced topic, but I've listed few important and relevant functions below.

Reading non-XML input:

- **unparsed-text(href)** returns the contents of the file found at *href* as a string.

Parsing input using regular expressions:

- **tokenize(input, regex_pattern)** returns a sequence of strings from the *input* string using the *regex_pattern* to break the input string into individual pieces.
- **replace(input, regex_pattern, replace)** returns an updated *input* string, where each occurrence of the *regex_pattern* in the input string is replaced with the *replace* string.
- **match(input, regex_pattern)** returns the boolean value (either true or false), depending on whether the *input* string matches the *regex_pattern* or not.
- **analyze-string(select="expression" regex="pattern")** returns a sequence of all the strings from the select *expression* that match the regex *pattern*. It is followed by one or both of the instructions: `<xsl:matching-substring>` and/or `<xsl:non-matching-substring>`, each of which processes the appropriate substrings from the `analyze-string` instruction.

Processing Non-XML Input

16

XQuery 1.0

XQuery 1.0 (*XML Query Language*) is the third major language resulting from the eight W3C Recommendations published in January, 2007. Like XSLT 2.0 (Chapter 14), XQuery is used to select content from an XML data source, transform that content as directed, and then return this new content as either XML, HTML, or some other format. XQuery uses the XPath 2.0 language (Chapter 15) to select XML source content and to manipulate that content if necessary, just like XSLT 2.0. In fact, most of the things that you can do with XSLT 2.0, you can also do with XQuery 1.0.

XQuery does differ from XSLT 2.0 in a few significant ways; including, most noticeably, that it does not use XML syntax. This actually makes for a more compact and easily learned language, especially for XML novices or those with previous programming experience. Interestingly enough, one of the other eight published Recommendations is a language that uses XML syntax for XQuery queries, called XQueryX. It is, however, a verbose and unwieldy language, and is only really usable by XML software tools, not by people.

As with XSLT 2.0 and XPath 2.0, in order to see this chapter's examples work (or to write XQuery yourself), you will need an XQuery processor. If you don't have one already, see Appendix A, *XML Tools,* for a list of options.

For additional XQuery information, visit the W3C's XQuery Working Group site at: *www.w3.org/XML/Query*.

XQuery 1.0 vs. XSLT 2.0

Both XQuery 1.0 and XSLT 2.0 can be used to query XML data sources. They are both built on XPath 2.0 expressions, and they use the same data model, XDM. In both languages, you can create user-defined functions, and you can use XML Schema to validate XML source content, as well as XML output content.

Given this, at the basic level, the choice to use XQuery 1.0, as opposed to XSLT 2.0, is a matter of taste and experience. XSLT 2.0 uses XML syntax and extends XSLT 1.0, a language with which you may have some experience. On the other hand, XQuery does not use XML syntax, and is more similar in structure to SQL (*Structured Query Language*), another language with which you may be familiar.

With basic queries and transformations, both languages are equally competent **(Figures 16.1 and 16.2)**. However, a well-known study showed that with no previous knowledge, XQuery is easier to learn than XSLT 2.0. But, as the transformation requirements increase in complexity, the better choice becomes XSLT 2.0. It has better support for grouping data, formatting numbers and dates, and schema-type validation.

Even still, XQuery is gaining significant momentum. One of the major reasons is that XQuery was designed with the idea of directly querying databases. And, major database developers such as IBM, Microsoft, and Oracle have mechanisms enabling XQuery to view their databases like any other XML source.

The bottom line is that the choice of whether to use XQuery 1.0 or XSLT 2.0, can be subjective. I suggest that for complex queries, you use XQuery, and for complex transformations, you use XSLT 2.0. Moreover, most XML processing infrastructures allow for a mixture of languages, and you will likely be best served by using both languages, each where most appropriate.

```
xslt
...
<p>These ancient wonders are
 <ul>

  <xsl:for-each select="
    ancient_wonders/wonder/name
    [@language='English']">

   <li>
     <xsl:value-of select="."/>
   </li>

  </xsl:for-each>

 </ul>
 </p>
...
```

Figure 16.1 *This excerpt of XSLT uses XPath to retrieve a sequence of ancient wonder names whose* language *attribute equals 'English'. It then uses the* xsl:for-each *construct to loop over all the names and display each of them in an HTML bulleted list.*

```
xquery
...
<p>These ancient wonders are:
 <ul>

  {
   for $x in
     doc("wonders-master.xml")
     /ancient_wonders/wonder/name
     [@language='English']

   return
     <li>
     {data($x)}
     </li>
  }

 </ul>
</p>
...
```

Figure 16.2 *This XQuery excerpt generates the exact same HTML as the XSLT shown in Figure 16.1. Here, a loop is created where XPath returns each of the* wonder *nodes whose* language *attribute equals 'English,' and sets the variable* $x*. Then, each time through the loop, the data value of the variable* $x *is output in an HTML bulleted list.*

```
xquery
xquery version "1.0";

"Hello World!"
```

```
output
Hello World!
```

Figure 16.3 *In the XQuery document above, I declared that I'm using XQuery version 1.0. Then, I typed in a literal string, which will be output as shown when the document is processed.*

```
xquery
xquery version "1.0";

"Everyone count down:",

reverse(1 to 10),

"Blastoff!"
```

```
output
Everyone count down:
10 9 8 7 6 5 4 3 2 1 Blastoff!
```

Figure 16.4 *In the example above, the three XQuery expressions are separated by commas. The second expression constructs a sequence, which is then reversed using the built-in* reverse() *function.*

```
xquery
xquery version "1.0";

<countdown>
  {reverse(1 to 10)}</countdown>
```

```
output
<countdown>10987654321</countdown>
```

Figure 16.5 *In this example, I am constructing an XML element called* countdown. *Notice the use of the curly braces, which delimit the enclosed expression. This expression is then evaluated, and replaced by its value in the output.*

Composing an XQuery Document

An XQuery document is a text-only file and begins with a version declaration **(Figure 16.3)**. It does not start with the standard XML declaration, because it is not an XML document itself. An XQuery document is saved with either an `.xquery` or `.xq` extension. I use the latter in this chapter.

To compose an XQuery document:

1. At the top of your document, type **xquery**.
2. Then, type **version "1.0"**.
3. Next, type **;** (a semi-colon).
4. Finally, write an XQuery expression, or multiple XQuery expressions, separated by commas.

✔ Tips

- An XQuery expression can be a numeric or string literal **(Figure 16.3)**; a sequence constructor **(Figure 16.4)**; an element constructor **(Figure 16.5)**; a built-in or user-defined function *(see page 216)*; or one of the built-in expressions, such as a conditional expression *(see page 214)* or a FLWOR expression *(see page 212)*.
- Comments in XQuery use the same syntax as XPath 2.0. **(:** is used to start the comment, and **:)** is used to end it. And, like XPath 2.0, they can be nested.
- When using element constructors **(Figure 16.5)**, curly braces (**{ }**) are used to distinguish expressions from literal text. These *enclosed expressions* are evaluated first before being output.
- Although XQuery does not use XML syntax, it is case sensitive, and all XQuery instructions are written in lowercase.

Identifying an XML Source Document

To process XML source documents with either version of XSLT, you would use the XML processing directive `xml-stylesheet`. This directive enables you to identify the path to the XML source document. For XQuery, however, there isn't an XML processing directive. To identify the XML source for an XQuery document, you can use the `doc()` function.

To identify an XML source document:

1. Type **doc(**.
2. Then, type **doc_uri**, where *doc_uri* is the path to the XML source document.
3. Finally, type **)** to end the function **(Figure 16.6)**.

✔ Tips

- Some XQuery processors require that you identify the XML source document when you process your XQuery (and not in the XQuery code itself). In this case, you will need to replace the *doc_uri* in the `doc()` function with **.** (a period). This is a representation of the current context, which you will need to use instead of a URI.
- Regardless of the XQuery processor you use, XQuery can actually use more than one XML source document *(see page 215)*.

xquery

```
xquery version "1.0";

doc("wonders-master.xml")
```

output

```
<?xml version="1.0" encoding="UTF-8"?>
<!-- Note: For many of the wonders,
  the experts do not agree on precise
  dates or construction dimensions.
  In these cases, I chose a year or
  dimension in the middle of the
  range so all attributes could be
  numeric. -->
<ancient_wonders>
 <wonder>
  <name language="English">
    Colossus of Rhodes</name>
  <name language="Greek">
    Κολοσσὸς της Ρόδου</name>
  <location>Rhodes, Greece</location>
  <height units="feet">107</height>
  <history>
   <year_built era="BC">
     282</year_built>
   <year_destroyed era="BC">
     226</year_destroyed>
   <how_destroyed>
     earthquake</how_destroyed>
   <story>In 294 BC, the people of
     the island of Rhodes began
     building a colossal statue ...
```

Figure 16.6 *In the XQuery example above, I have identified the XML source document to be the* wonders-master.xml *document, something you should be familiar with by now. The* doc() *function returns the node tree of the current context as a sequence.*

```
xquery
xquery version "1.0";

doc("wonders-master.xml")
  /ancient_wonders/wonder/location
```

```
output
<location>Rhodes, Greece</location>
<location>Giza, Egypt</location>
<location>Al Hillah, Iraq</location>
<location>Olympia, Greece</location>
<location>Ephesus, Turkey</location>
<location>Bodrum, Turkey</location>
...
```

Figure 16.7 *In the example above, I use the* doc() *function to retrieve the document node from the* wonders-master.xml *source document. Then, I use the location path* /ancient_wonders/wonder/location *to retrieve each wonder's* location *element.*

```
xquery
xquery version "1.0";

doc("wonders-master.xml")
  /ancient_wonders/wonder/location
  [contains(., "Turkey")]
```

```
output
<location>Ephesus, Turkey</location>
<location>Bodrum, Turkey</location>
```

Figure 16.8 *In this example, I have added a predicate to select only those location elements that contain the string "Turkey."*

```
xquery
xquery version "1.0";

doc("wonders-master.xml")
  /ancient_wonders/wonder/name
  [contains(../location, "Turkey")]
```

```
output
<name language="English">Temple of
  Artemis at Ephesus</name>
<name language="Greek">
  Ἀρτεμίσιον</name>
<name language="English">Mausoleum at
  Halicarnassus</name> ...
```

Figure 16.9 *Here, I have altered the path expression and predicate to return the* name *elements which have a* location *element containing the string "Turkey."*

Using Path Expressions

To select content from an XML data source, XQuery uses the XPath language syntax **(Figure 16.7)**. The XML source document is first converted into an XML node tree. Then, based on the location path you provide, the XML tree is searched to find the information requested. As discussed in Chapter 3, the location path describes the position of the desired content relative to the position of the current context.

To use a path expression:

1. First, identify the XML source document using the `doc()` function described on page 210.
2. Next, type any valid XPath expression. This expression will be used with the node tree generated from the XML source document, retrieved by the `doc()` function in Step 1.

✔ Tips

- Some XQuery processors require that you select the XML source document when you process your XQuery. In this case, you will need to change the *doc_uri* in the doc() function to a representation of the current context, which is **.** (a period).
- Like all XPath expressions, those used in XQuery can take predicates, and XQuery predicates can also use functions **(Figures 16.8 and 16.9)**.

Writing FLWOR Expressions

The FLWOR expression (pronounced "flower") is unique to XQuery **(Figure 16.10)**. It is similar to XSLT's `xsl:for-each` instruction and is an extension of the XPath 2.0 `for` expression. Also, the FLWOR expression is loosely based on the SQL Select statement, and its name is an acronym of each of its five keywords: *for*, *let*, *where*, *order*, and *return*.

To write a basic FLWOR expression:

1. Type **for**.
2. Then, type **$range_var**, where *range_var* will be set to each of the items returned in the expression in Step 4 below. This is sometimes called the *range variable*.
3. Next, type **in**.
4. Specify the expression, which is the sequence of items used to set the range variable in Step 2 above. This is sometimes called the *binding sequence*.
5. Then, type **where**.
6. Specify the expression, which will filter the range variables set by the binding sequence in Steps 2 and 4 above. This is usually called the *where clause*.
7. Next, type **return**.
8. Finally, specify the *return clause*. This expression is evaluated once for each range variable set by the binding sequence and filtered by the where clause (Steps 2, 4, and 6, respectively).

✔ Tip

- In a FLWOR expression, the where clause shown in Steps 5 and 6 is optional.

xquery

```
xquery version "1.0";

for $wndr in
  doc("wonders-master.xml")
  /ancient_wonders/wonder

where
  contains($wndr/location, "Turkey")

return $wndr/name
```

output

```
<name language="English">Temple of
  Artemis at Ephesus</name>
<name language="Greek">
  Ἀρτεμίσιον</name>
<name language="English">Mausoleum at
  Halicarnassus</name> ...
```

Figure 16.10 *The FLWOR expression above sets the range variable* $wndr *to each of the* wonder *elements in the XML source document,* wonders-master.xml. *The where clause then filters the sequence of* $wndr *variables to only include those which have a* location *element containing the string "Turkey." Then, the return clause outputs each of these* name *elements. You'll see from the output that this FLWOR expression generates the exact same result as the example in Figure 16.9.*

xquery

```
xquery version "1.0";

for $wndr in
  doc("wonders-master.xml")
  /ancient_wonders/wonder

where
  contains($wndr/location, "Turkey")

return $wndr/name[@language='English']
```

output

```
<name language="English">Temple of
  Artemis at Ephesus</name>
<name language="English">Mausoleum at
  Halicarnassus</name>
```

Figure 16.11 *In this example, I've added a predicate to the return clause, only outputting the* name *elements with a* language *attribute of 'English.'*

Writing FLWOR Expressions

```
xquery
xquery version "1.0";

for $wndr in
  doc("wonders-master.xml")
  /ancient_wonders/wonder
where
  contains($wndr/location, "Turkey")
order by
  $wndr/name[@language='English']
return $wndr/name[@language='English']
```

```
output
<name language="English">Mausoleum at
  Halicarnassus</name>
<name language="English">Temple of
  Artemis at Ephesus</name>
```

Figure 16.12 *Here, I'm using an order by clause to sort the final sequence by each wonder's English name.*

```
xquery
xquery version "1.0";

for $wndr in
  doc("wonders-master.xml")
  /ancient_wonders/wonder
let $src := $wndr/source
where
  contains($wndr/location, "Turkey")
order by
 $wndr/name[@language='English']
return
  ($wndr/name[@language='English'],
  $src)
```

```
output
<name language="English">
  Mausoleum at Halicarnassus</name>
<source sectionid="141"
  newspaperid="21"/>
<source sectionid="2"
  newspaperid="19"/>
<name language="English">
  Temple of Artemis at Ephesus</name>
<source sectionid="92"
 newspaperid="19"/>
```

Figure 16.13 *The let clause sets* $src *to the* source *element(s) for each wonder in the for clause (also filtered by the where clause). These* source *elements are output with each wonder's English* name *element. The parentheses and comma separator in the return clause create a single sequence of the two expressions shown. This is used because return clauses can only output a single expression.*

The other optional clause in the FLWOR expression is the *order by clause*. It sorts the final sequence of items before it's output by the return clause **(Figure 16.12)**.

To include the order by clause:

1. Immediately before the return clause shown in Steps 7 and 8 on page 212, type **order by**.
2. Finally, specify the expression which will order the final sequence of items to be output by the return clause.

The last clause in the FLWOR expression is the *let clause* **(Figure 16.13)**. It, like the for clause, generates an ordered sequence of items. The difference between the two is that for each item in the sequence generated by the for clause, only one item is created for the variable in the let clause, even if this variable is set to a sequence itself.

To include the let clause:

1. Before the return clause and both the optional where clause and order by clause (if they are included), type **let**.
2. Then, type **$instance_var**, where *instance_var* will be set to the entire result of the expression in Step 4 below.
3. Next, type **:=** (a colon and an equals sign).
4. Finally, specify the expression which will set the instance variable in Step 2 above. This is sometimes called the *binding sequence*.

✔ Tips

- You can have as many, or as few, for clauses and let clauses as you wish, but you must have at least one of either for the FLWOR expression to be valid.
- Sometimes, the variable set in the for clause is used in the let clause expression. This creates something like the SQL *join clause,* and is discussed more on page 215.

Testing with Conditional Expressions

Conditional expressions in XQuery 1.0 use the same if-then-else syntax as those in XPath 2.0. These expressions **(Figure 16.14)** provide the ability to test a condition and output different results based on the boolean value (true or false) of the condition.

To test with a conditional expression:

1. Type **if (**.
2. Specify the boolean expression which is the condition on which you wish to test.
3. Then, type **)** to end the *test expression*.
4. Next, type **then**.
5. Specify the expression whose value will be returned if the boolean expression in Step 2 is true. This is called the *then-expression*.
6. Then, type **else**.
7. Finally, specify the expression whose value will be returned if the boolean expression in Step 2 is false. This is called the *else-expression*.

✔ Tips

- You may use any valid expression for the then-expression and the else-expression. In fact, these expressions may even be new if-then-else expressions **(Figure 16.14)**. Doing so creates what is called a *nested* if-then-else structure.
- Parentheses are required around the test expression. Parentheses are optional around the then-expression and the else-expression.
- If you do not need an else-expression, you still must include one. Just use **else()**, which returns an empty sequence **(Figure 16.14)**. Notice that in this case, parentheses are required.

xquery

```
xquery version "1.0";

<destruction>
{
 for $wndr in
   doc("wonders-master.xml")
   /ancient_wonders/wonder

 return
  if ($wndr/history/how_destroyed
    ="earthquake")
  then
   <quake>
     {data($wndr/name
     [@language='English'])}
   </quake>

  else
   if ($wndr/history/how_destroyed
     ="fire")
   then
    <fire>
      {data($wndr/name
      [@language='English'])}
    </fire>
   else ()
}
</destruction>
```

output

```
<destruction>
 <quake>
   Colossus of Rhodes</quake>
 <quake>
   Hanging Gardens of Babylon</quake>
 <fire>
   Statue of Zeus at Olympia</fire>
 <fire>
   Temple of Artemis at Ephesus</fire>
 <quake>
   Mausoleum at Halicarnassus</quake>
 <quake>
   Lighthouse of Alexandria</quake>
</destruction>
```

Figure 16.14 *In the XQuery example, the conditional expression tests how each wonder was destroyed, and returns a new element (*<quake> *or* <fire>*) with that wonder's English name. Remember, the enclosed expression inside the curly braces is evaluated first before being output.*

```
xml
<earthquakes>
 <occurrence>
  <epicenter>Abu Qir, Egypt
    </epicenter>
  <cities_affected>
   <city>Abu Qir, Egypt</city>
   <city>Alexandria, Egypt</city>
   <city>Damanhur, Egypt</city>
  </cities_affected>
  <date>1323-01-09</date>
  <magnitude>6.1</magnitude>
 </occurrence>
...
```

Figure 16.15 *I have created an xml file containing (100% fictitious) information about earthquakes that occurred in the 14th and early 15th centuries. It is called* earthquake_data.xml.

```
xquery
xquery version "1.0";

for $wndr in
  doc("wonders-master.xml")
  /ancient_wonders/wonder

for $quake in
  doc("earthquake_data.xml")
  /earthquakes/occurrence

where $quake[cities_affected/city
  = $wndr/location]

return (data($wndr/name
  [@language='English']),
  data($quake/date))
```

```
output
Mausoleum at Halicarnassus 1402-11-18
Mausoleum at Halicarnassus 1404-03-13
Mausoleum at Halicarnassus 1404-03-23
Lighthouse of Alexandria 1323-01-09
```

Figure 16.16 *In the example above, the first data source is* wonders-master.xml. *The second data source is* earthquake_data.xml. *The where clause joins these two data sources by matching the* cities_affected/city *with the wonder's* location. *This results in a list of wonders which were affected by earthquakes in the 14th and 15th centuries, and the dates of each earthquake.*

Joining Two Related Data Sources

Oftentimes, the information with which you are working is contained in multiple XML data sources. XQuery allows you to query information in multiple files simultaneously using a FLWOR expression.

For example, a clothing store might have an XML file listing its products: product id, name, price, and description; and another XML file listing its orders: order id, product id, quantity purchased, and customer information. Using the product id as the primary relationship between the two files, you could use an XQuery FLWOR expression to calculate the total cost of an order by multiplying the quantity of each product purchased (in the orders file) by the price of the product itself (in the products file).

To join two related data sources:

1. Write the for clause which refers to the first data source.
2. Then, write a second for clause, and refer to the second data source. The relationship between both data sources will be defined in Step 3 below.
3. Finally, in the where clause of the FLWOR expression, use the range variables from both for clauses in Steps 1 and 2 to define the relationship between the data sources **(Figure 16.16)**.

✔ Tip

- There are actually many different ways to join related data sources. You could use let clauses instead of one or both for clauses; you could write a second FLWOR expression as the return clause for the first FLWOR expression; you could use predicates instead of a where clause, etc. The idea is the same; joining two related data sources requires items in the first data source that relate to (and are often equal to) items in the second data source.

Creating and Calling User Defined Functions

A User Defined Function (UDF) in XQuery acts just like a built-in XQuery function, except that you define its name, input, what it does with the input, and what it outputs.

To create a User Defined Function:

1. Immediately after the version declaration *(see page 209)*, type **declare function**.
2. Then, type **local:UDF_name(**, where *UDF_name* is the name of your function.
3. Next, type **$param_name** to identify any input parameters, where *param_name* will refer to this parameter within your UDF.
4. Repeat Step 3 for each input parameter you want, separated by a comma, and finish the parameter listing with an **)**. You may also have no input parameters and skip Step 3.
5. Type **{**.
6. Then, write your XQuery expression. If you have defined any input parameters in Steps 3 and 4, use them in this expression.
7. Finally, type **};** to complete the function.

To call your User Defined Function:

1. Anywhere an XQuery function is expected, type **local:UDF_name(**, where *UDF_name* matches the one you used in Step 2 above.
2. Type the value(s) of any input parameters defined in Steps 3 above, separated by a comma. If there are no input parameters declared, you will skip this step.
3. Finally, type **)** to finish calling your UDF.

✔ Tip

- XQuery provides a namespace (`local:`) to prevent conflicts between UDF names and the names of functions in the default namespace. You may also declare and use a different namespace for your UDFs.

```
xml
<richter>
 <quake>
  <magnitude>1.0</magnitude>
  <energy>50 lbs</energy>
  <example>Blast at construction
    site</example>
 </quake>...
```

Figure 16.17 *This xml file, called* richter_scale.xml, *contains information about the energy released by earthquakes of different Richter scale magnitudes.*

```
xquery
xquery version "1.0";

declare function local:richter($mag)
{
 let $mag_normalized :=
   ((round($mag * 2)) div 2)
   cast as xs:decimal
 for $r in
   doc("richter_scale.xml")
   /richter/quake
 let $r_dec := (data($r/magnitude))
   cast as xs:decimal
 where $r_dec = $mag_normalized
 return
  (data($r/energy), data($r/example))
};
for $wndr in
  doc("wonders-master.xml")
 /ancient_wonders/wonder
...
return (data($wndr/name
  [@language='English']),
  data($quake/date),
  local:richter(
  data($quake/magnitude)))
```

```
output
Mausoleum at Halicarnassus 1402-11-18
200 million tons Estimated energy
released by Krakatoa volcano in 1883
Mausoleum at Halicarnassus 1404-03-13
80,000 tons Large hurricane
Mausoleum at Halicarnassus 1404-03-23
32 million tons Largest Thermonuclear
Weapon ...
```

Figure 16.18 *The UDF named* richter *has an input parameter named* $mag. *The UDF rounds* $mag *to the nearest 0.5 increment, and returns the amount of energy released by an earthquake of that magnitude and an example of that energy in another context. The calling expression* local:richter(...) *is part of the return clause of the FLWOR clause from Figure 16.16.*

USA	36	38	36
China	51	21	28
Russian Fed.	23	21	28
Great Britain	19	13	15
Australia	14	15	17
Germany	16	10	15
France	7	16	17
South Korea	13	10	8
Italy	8	10	10
Ukraine	7	5	15

Figure 16.19 *This excerpt is from a database table that contains the medals earned by country during the 2008 Summer Olympics. The table's name is* medals *and is in a database called* olympics. *The field names are* country, gold, silver, *and* bronze.

xquery

```
xquery version "1.0";

let $cntry_medals :=
  collection("olympics.medals")/*
let $total_gold :=
  sum(data($cntry_medals/gold))
let $total_silver :=
  sum(data($cntry_medals/silver))
let $total_bronze :=
  sum(data($cntry_medals/bronze))
let $total_medals := $total_gold +
  $total_silver + $total_bronze
return
(
 "Total gold medals awarded:",
   $total_gold,
...
 "Total medals awarded:",
   $total_medals
)
```

output

```
Total gold medals awarded: 302
Total silver medals awarded: 303
Total bronze medals awarded: 353
Total medals awarded: 958
```

Figure 16.20 *This example uses the* collection() *function to set* $cntry_medals *to the sequence of rows from the* medals *table in the* olympics *database. While technically a FLWOR expression, there is no for clause in the XQuery document. Had the first line been a for clause instead of a let clause, the sum calculations would have only taken place on a row-by-row basis, not on the entire node tree.*

XQuery and Databases

XQuery was specifically designed to be able to query a wide array of XML data sources. To accomplish this, before a query can be processed, all data sources are converted into an XML node tree. XQuery doesn't care whether that data source is some random file, an XML document, or a relational database.

Since the inception of XQuery, database developers have been writing extensions for shuttling data back and forth between their databases and XML documents. In this way, these databases were able to export data in XML format, as well as convert (or *shred*) XML data into relational format. However, using an *XML-enabled database* only works well if the XML data is easily converted into the "rows and columns" structure of a relational database. Moreover, shredding XML for storage in the database, and then putting it back together as XML, is often an inefficient and costly process.

To address these drawbacks, a new type of database was developed. It was designed to support standard database features, but store its data in a native XML format. And, while many users are not interested (or are not in a position), to change their database application, many others have started using *Native XML Databases.*

The XQuery specification, however, does not say how to create a database connection. Most XQuery processors use the `collection()` function. Like the doc() function, collection() takes a URI argument and returns a sequence of nodes **(Figure 16.20)**. Even still, different processors interpret the URI in different ways, so you'll need to consult your processor's documentation for specifics.

In addition to the XQuery Working Group site at: *www.w3.org/XML/Query*, a good resource for information about XML and databases (albeit a little out of date) can be found at: *www.rpbourret.com/xml/*.

Part 7: XML in Practice

17

Ajax, RSS, SOAP, and More

Through reading this book, hopefully you have come to understand that XML is not a markup language itself. Rather, you now understand that XML is a specification for creating markup languages, and thus, its inherent extensibility.

In this chapter, I will identify and breakdown some of the more widespread uses of XML today. In one case, XML is simply being used as a data container; in another case, the custom markup language that was created has already been extended further by those who are using it. In yet another case, there are two XML standards fighting to become *the* standard. And, in many of the examples, XML has been an integral part of the creation of a new technology.

The examples that I have included are not nearly as extensive as those found in the rest of the book. That's because the intention of this chapter is not to teach you how to develop in each use of XML; each one could have a chapter and much more devoted to it. Rather, the examples are meant to give you a flavor of the specific implementations, and how XML is really being used in practice.

In February 1998, XML became an official W3C Recommendation. The working group members must certainly have thought they had a great idea, but I don't imagine that they could foresee what it could become.

This chapter is about what XML has become.

Please note: If you want to follow the examples in this chapter more closely, see pages 240–241 at the end of this chapter for some guidance.

Ajax Basics

Ajax (sometimes written as AJAX) stands for *Asynchronous JavaScript and XML*. It is a Web-based technique that creates a more seamless user experience when a Web page is updated based on user input. For instance, a page not using Ajax **(Figure 17.1)** will take user input and submit it to a script on the Web server for processing. This is often the result of the user clicking a submit button or selecting something in a pull-down menu. The user input is then processed by the server, and a new HTML page is created. This new page is returned to the browser, and the existing page is refreshed.

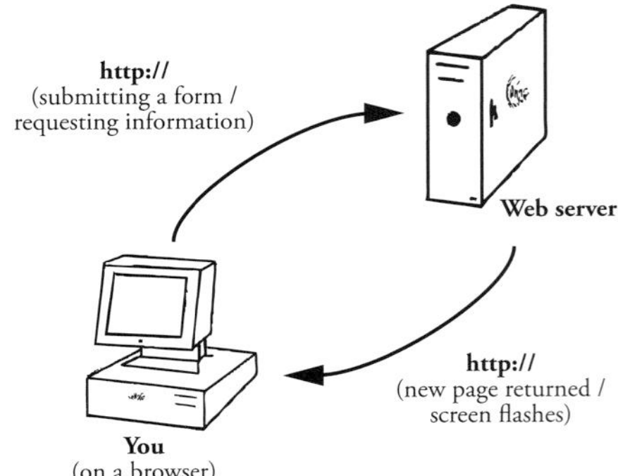

Figure 17.1 *Without Ajax, data is submitted to a Web server, processed, and then returned as a new page.*

A Web page using Ajax **(Figure 17.2)** also takes user input, and submits it to a script on the Web server. This is triggered in the same manner as above; however, the user input is sent to the Web server differently (this is discussed in more detail a little later). The user input is then processed by the server, but instead of creating a new HTML page, only new data is created. This new data is returned to the browser (again via a different mechanism than in the non-Ajax experience). Then, instead of refreshing the page, the existing page is simply updated with the new data.

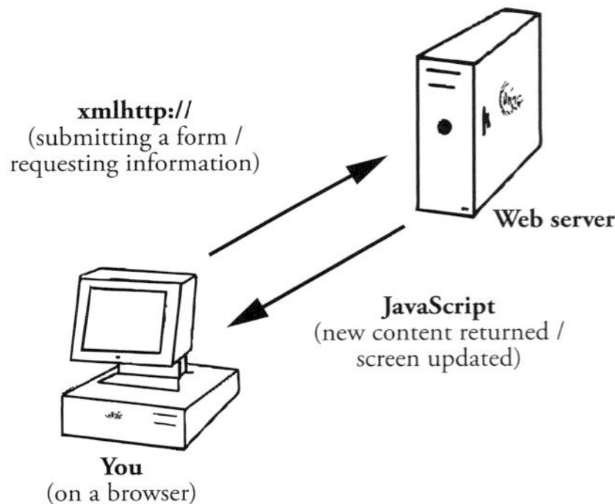

Figure 17.2 *Here, data is submitted to, and returned from, the Web server. However, using Ajax, the content is updated without a new page loading in the browser.*

The Technology of Ajax

Ajax is not a language. It is a specific way of using existing languages to create a more interactive Web experience. It is the combination of HTML (used to display the Web page), XML (used to exchange data between the server-side script and the Web page), and JavaScript (used to update the HTML page with new data and bind the entire process together).

The foundational component of Ajax is the *XMLHttpRequest* object. It facilitates the exchange of data between the Web page and the script on the server. The XMLHttpRequest object is supported by most current browsers. And, for older browsers, there are other objects that can be used in its place **(Figure 17.3)**.

javascript

```
function GetXmlHttpObject() {
 var xmlHttpObject = false;
 try {
  // Most browsers today
  xmlHttpObject = new
    XMLHttpRequest();
 }
 catch (e) {
   // Internet Explorer 5 and 6
   xmlHttpObject = new
     ActiveXObject("Msxml2.XMLHTTP");
 }
 return xmlHttpObject;
}
```

Figure 17.3 *This JavaScript function returns the* XMLHttpRequest *object used with Ajax. It supports most current browsers, as well as IE 5 and 6.*

```javascript
function RequestAjax(url) {
 var xmlHttp = GetXmlHttpObject();
 if (xmlHttp) {
  xmlHttp.onreadystatechange =
    function() {
     if (xmlHttp.readyState == 4)
     ProcessAjax(xmlHttp.responseXML);
    }
  xmlHttp.open("GET", url, true);
  xmlHttp.send(null);
 }
 else
  alert ("Your browser is old or
    doesn't support Ajax.");
}
```

Figure 17.4 *This JavaScript function uses the* XMLHttpRequest *object to set up the structure for the asynchronous communication. When the Web server is ready, the* ProcessAjax *function is called with the Web server's updated data (*xmlHttp.responseXML*).*

```html
<script language="JavaScript">
 function SelectWonder(value) {
  if (value != 0)
   RequestAjax(
     "getWonder.asp?id=" + value);
 }
...
<form>
Ancient Wonders:
 <select name="wonders" onchange=
   "SelectWonder(this.value)">
 <option value="0" default>
   Select a Wonder
 <option value="1">Colossus of Rhodes
...
```

Figure 17.5 *The* SelectWonder() *function is called when a wonder is selected. It sends the server-side script URL with the selected wonder's option value to the* RequestAjax() *function.*

```html
function ProcessAjax(ret_xml) {
 var xmlDoc = ret_xml.documentElement;
 var xmlName = xmlDoc.
   getElementsByTagName("name")[0].
   childNodes[0].nodeValue;
...
```

Figure 17.6 *The* ProcessAjax() *function is called when data is returned from the server. It parses the returned XML and displays it as directed on the page.*

The XMLHttpRequest object exchanges data between the Web page and the server-side script asynchronously. This means that the browser isn't stopped while waiting for the server to return the updated data. Consequently, the data exchange happens without interfering with the display or functionality of the existing page.

Once the XMLHttpRequest object has been created, there are three steps required for the data exchange to take place **(Figure 17.4)**. The first is to create the "retrieving function," which will be called when the Web server is ready to send the updated data. For this, the `onreadystatechange` property is used.

Once the retrieving function is declared, the next step is to identity the URL of the server-side script, which is done using the `open` property. The final step is to send the request to the server using the `send` property, which can include content, variables, or be `null`.

Using Ajax

To use this Ajax foundation, the HTML page needs to call the `RequestAjax()` function from Figure 17.4. When it does, it must include the server-side script's URL and the data to be processed **(Figure 17.5)**.

The HTML page will also need to have a `ProcessAjax()` function, which is called when data is returned from the server **(Figure 17.6)**. It parses the XML returned by the server, and uses JavaScript to display it as needed on the Web page.

✔ Tips

- The names of the functions and parameters shown here were created by me; they are not required names. The one exception is the *XMLHttpRequest*`()` function. It and its properties must be named as shown.
- The examples shown here can be seen in action on my Web site at: *www.kehogo.com/examples/wonders-ajax.html*.

Ajax Examples

Ajax is not that new. In fact, the underlying concepts go back as far as 1996 (which, in Internet time, is a long time ago).

The term Ajax was actually first used in an essay by Jesse James Garrett in 2005. The essay, in conjunction with Google Lab's Beta release of Google Suggest, is believed to have brought about the wider recognition of the Ajax concept. Here are some examples of Ajax in action.

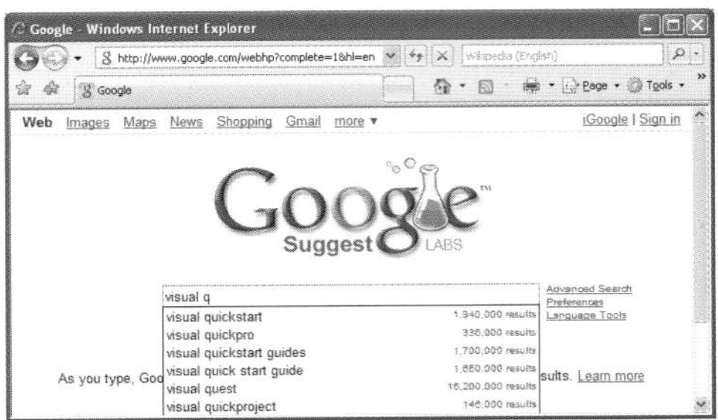

Figure 17.7 *Having typed in "visual q," Google Suggest offers a set of suggestions for me to search.*

Google Suggest

The idea behind Google Suggest (which has since become a built-in feature of Google's standard search service), was to use Ajax to offer search suggestions, based on what was being typed. Using Ajax, each key press in the Google search field would be sent to Google's server, and the data returned would be (typically) the most popular searches, based on the string of characters already typed **(Figure 17.7)**.

Netflix: Star Ratings

Although not the first site to use Ajax for data submissions, Netflix (an online movie rental company) offers a star rating interface that has earned it accolades in the Web community.

Figure 17.8 *The 4.4 red stars show the average rating.*

As a Netflix member, you have the ability to rate every movie. Before you do so, each movie displays the average of all Netflix members' ratings for that movie. The rating is displayed using red stars; the more stars shown, the higher the rating **(Figure 17.8)**.

You can mouse over the stars to see their meanings (two stars: "Didn't Like It", four stars: "Really Liked It," etc.). Then, by clicking on a specific star, you give the movie your rating. Upon your click, information is sent to the Netflix server via Ajax and the rating area is updated, all without causing the page to refresh. Now the movie displays your rating in yellow stars, instead of the average rating of all Netflix members **(Figure 17.9)**.

Figure 17.9 *Mousing over the stars shows their meaning. I clicked on the 5th star, meaning I loved it.*

Figure 17.10 *Tracking Apple Inc.'s stock activity on Yahoo! Finance's stock quote page.*

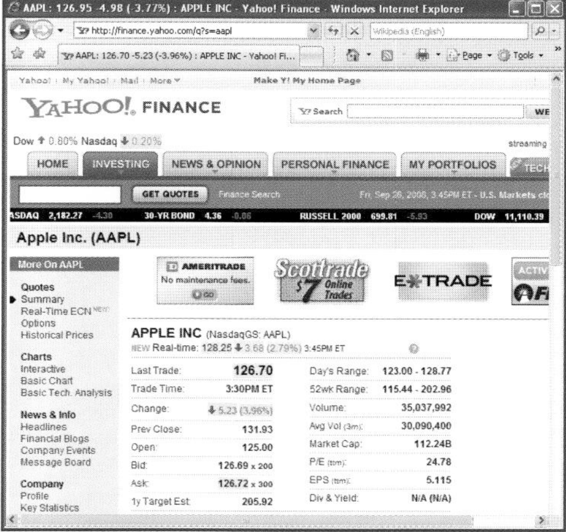

Figure 17.11 *In real-time (at 3:45 p.m. ET), Apple's stock price traded down to $128.25 per share, a 2.79% decrease on the day.*

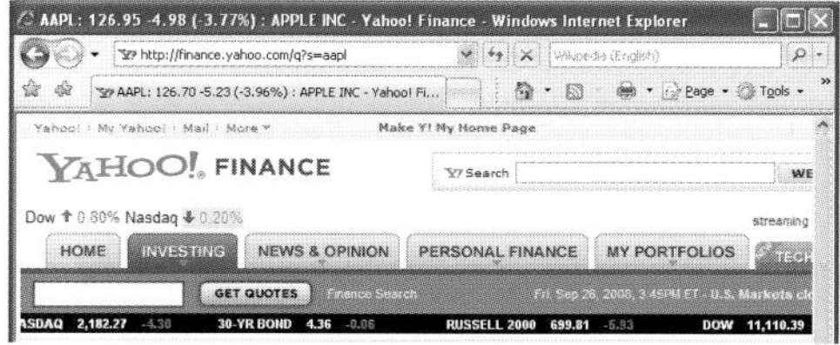

Figure 17.12 *The NASDAQ traded down to be –0.20% on the day.*

Yahoo! Finance

In the previous examples, a user action triggered the Ajax data exchange. However, that is not always necessary.

In the case of the Yahoo! Finance stock quote page **(Figure 17.10)**, and the quote pages on many other financial sites, the Ajax exchange is only one-way, from the server to the browser. The triggering event is a completed trade of the stock being viewed. (In some cases the data is delayed 20 minutes. And, in other cases, it's real-time, but the functionality is the same.)

When a stock is traded, if any of the data reported on that stock (price, price movement, volume traded, etc.) has changed, it gets updated on the page. Once again, because of the use of Ajax, the change happens without the page needing to be refreshed.

On the Yahoo! Finance pages, there is a colored background rectangle that flashes behind the new data to indicate a change. The rectangle is green if the change in the data is positive, and red if the change is negative **(Figure 17.11)**. This is true for all the data on the page, including the major market indices, such as the Dow and NASDAQ **(Figure 17.12)**.

✔ Tip

- It's interesting to note that Ajax has become more of a concept, as opposed to a specific use of JavaScript and XML. In other words, Web developers are creating the same Ajax-like user experience, without using Ajax technologies. In some instances, JavaScript has been replaced with VBScript for the client-side functionality. At other times, iFrames have been used to send and receive data asynchronously between the browser and the server (Google Maps was initially launched using iFrames). And, in still other cases, the data sent back from the server can be anything from HTML to plain text, using no XML at all.

RSS Basics

RSS *(Really Simple Syndication)* is a file format that allows Web sites to easily make their content available to readers, such as yourself. The content is packaged into what is called an *RSS feed* or *RSS channel* **(Figure 17.13)**. To see this content, you subscribe to an RSS feed. Then, you can view the RSS feed using an *RSS Reader* or an *RSS Aggregator*.

RSS and its orange icon have become quite ubiquitous, showing up on everything from espn.com and nytimes.com, to practically anyone's blog site. RSS allows you to subscribe to news articles **(Figure 17.14)**, calendar events, blog postings, podcasts, and even newly uploaded photos called photostreams.

RSS Readers are everywhere as well. Besides the many readers you can purchase, or download for free, both Google and Yahoo! offer free RSS Readers of their own. Even the major Web browsers now have built-in RSS Readers, making it more convenient than ever to subscribe to and view RSS feeds **(Figure 17.15)**. And once you've subscribed to an RSS feed, you won't need to go back to the Web site that provides the feed. You can simply open your RSS Reader and view all the most up-to-date content from that site, based on the feed to which you subscribed.

The RSS specification has a 10+ year history, with different versions, including RSS 0.91, RSS 1.0, and RSS 2.0. Currently, the trend is moving toward RSS 2.0, and that's what I'll be focusing on in this section.

✔ Tip

- A version of the RSS 2.0 specification can be found at: *http://cyber.law.harvard.edu/rss/rss.html*.

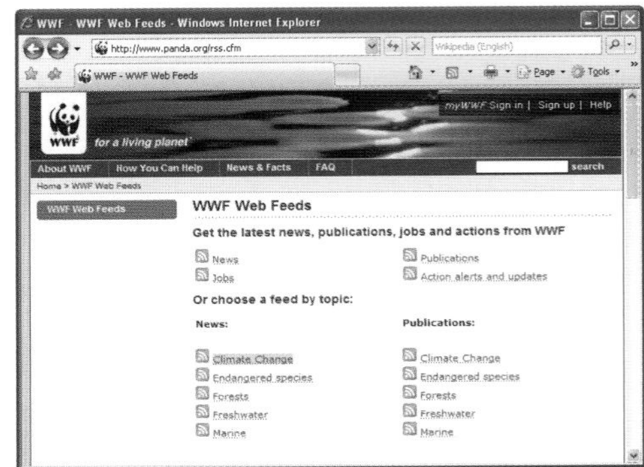

Figure 17.13 *This is the RSS subscription page on the WWF Web site. Clicking the* Climate Change *link shows the content for that RSS feed, and gives the user an option to subscribe to it.*

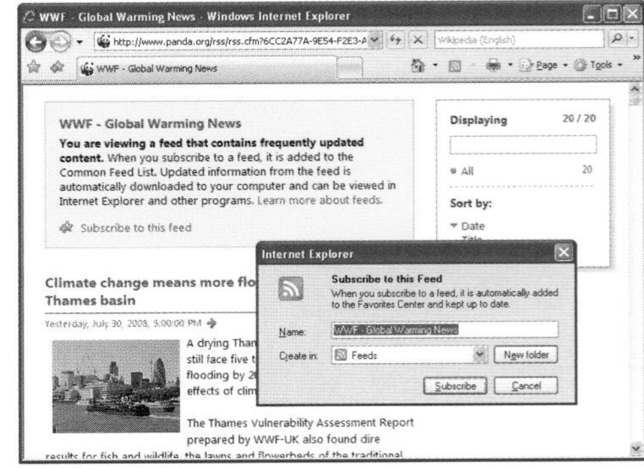

Figure 17.14 *Subscribing to the* Climate Change / Global Warming News *RSS feed, I can use my own RSS reader, or the one built into most browsers today.*

Figure 17.15 *The view of the Global Warming News RSS feed, as seen in Internet Explorer 7's RSS reader.*

```xml
<?xml version="1.0"?>
<rss version="2.0">

</rss>
```

Figure 17.16 *An RSS file is written in XML. Its root element is* rss *and contains a single attribute,* version.

```xml
<?xml version="1.0"?>
<rss version="2.0">
 <channel>
  <title>
    WWF - Global Warming News</title>
  <link>http://www.panda.org/</link>
  <description>News, publications
    and job feeds from WWF - the
    global conservation organization
  </description>
 </channel>
</rss>
```

Figure 17.17 *The* rss *element has one child element called* channel, *with three children* (title, link, *and* description), *and other optional child elements. The* channel *element contains content about the feed itself.*

```xml
<?xml version="1.0"?>
<rss version="2.0">
 <channel>
...
  <item>
   <title>Climate change means more
     floods for a drying Thames
     basin</title>
   <link>http://www.panda.org/about_
     wwf/what_we_do/climate_change/
     news/index.cfm?uNewsID=142541
   </link>
   <description>.,..A drying Thames
     river basin in the UK would
     still face five times the
     current risk of flooding by
     2080, ...</description>
   </item>
 </channel>
</rss>
```

Figure 17.18 *The actual content of an RSS feed is in the* item *element, a child of the* channel *element. It, like the* channel *element, has three children* (title, link, *and* description), *and other optional child elements as well.*

RSS Schema

The RSS 2.0 format is specified using XML. This means that when writing an RSS document, all the rules about writing XML documents apply *(see Chapter 1)*.

The root element of an RSS file is the `rss` element (`rss` is written in all lowercase, as XML is case-sensitive). It has a `version` attribute, and since I am writing for RSS 2.0, the value of the attribute must be "2.0" **(Figure 17.16)**.

The `rss` element has one child element, called `channel`. It is a required element and contains information describing the RSS feed. It has three required child elements: `title`, `link`, and `description` **(Figure 17.17)**. It also has a few optional child elements, including: `category` (which RSS Readers use to group feed content), and `image` (which is the URL of an image to be displayed when the feed is presented).

The most important child element of `channel` is the `item` element. Although technically optional, if there are no `item` elements, there is no content in the feed. The item element, like the `channel` element, has three required child elements: `title`, `link`, and `description` which describe the item content **(Figure 17.18)**. As well, it has a number of additional, optional child elements including, `enclosure` (which points to a media file such as a video or audio file that is related to the item).

✔ Tip

- There is no formal namespace for RSS 2.0. This is to support backward compatibility so that a version 0.91 or 0.92 file is also a valid 2.0 file. However, individuals have written their own schemas based on the specification. Some examples can be found at: *www.silmaril.ie/software/rss2.dtd* and *www.thearchitect.co.uk/schemas/rss-2_0.xsd*.

Extending RSS

Since RSS is an XML format, it is inherently extensible. Additional XML schemas have been written, called *RSS modules*, taking advantage of this extensibility. These extensions, declared through XML namespaces, add functionality to RSS, without modifying its core structure.

It's not enough, however, to just extend RSS. An RSS Reader must be aware of the extension and how to use the additional information. And, while new modules can be created, only the ones deemed interesting or significant will get developers to update their RSS Readers.

Here are three widely used extensions to RSS:

Media RSS module

Yahoo! Search developed an RSS module, called Media RSS. This module adds additional elements and attributes to better support multimedia files in RSS feeds **(Figure 17.19)**.

- The namespace declaration for the Media RSS module is defined to be **xmlns:media="http://search.yahoo.com/mrss/"**. Documentation about the module can be found at this URL as well.
- `media:content` is the primary element introduced by this module, and is typically a child of the RSS element `item`.
- It has many optional attributes, some of which are: `url`, `type`, `height`, `width`, `medium`, `framerate`, and `duration`.
- The module provides additional optional elements that are also typically children of `item`. Some of these are: `media:title`, `media:description`, `media:keywords`, `media:credit`, `media:category`, and `media:copyright`. Also, a few of these elements have attributes of their own.

```xml
<?xml version="1.0"?>
<rss version="2.0" xmlns:media=
  "http://search.yahoo.com/mrss/">
...
 <item>
  <title>Daylily</title>
  <link>http://www.flickr.com/photos
    /larigan/2721793930/</link>
  <description> ... Daylily"
  </description>
  <media:content url="http://farm4.
    static.flickr.com/3105/2721793930_
    e71f7a6ff7_m.jpg" type="image
    /jpeg" height="166" width="240"/>
  <media:title>Daylily</media:title>
  <media:description type="html">
    &lt;p&gt;Hemerocallis&lt;/p&gt;
  </media:description>
  <media:credit role="photographer">
    larigan.</media:credit>
  <media:category scheme=
    "urn:flickr:tags">yellow daylily
    hemerocallis larigan phamilton
  </media:category>
 </item>
...
```

Figure 17.19 *This excerpt is from an RSS feed of pictures (a photostream) from a photo sharing Web site called flickr.com. The RSS file uses the Media RSS module to include additional information about the picture, such as photographer credits and a set of categories that are flickr tags.*

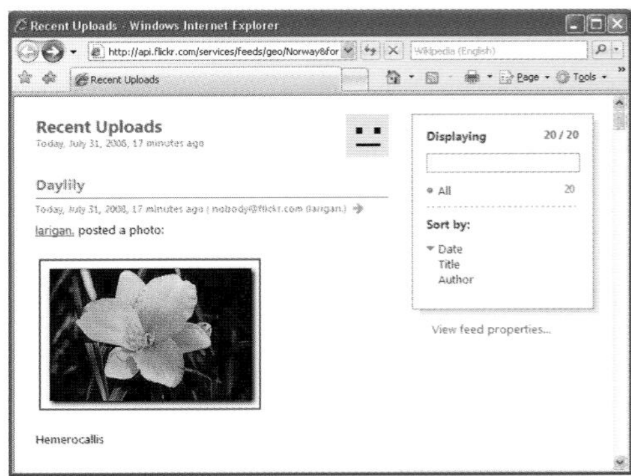

Figure 17.20 *This is the display of the RSS photostream feed, shown in Figure 17.19 above.*

blogChannel RSS module

The very first RSS module available for extending RSS 2.0 was written by Dave Winer, one

```xml
<?xml version="1.0"?>
<rss version="2.0" xmlns:itunes=
  "http://www.itunes.com/dtds
   /podcast-1.0.dtd">
...
 <item>
  <title>Nature: 31 July 2008</title>
  <itunes:duration>
    00:30:40</itunes:duration>
  <itunes:author>
    Nature</itunes:author>
   <itunes:subtitle>The origins of
     snake fangs, an ethane lake on
     Saturn's largest moon, the
     genetics of schizophrenia and
     an ancient Greek computer.
   </itunes:subtitle>
...
```

Figure 17.21 *An excerpt of an RSS podcast feed, from nature.com.*

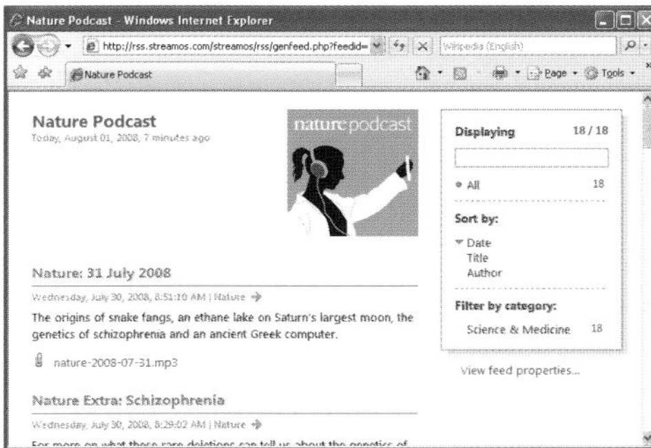

Figure 17.22 *The display in IE7s' RSS Reader of the RSS podcast stream shown in Figure 17.21 above.*

Figure 17.23 *The display in iTunes of the same RSS podcast stream referenced in Figure 17.22 above.*

of the pioneers of RSS itself. The blogChannel RSS module adds new elements to RSS, providing additional functionality for bloggers and their readers.

- The namespace declaration for the blogChannel RSS module is defined to be **xmlns:blogChannel="http://backend.userland.com/blogChannelModule"**. Documentation about the module can be found at this URL as well.
- The four new elements introduced by this module are children of the RSS `channel` element. They are: `blogChannel:blogRoll`, `blogChannel:mySubscriptions`, `blogChannel:blink`, and `blogChannel:changes`.

Podcasting and iTunes

A podcast, like any other RSS feed, is a syndicated group of files available for download or subscription **(Figure 17.21)**. You can use a standard RSS Reader for a podcast feed **(Figure 17.22)**, but most people use a *podcatching client*, the most popular of which is Apple's iTunes **(Figure 17.23)**.

In addition to standard RSS, there is an iTunes Podcasting namespace that better supports listing and placement on the iTunes interface.

- The declaration for the iTunes Podcasting namespace is defined to be **xmlns:itunes="http://www.itunes.com/dtds/podcast-1.0.dtd"**. Documentation about the namespace can be found at: *www.apple.com/itunes/whatson/podcasts/specs.html*.
- The new elements can often be children of both `channel` and `item`, some of which are: `itunes:author`, `itunes:block`, `itunes:duration`, `itunes:explicit`, `itunes:category`, `itunes:subtitle`, and `itunes:summary`.

SOAP and Web Services

SOAP stands for *Simple Object Access Protocol.* (Technically, with version 1.2, that definition was dropped, yet most people still use it anyway.) In either case, SOAP is an XML-based messaging framework. In the same way that a person can request a stock price or an item's inventory from a server, SOAP supports server-to-server communication. Specifically, it allows for platform- and language-independent communication between different applications, typically running on different servers.

SOAP's support of this type of interoperability has made it an important part of what the W3C calls a *Web Service.* A Web Service is a set of functions that can be accessed and executed over a network. While generic in its definition, a Web Service usually refers to the exchange of XML messages using the SOAP framework.

SOAP's core functionality is to support this exchange of XML messages from one application to another. SOAP is a lightweight protocol because, for the most part, a SOAP message is basically an XML file in a SOAP wrapper. And, this wrapper, often referred to as the SOAP envelope **(Figure 17.24)**, adds very little overhead to the messaging process.

The exchange of SOAP messages is most frequently done over the Internet via HTTP. A client application sends a SOAP message as an HTTP request, and the server sends back its SOAP message as an HTTP response. Because the SOAP message exchange works using HTTP, it allows for easier communication between computers on different networks than was previously possible. This is one of the biggest advantages of using SOAP over other remote communication frameworks.

✔ Tip

■ The SOAP Version 1.2 specification can be found at: *www.w3.org/TR/soap12.*

xml
```
<?xml version="1.0"?>
<soap12:Envelope xmlns:soap12="http://
  www.w3.org/2003/05/soap-envelope">
 <soap12:Body>

...

 </soap12:Body>
</soap12:Envelope>
```

Figure 17.24 *The SOAP wrapper, or envelope, is actually two elements:* Envelope *and* Body. *Notice that the* Envelope *element is qualified with the SOAP namespace prefix* soap12:.

```xml
<?xml version="1.0"?>
<soap12:Envelope xmlns:soap12="http://
  www.w3.org/2003/05/soap-envelope">
 <soap12:Body>
  <sayHello xmlns="http://
    www.kehogo.com/ns/hello">
   <name>Kevin</name>
  </sayHello>
 </soap12:Body>
</soap12:Envelope>
```

Figure 17.25 *This SOAP request message is calling the procedure* sayHello *and passing the* name *parameter with the value "Kevin."*

```xml
<?xml version="1.0" encoding="utf-8"?>
<soap12:Envelope xmlns:soap="http12://
  www.w3.org/2003/05/soap-envelope"
  xmlns:xsi="http://
  www.w3.org/2001/XMLSchema-instance"
  xmlns:xsd="http://
  www.w3.org/2001/XMLSchema">
 <soap12:Body>
  <sayHelloResponse xmlns="http://
    www.kehogo.com/ns/hello">
   <sayHelloResult>Hello Kevin (and
     World). It's Sunday, September
     21, 2008, 10:20 PM, and I've
     been expecting you.
   </sayHelloResult>
  </sayHelloResponse>
 </soap12:Body>
</soap12:Envelope>
```

Figure 17.26 *This SOAP message is the response to the request message in Figure 17.25 above. It is returning the result of the* sayHello *procedure, using the* sayHelloResponse *element.*

SOAP Message Schema

The SOAP framework is based on the XML language, which means that all the rules about writing XML documents apply to SOAP messages. The root element of a SOAP message is the `Envelope` element (written in title case). It must declare the SOAP namespace, which defines the elements and attributes of a SOAP message. There is no standard namespace prefix, so I use `soap12:` *(see Figure 17.24).*

A SOAP message has an optional `Header` element which, if present, must be the first immediate child of the `Envelope` element. It allows application-specific communication between the client and the server, beyond the actual SOAP message itself.

The `Body` element is a required child element of the `Envelope` element and contains the actual SOAP message content. In a request message, the `Body` element's children correspond to the operation being called, and its grandchildren correspond to the operation's parameters **(Figure 17.25)**. In a response message, the word "Response" is typically appended to the `Body` element's children (the operation elements) and its grandchildren are the operation's result values **(Figure 17.26)**. The `Body` element must be the first, or second, child element of the `Envelope` element, depending on whether or not the `Header` element is present.

✔ Tips

- Notice in Figures 17.25 and 17.26 that the descendant elements of the `Body` element are namespace-qualified using the URI: *www.kehogo.com/ns/hello*. This will often be the case, as the elements of your Web Service will likely not belong to the SOAP namespace itself.
- The SOAP-based Web Service shown in these examples can be found on my Web site at: *www.kehogo.com/examples/hello_world.asmx*.

WSDL

WSDL or *Web Services Description Language*, is an XML language for describing how to interface with Web Services. Where SOAP provides the message exchange framework for a Web Service, WSDL (often pronounced "wizdel") documents the messages that can be sent.

WSDL is not needed for the exchange of Web Service messages—this can happen using SOAP exclusively. However, with WSDL, requesting applications are given technical information about the Web Service which supports an easier, more automated, and less error prone exchange.

WSDL Schema

A WSDL document is an XML document, and its root element is `definitions` (written in all lowercase). You'll need to declare the WSDL namespace and its binding namespace for SOAP. You may also need to declare the XML Schema namespace, and the namespace in which you have defined the elements for your Web Service **(Figure 17.27)**.

The `definitions` elements has five major child elements (in sequence): `types`, `message`, `portType`, `binding`, and `service`. The center hub of them all is the `portType` element. It describes the available operations and the messages each expects **(Figure 17.28)**. It is the equivalent of a description of the application's library, and each operation contains the equivalent of a list of specific function calls.

The `types` and `message` elements work hand in hand **(Figure 17.29)**. The `message` element identifies the messages each operation expects, and the parameters each message will contain. These parameters reference the elements defined for your Web Service, and their definitions are found in the `types` element.

The `binding` element defines the transport protocol of the SOAP message exchange (which is typically done via HTTP, but can be done via SMTP, FTP, or other transport protocols).

```xml
<?xml version="1.0"?>
<definitions xmlns="http://
    schemas.xmlsoap.org/wsdl/"
   xmlns:soap12="http://
    schemas.xmlsoap.org/wsdl/soap12/"
...
```

Figure 17.27 *The WSDL root element contains namespace declarations for WSDL and for binding with SOAP. As the default namespace, the WSDL namespace won't require a namespace prefix.*

```xml
<portType name="hello_world">
 <operation name="sayHelloRequest">
  <input message="tns:hello_in"/>
  <output message="tns:hello_out"/>
 </operation>
</portType>
```

Figure 17.28 *In this excerpt, the* portType *element is defining the* sayHelloRequest *operation of this Web Service. It is expecting an input message called* hello_in, *and will return a response message called* hello_out, *both of which are defined below.*

```xml
<types>
 <xs:schema
   targetNamespace="http://
   www.kehogo.com/ns/hello">
  <xs:element name="sayHelloRequest">
   <xs:complexType>
    <xs:sequence>
     <xs:element name="name"
       type="xs:string"/>
     </xs:sequence>
...
</types>

<message name="hello_in">
  <part name="parameters"
    element="tns:sayHelloRequest"/>
 </message>
 <message name="hello_out">
  <part name="parameters"
    element="tns:sayHelloResponse"/>
</message>
```

Figure 17.29 *The* types *element defines the* sayHelloRequest *and* sayHelloResponse *(not shown) elements used by the Web Service. These XML elements are parameters in the* hello_in *and* hello_out *messages respectively.*

```
x m l
<binding name="hello_binding12"
  type="tns:hello_world">
 <soap12:binding transport="http://
   schemas.xmlsoap.org/soap/http"/>
  <operation name="sayHelloRequest">
   <soap12:operation soapAction=
     "http://www.kehogo.com/ns/hello/
     sayHello">
   <input>
    <soap12:body use="literal"/>
   </input>
   <output>
    <soap12:body use="literal"/>
   </output>
  </operation>
 </binding>
```

Figure 17.30 *This* binding *element says to use SOAP via HTTP, and that the SOAP* body *will contain the XML Schema-defined elements from the WSDL* types *element.*

```
x m l
<service name="xml2e_example">
...
 <port name="hello_world12"
   binding="tns:hello_binding12">
  <soap12:address
    location="http://www.kehogo.com/
    examples/hello_world.asmx"/>
 </port>
</service>
```

Figure 17.31 *The* service *element connects the* portType *element and the* binding *element, effectively defining the public use of the Web Service.*

Then, for each named operation, you define how the messages appear inside the SOAP `body` element. For example, `use="literal"` means to use the schema-defined elements from the WSDL `types` element **(Figure 17.30)**.

Finally, the `service` element puts together the pieces of the Web Service by connecting the `portType`, defined in Figure 17.28, with the `binding`, defined in Figure 17.30. And, it identifies the public URI of the Web Service itself **(Figure 17.31)**.

UDDI

The final part of what are considered to be the three standards of a Web Service is called UDDI (*Universal Description, Discovery, and Integration*). It was written as an XML-based registry of SOAP-based Web Services, and provides each service's corresponding WSDL file to applications requesting such information.

A public registry called the UDDI Business Registry (UBR) was announced in September 2000. It was created as a proof of concept, with the intention of improving the UDDI specification, as well as the applications that used it.

In January 2006, major supporters of the UBR announced that they would no longer publish to the registry. While still providing Web Services internally and to clients, these organizations felt that the UBR had served its purpose, and it has since become obsolete.

✔ Tips

- The WSDL file from these examples (and its corresponding SOAP Web Service) can be found on my Web site at: *www.kehogo.com/examples/hello_world.wsdl*.
- These pages have used WSDL Version 1.1. Its specification is at: *www.w3.org/TR/wsdl*, and its XML Schema is at: *http://schemas.xmlsoap.org/wsdl/*. In June 2007, the W3C released version 2.0, and its adoption success has yet to be determined.

KML Basics

KML (*Keyhole Markup Language*) is an XML markup language for annotating maps using placemarks, polygonal shapes, paths, descriptions, and the like. It was initially developed for use with Google Earth (an application often run on your local computer) **(Figure 17.32)**. Since then, it has been adopted for use by many other map-related applications.

Figure 17.32 *Google Earth's interface zoomed in to focus on the Mediterranean Sea.*

Annotating a map using KML (like an XML file) can be done by hand in an XML editor. It's more likely, however, that you would generate a KML file by using one of the KML mapping tools. You would do this by first annotating a map in Google Earth or Google Maps online at: *http://maps.google.com/* **(Figure 17.33)**. Then, you would copy the KML generated by the tool to a text editor and save the file with a `.kml` extension. If you prefer, you can edit that file to gain even more control over the annotation elements that were generated by the tool.

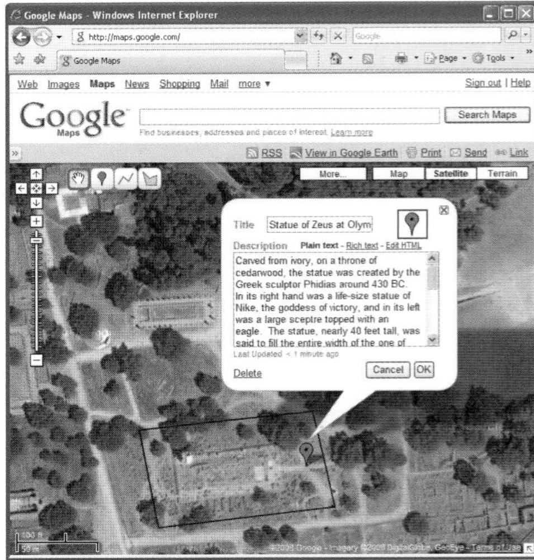

Figure 17.33 *A placemark and polygonal outline for the Statue of Zeus at Olympia using Google Maps.*

There are other applications that use KML. For example, you can *geotag* (add geographic information to something) your photos on the photo sharing site, flickr.com. Then you can share those photos using KML. When this KML file is viewed, each photo that you geotagged would be placed in that location on the map **(Figure 17.34)**.

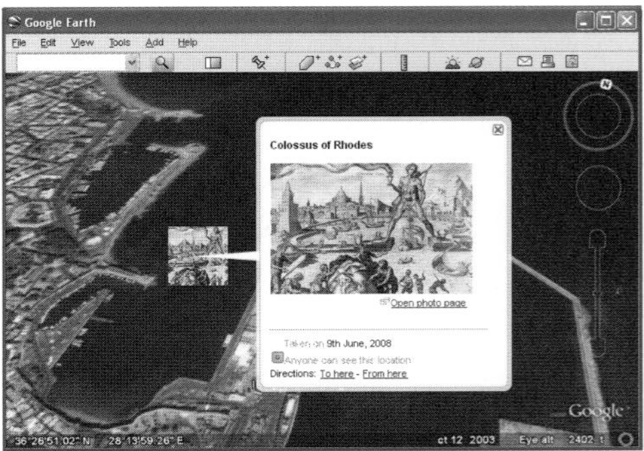

Figure 17.34 *A geotagged photo from flickr.com.*

✔ Tips

- You can download a copy of Google Earth from: *http://earth.google.com/*.
- KML Version 2.2 is an official standard of the OGC (*Open Geospatial Consortium*), an international standards organization similar to the W3C. You can read about this version of KML and download the specification at: *www.opengeospatial.org/standards/kml*.

```
xml
<?xml version="1.0"?>
<kml xmlns="http://
  www.opengis.net/kml/2.2">
 <Placemark>
  <name>Great Pyramid of Giza</name>
  <Point>
   <coordinates>
    31.134224,29.979769,0
...
```

Figure 17.35 *A KML file with a* Placemark *element.*

Figure 17.36 *The KML output from Figure 17.35 as seen in Google Earth.*

```
xml
...
<Style id="purple_poly">
 <PolyStyle>
   <color>669900aa</color>
...
<Style id="arrow_icon">
 <IconStyle>
  <color>ff33aa22</color>
...
```

Figure 17.37 *Adding placemark styles for a purple polygon for the pyramid, and a green arrow instead of the default yellow pushpin.*

Figure 17.38 *The KML output from Figure 17.37 as seen in Google Earth.*

A Simple KML File

The root element of a KML file is the `kml` element (written in all lowercase). As part of the root element, the kml namespace is declared, and is typically done without the `kml:` prefix.

Placemarks

The most common annotation used with kml files is a *placemark*. The most common placemark is a pushpin graphic marking a location. When used in this manner, the `Placemark` element will often have the child elements: `name`, and `Point` (`Point` is the longitude, latitude, and altitude above the surface of the placemark on the map) **(Figure 17.35)**.

Placemarks can also be styled using a `styleURL` element, which can refer to the URL of a kml style document, or an inline style defined with a `Style` element. In either case, the `Style` element will have child elements for each type of object it is styling, such as `IconStyle` or `PolyStyle` (which is used below). Within each object style, there can be child elements for `color`, `scale`, `icon`, and others.

In addition to the pushpin, placemarks can also be lines, polygonal shapes, and even 3D objects. A polygonal shape element (`Polygon`), must have an outer boundary child element (`outerBoundaryIs`), which contains the longitude, latitude, and altitude of a minimum of four points, thereby creating a closed shape. And, as noted above, polygons can be styled using the `PolyStyle` element **(Figure 17.37)**.

✔ Tips

- The XML Schema for the KML language can be found at: *http://schemas.opengis.net/kml/2.2.0/ogckml22.xsd*.
- A detailed KML file of all the wonders can be found at: *www.kehogo.com/examples/wonders.kml*. You can view it in Google Maps, or you can type this URL directly into the Google Maps search field.

ODF and OOXML

Both ODF (*Open Document format*) and OOXML (*Office Open XML*) are file formats for office productivity documents, such as spreadsheets, presentations, word processing, and more. They were both started at large corporations, and have since been published as open standards by organizations, like the W3C.

Both standards create a separation between content and presentation, and store these elements in separate files. Consequently, a single document generated by either format is actually compressed and contains multiple files and folders. Besides binary data, such as images and audio, the format for these files is XML.

The fact that office productivity applications can store their data as XML is a monumental change. Instead of the proprietary formats used just a few years ago, this data is now stored in an open, platform-independent format. This provides greater accessibility to the underlying data, and opens up the possibility of creating other complementary tools and applications.

ODF

In 2002, Sun Microsystems began working with OASIS (an international standards organization) to create an open standard based on the XML format used by OpenOffice.org (an open source office productivity suite). In 2005, ODF was approved as an OASIS standard, and in 2006, it became an ISO (*International Organization for Standardization*) standard.

ODF packages its files and folders using the JAR file format. Besides data files, each document's information is stored in one of a few XML files, with `content.xml` being the file that contains the actual content **(Figure 17.39)**.

There are many applications that support the ODF standard. Of course, OpenOffice.org's default format is ODF. As well, Lotus Symphony, WordPerfect, and Google Docs all have extensive support for the standard.

```xml
<?xml version="1.0" encoding="UTF-8"?>
<office:document-content xmlns:office=
  "urn:oasis:names:tc:opendocument:
  xmlns:office:1.0" xmlns:style="
  urn:oasis:names:tc:opendocument:
  xmlns:style:1.0" xmlns:text="
  urn:oasis:names:tc:opendocument:
  xmlns:text:1.0" xmlns:table="urn:
  oasis:names:tc:opendocument:xmlns:
  table:1.0" xmlns:draw="urn:oasis:
  names:tc:opendocument:xmlns:
  drawing:1.0" xmlns:fo="urn:oasis:
  names:tc:opendocument:xmlns:
  xsl-fo-compatible:1.0"
  ...
  office:version="1.1">
 <office:scripts/>
 <office:font-face-decls>
  <style:font-face style:name=
  "Tahoma1" svg:font-family="Tahoma"/>
  <style:font-face style:name="
  Times New Roman" svg:
  font-family="&apos;Times New
  Roman&apos;" style:font-family-
  generic="roman" style:font-
  pitch="variable"/>
...
 </office:font-face-decls>
 <office:automatic-styles/>
 <office:body>
  <office:text>
   <text:sequence-decls>
    <text:sequence-decl
      text:display-outline-level="0"
      text:name="Illustration"/>
    <text:sequence-decl text:display-
      outline-level="0" text:name=
      "Table"/>
    <text:sequence-decl text:display-
      outline-level="0" text:name=
      "Text"/>
    <text:sequence-decl text:display-
      outline-level="0" text:name=
      "Drawing"/>
   </text:sequence-decls>
   <text:p text:style-name="
     Standard">Hello World!</text:p>
  </office:text>
 </office:body>
</office:document-content>
```

Figure 17.39 *The* content.xml file *from an ODF package. This file, along with other XML files in the package, produces a word processing document that has Hello World! in it.*

```xml
<?xml version="1.0" encoding="UTF-8"
  standalone="yes"?>
<w:document xmlns:ve="http://
  schemas.openxmlformats.org/
  markup-compatibility/2006"
  xmlns:o="urn:schemas-microsoft-com
  :office:office" xmlns:r="http://
  schemas.openxmlformats.org/
  officeDocument/2006/
  relationships" xmlns:m="http://
  schemas.openxmlformats.org/
  officeDocument/2006/math"
  xmlns:v="urn:schemas-microsoft-com:
  vml" xmlns:wp="http://schemas.
  openxmlformats.org/drawingml/2006/
  wordprocessingDrawing"
  xmlns:w10="urn:schemas-microsoft-
  com:office:word" xmlns:w="http://
  schemas.openxmlformats.org/
  wordprocessingml/2006/main"
  xmlns:wne="http://schemas.
  microsoft.com/office/word/2006/
  wordml">
 <w:body>
  <w:p w:rsidR="00A27C68"
    w:rsidRDefault="00A27C68">
   <w:r>
    <w:t>Hello World!</w:t>
   </w:r>
  </w:p>
  <w:sectPr w:rsidR="00A27C68">
   <w:pgSz w:w="12240" w:h="15840"/>
   <w:pgMar w:top="1440"
     w:right="1440" w:bottom="1440"
     w:left="1440" w:header="720"
     w:footer="720" w:gutter="0"/>
   <w:cols w:space="720"/>
   <w:docGrid w:linePitch="360"/>
  </w:sectPr>
 </w:body>
</w:document>
```

Figure 17.40 *The* document.xml file *from an OOXML package. Like the example in Figure 17.39, this file, along with other XML files in the package, produces a word processing document that has Hello World! in it. And, while you may be able to understand both files, manually creating either one is not something I'd recommend trying.*

OOXML

In 2005, Microsoft announced that it would work with Ecma International (a standards organization) to create an open standard based on the XML format used with the Office 2003 suite. In 2006, OOXML was approved as an Ecma standard (a 6,000 plus page specification!), and in 2008, it became an ISO standard.

OOXML packages its files and folders using the ZIP file format. Unlike ODF, each document's information is stored in differently named XML files, based on the custom markup language in which it was written, such as WordProcessingML **(Figure 17.40)**, SpreadsheetML, PresentationML, and others.

There are many applications on the market that support OOXML. Of course, it is Office 2007's default format. WordPerfect has extensive support for OOXML, and Apple's iWork suite offers read-only support. There is also OpenXML Writer, an open source text editor created specifically for working with OOXML.

Comparison and Controversy

There is controversy over the process by which OOXML became an ISO standard. You can search online and find different opinions from each of the standard's camps. As well, you will find information about which standard will "win," or if there will be a winner at all.

Many think that because of OOXML's strong tie to Microsoft Office, ODF has a long row to hoe. Others think that OOXML's specification is so bloated (nearly eight times longer than ODF's), that creating compliant applications and tools is simply too cumbersome. To complicate matters, earlier this year, Microsoft announced that it would add native support for ODF in Office 2007's upcoming Service Pack.

Regardless of the outcome, with their underlying data model changing to XML, productivity applications are clearly entering a new era in their product lifecycle.

eBooks, ePub, and More

In 1971, Michael Hart began making available free, electronic text copies of public domain books, including the Bible and the works of Shakespeare and Mark Twain. Since 1971, Hart's vision (*Project Gutenberg*) has accumulated more than 25,000 free electronic books.

Electronic books (also referred to as eBooks or e-Books), are books that use electronic files instead of paper. eBooks can be read on personal computers or special eBook readers, which have features such as "dog-earring" pages, highlighting book content, and looking up words in an included dictionary. And, while the market for eBooks is nothing compared to the market for paper books, the industry is nevertheless growing rapidly.

ePub

Besides plain text, eBooks can be published in many different formats. And, the format war has certainly begun. One format that has gained large support in the electronic publishing industry is *ePub*. Its specification is an open standard of the IDPF, the industry's standards organization. As an XML-based format, ePub uses XHTML for the book's content, and XML for the book's structure, table of contents, etc. Also, like the office productivity formats, these files are then compressed using a ZIP format for final delivery.

A compressed ePub file contains a few required files, and one required folder. The first required file must be named `mimetype`, and must contain the exact single line of text shown in Figure 17.41, describing the MIME type of the ePub file. It literally must be the first file in the compressed ePub file, or the ePub file will not be considered valid.

The one required folder is named `META-INF`, and it must contain an XML file named `container.xml` **(Figure 17.42)**. Its purpose is to tell the eBook reader where to find the

```
mimetype
application/epub+zip
```

Figure 17.41 *The contents of the* mimetype *file. This file never changes, and must always be the first file in the compressed ePub file.*

```
xml
<?xml version="1.0"?>
<container version="1.0" xmlns="
  urn:oasis:names:tc:opendocument:
  xmlns:container">
 <rootfiles>
  <rootfile
    full-path="content.opf"
    media-type="application/oebps-
    package+xml"/>
 </rootfiles>
</container>
```

Figure 17.42 *This is the* container.xml *file. The* rootfile *element identifies the path to the file that describes the eBook's structure. Although you can change its content (unlike the* mimetype *file), unless you choose to reorganize the remaining files, there's really no purpose in doing so.*

```xml
<?xml version="1.0" encoding="UTF-8"?>
<package xmlns="http://
  www.idpf.org/2007/opf" ...>
 <metadata>
  <dc:creator>
    Goldberg, Kevin Howard</dc:creator>
  <dc:title>Seven Wonders of the
    Ancient World</dc:title>
  <dc:language>en</dc:language>
  <dc:identifier id="ePUBid">
    wonders_v01</dc:identifier>
 </metadata>
 <manifest>
  <item id="ncx" href="toc.ncx"
    media-type="text/xml"/>
  <item id="main"
    href="ancient_wonders.htm"
    media-type="application/xhtml+xml"/>
  <item id="herodotus"
    href="images/herodotus.jpg"
    media-type="image/jpeg"/>
 </manifest>
 <spine toc="ncx">
  <itemref idref="main"/>
 </spine>
</package>
```

Figure 17.43 *The* content.opf *file describes the eBook structure and the files that it contains.*

```xml
<?xml version="1.0" encoding="UTF-8"?>
<ncx xmlns="http://www.daisy.org/
  z3986/2005/ncx/" version="2005-1"
  xml:lang="en">
...
 <docTitle>
  <text>Seven Wonders of the Ancient
    World</text>
 </docTitle>
 <docAuthor>
  <text>Goldberg, Kevin Howard</text>
 </docAuthor>
 <navMap>
  <navPoint id="navpoint-1"
    playOrder="1">
   <navLabel>
    <text>Intro</text>
   </navLabel>
   <content
     src="ancient_wonders.htm"/>
  </navPoint>
 </navMap>
</ncx>
```

Figure 17.44 *This* .ncx *file is essentially some eBook metadata, along with a linkable table of contents.*

file that describes the eBook's structure. This information is found in the `rootfile` element's `full-path` attribute.

The `container.xml` file, the `META-INF` folder, and the `mimetype` file, are all written according to one of ePub's three sub-specifications, the OCF (*OEBPS Container Format*), which is derived from the Open eBook format.

The file referred to in `container.xml` that describes the eBook's structure is often called `content.opf`. It is written according to the second of ePub's three sub-specifications, the OPF (*Open Package Format*). This `.opf` file is required and has the following elements: `metadata` (containing metadata about the eBook), `manifest` (containing a list of all the files in the ePub compressed file), and `spine` (containing the order in which the files are to be presented) **(Figure 17.43)**.

In most cases, there is also an `.ncx` file, which contains the table of contents. It is referred to by the `.opf` file in both the `manifest` and the `spine`'s `toc` attribute. It contains elements for the document title and author, as well as a navMap element, which describes the content's play order **(Figure 17.44)**.

The final required file is the eBook's content itself, which is governed by ePub's third sub-specification, the OPS (*Open Publication Structure*). This can be a single file with bookmarks concluding each chapter, or each chapter can be in a separate file. The content is typically written in XHTML Version 1.1 (without forms, server-side image maps, events, and scripting), and can use a subset of CSS 2.1.

✔ Tip

- The ePub format is an open standard comprised of three other IDPF standards. Information about all three standards can be found at: *www.idpf.org/2007/ops/OPS_2.0_final_spec.html.*

Tools for XML in Practice

Besides an XML editor and a browser, there are some other tools that will be useful in working with this chapter's examples. Note: When it comes to creating your own examples, this list is inadequate. So, unless you like to tinker, I recommend finding a book or an online tutorial.

Ajax

To see Ajax in action, go to the examples listed in the book, or refer to the ones on my Web site. If you want to edit the examples, or create some of your own, you'll need an HTML/JavaScript editor. You'll also need a Web server on which to run the HTML and JavaScript that you create. Using a scripting language (such as .asp) is not required, but it is usually how the server-side script is created.

RSS

To view RSS at work, you can use your browser's built-in RSS Reader (most current browsers have one). You could also use the Yahoo! (*http://my.yahoo.com/*) or Google (*www.google.com/ig*) custom Home pages, or simply download an RSS Reader from the Internet.

If you want to create an RSS feed of your own, you'll need an XML editor to start. You'll also need a Web server on which to serve your RSS feed. You'll probably want to use one of the book's examples as a starting point (or a feed you can find online), and edit that. When you think you're ready, you can validate your feed at: *http://aggregator.userland.com/validator*.

SOAP and WSDL

To experience SOAP or WSDL, you'll need a client application. Some of the XML editors listed in Appendix A support SOAP/WSDL. You could also use a free online tool, such as *www.soapclient.com/soaptest.html*. Then, use the examples on the book's companion Web site.

To create a Web Service, I used the Microsoft .NET Web Service template and then modified it using an editor. Other scripting languages provide Web Service templates as well.

KML

To view the results of a KML file, download Google Earth at: *http://earth.google.com/*. Then, use the examples on my Web site.

If you want to edit my examples, or create some of your own, you can use Google Maps, Google Earth, or edit directly in an XML editor.

ODF and OOXML

To see the inner workings of an ODF or an OOXML file, you'll need to create a document in that format. For ODF, one option is to use the productivity suite at *www.openoffice.org/*. For OOXML, some options include Microsoft Office 2007, or OpenXML Writer at *www.openxml.biz/OpenXMLWriter.html*.

Once you've created a file in either format, rename the file's extension to `.zip`. Then, open that file using a ZIP application. When opened, you will see that it contains a number of XML files as described in this chapter, and you can extract and view them all as you like.

ePub

To read the book in an ePub file, you'll need to download an eBook in the ePub format, as well as an eBook reader, such as Mobipocket Reader at: *www.mobipocket.com/en/DownloadSoft/*, or Adobe Digital Editions at: *www.adobe.com/products/digitaleditions/*.

To see the inner mechanics of an ePub file (just as with files in the ODF and OOXML formats), rename it with a `.zip` extension and open it using a ZIP application to see its contents. You can extract and view any of the component files. You can also edit any file and see your changes in an eBook reader. To do so, after editing, recompress all the ePub's contents with a ZIP application, and then rename the compressed file with an `.ePub` extension.

APPENDICES

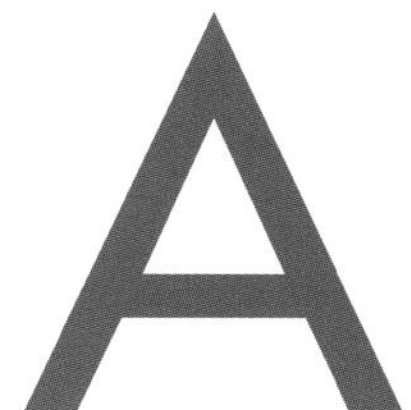

XML Tools

When the first edition of this book was written, many people were writing XML using simple text editors, such as Notepad for Windows, and TextEdit for the Mac. Then, in order to validate or transform their XML, they were using command-line or Web-based applications, neither of which were necessarily easy to use or easy to fit into a business workflow.

Luckily, things have changed. For starters, the current Web browsers (including Mozilla Firefox, Internet Explorer, Opera, and Safari), have support for XML and XSLT. You also have the option to choose from dozens of XML editors that you can download from the Internet and use right now. Many of these editors are free to use, and some of the free ones are actually very good.

Most of the XML editors today can validate your XML using both DTD and XML Schema, and process your XML with XSLT style sheets. Also, most have additional features, including support for XSLT 2.0 / XPath 2.0, XSL-FO, XQuery, and more.

This appendix is not an exhaustive list of the XML editors or tools available today. And, since it's certainly possible that a good editor or tool was overlooked, or one has recently been released, I will keep a running list of editors and tools on the companion Web site for your reference.

XML Editors

The minimum requirements to include an XML editor in this list are as follows: be able to check for well-formed XML; validate against both a DTD and an XML Schema; perform an XSLT transformation; and support the Unicode character set (for the Greek text in the examples). There are a few other excellent XML editors, listed on page 248, if none of these are well-suited for you.

Feature	XML Copy Editor	EditiX XML Editor	Altova XMLSpy	oXygen XML Editor
Operating Systems supported:				
◆ Windows	Yes	Yes	Yes	Yes
◆ Macintosh	Yes[1]	Yes	No	Yes
◆ Unix / Linux	Yes	Yes	No	Yes
Free Version	Yes	Yes	No	No
Retail Version	No	Yes[2]	Yes[2]	Yes[2]
XSLT Preview	No	Yes[3]	Yes	Yes
XSL-FO Support	No	Yes[3]	Yes	Yes
XSLT 2.0 / XPath 2.0 Support	No	Yes	Yes	Yes
XQuery 1.0 Support	No	Yes	Yes	Yes
SOAP / WSDL Support	No	No	Yes	Yes
Auto-completion	Yes	Yes	Yes	Yes
Format Document	Yes	Yes	Yes	Yes
Collapse / Expand XML	Yes	No	Yes	Yes
Search & Replace:				
◆ Basic	Yes	Yes	Yes	Yes
◆ Multiple Documents	Yes	No	Yes	Yes
◆ Within Folders	No	No	Yes	Yes
Spell Check	Yes	No	Yes	Yes
Grid / Tree View of Content	No	Yes	Yes	Yes
Auto-creation of DTD	No	Yes[3]	Yes	Yes
Auto-creation of XML Schema	No	Yes[3]	Yes	Yes
Convert DTD to XML Schema	No	Yes	Yes	Yes
Convert XML Schema to DTD	No	No	Yes	No
Generate Sample from DTD	No	Yes[2]	Yes	No
Generate Sample from XML Schema	No	Yes[2]	Yes	Yes
New File Templates	Yes	Yes	Yes	Yes

1. The application should compile from the source code.
2. The retail versions all have free trial periods.
3. These features are only available in the retail version.

XML Copy Editor

URL: *http://xml-copy-editor.sourceforge.net*

OS Support: Windows, Unix / Linux, Macintosh (should compile from source code)

Version: 1.2.0

Free Version: Yes

Additional Features:

- Can handle files >10MB at an appropriate speed.
- Import / export Microsoft Word
- XML Tag locking
- RELAX NG validation
- Background validation
- For more info: *http://xml-copy-editor.sourceforge.net/index.php?page=features*

EditiX XML Editor

URL: *www.editix.com*

OS Support: Windows, Unix / Linux, Macintosh

Version: 2008, Service Pack 5

Free Version: Yes (and retail version)

Additional Features:

- Open XML / Open Document support
- XML file compare
- DTD / XML Schema documentation generator
- XPath builder / editor
- XSLT editor / debugger
- For more info: *www.editix.com/features.html*

Altova XMLSpy

URL: *www.altova.com/xmlspy*

OS Support: Windows

Version: 2008, Release 2

Free Version: No (retail version has free trial)

Additional Features:

- Open XML / Open Document support
- XML file compare
- WSDL editor and SOAP client /debugger
- XQuery editor / debugger / profiler
- XSLT 1.0/2.0 editor / debugger / profiler
- RELAX NG validation
- Relational / XML database integration
- For more info: *www.altova.com/matrix_x.html*

oXygen XML Editor

URL: *www.oxygenxml.com*

OS Support: Windows, Unix / Linux, Macintosh

Version: 9.3

Free Version: No (retail version has free trial)

Additional Features:

- Open XML / Open Document support
- XML file compare
- WSDL editor and SOAP client /debugger
- XQuery editor / debugger / profiler
- XSLT 1.0/2.0 editor / debugger / profiler
- RELAX NG validation
- Relational / XML database integration
- For more info: *www.oxygenxml.com/feature_matrix.html*

Additional XML Editors

XMLwriter XML Editor

URL: *www.xmlwriter.net*

OS Support: Windows

Version: 2.7

Free Version: No (retail version has free trial)

Additional Features:

- For more info: *www.xmlwriter.net/xmlwriter/features.shtml*

Stylus Studio

URL: *www.stylusstudio.com*

OS Support: Windows

Version: Release 2

Free Version: No (retail version has free trial)

Additional Features:

- For more info: *www.stylusstudio.com/xml_feature_overview.html*

Liquid XML Studio

URL: *www.liquid-technologies.com*

OS Support: Windows

Version: 2008 (v6)

Free Version: Yes (and retail version)

Additional Features:

- For more info: *www.liquid-technologies.com/Product_XmlStudio_Features.aspx*

WMHelp XMLPad

URL: *www.wmhelp.com/xmlpad3.htm*

OS Support: Windows

Version: 3.0.2a

Free Version: Yes

Additional Features:

- For more info: *www.wmhelp.com/xmlpad32.htm*

XMLmind XML Editor

URL: *www.xmlmind.com/xmleditor*

OS Support: Windows, Unix / Linux, Macintosh

Version: 4.1

Free Version: Yes (and retail version)

Additional Features:

- For more info: *www.xmlmind.com/xmleditor/features.html*

XML Tools and Resources

This list of XML tools is just a sampling of what you can find by searching the Web. The specifications are listed in the order in which they are discussed in the book.

Validation and Conversion Tools

- **XML Validator**
  www.stg.brown.edu/service/xmlvalid/
- **DTD Validator**
  www.validome.org/grammar/
- **XML Schema Validator**
  www.w3.org/2001/03/webdata/xsv
- **Convert XML to DTD / XML Schema; Convert DTD to XML Schema**
  www.hitsw.com/xml_utilities/

Specifications

- **XML 1.0**
  www.w3.org/TR/xml/
- **XSLT 1.0**
  www.w3.org/TR/xslt
- **XPath 1.0**
  www.w3.org/TR/xpath
- **XSL-FO (the same as XSL 1.1)**
  www.w3.org/TR/xsl/
- **DTD** (within the XML spec)
  www.w3.org/TR/xml/
- **XML Schema**
  www.w3.org/TR/xmlschema-0/
- **XML Namespaces**
  www.w3.org/TR/xml-names/
- **XSLT 2.0**
  www.w3.org/TR/xslt20/
- **XPath 2.0**
  www.w3.org/TR/xpath20/
- **XQuery 1.0**
  www.w3.org/TR/xquery/

Character Sets and Entities

B

An XML document may contain any character from the entire Unicode character set. This character set (equivalent to the ISO/IEC 10646 standard) is a universal character set (UCS), and represents nearly all the characters for all known world languages today.

In most cases, you can simply type a character into an XML document, and it will display as expected. However, if you want to use any accents, foreign language characters, or special symbols, this may not be the case. That's because not all computer applications store character information in the same way.

The method of storing the characters from a character set is called *character encoding*. And, if your XML document and the application displaying it do not use the same character encoding, then what you type may not be what is displayed. To avoid this, you can specify the character encoding of your document. Then, if the displaying application supports that encoding, the character will display as expected.

If this doesn't work, there are two other ways to have the character represented correctly. One is to use NCRs (*numeric character references*), which are short sequences of numbers that represent Unicode characters. For example, `Δ` represents the Greek letter Δ (Delta) .

Another way is to use entities, which are unique "words" that represent Unicode characters. In XML, there are five predefined entities *(see page 14)*, such as `>` which creates > (a greater than sign). Besides those options, entities can be created by using a DTD *(see Chapter 7)*.

Still Not Displaying Correctly?

Even after setting your XML document's character encoding, or entering your character using NCRs, your character still may not display correctly. That could be because your operating system doesn't support Unicode. Or, more likely, the font you are using cannot display that particular Unicode character.

Specifying the Character Encoding

Although all XML documents use the Unicode character set, the character encoding used by an XML document is not predetermined.

To specify the character encoding:

1. After the version in the XML declaration, type **encoding=**.
2. Then, type **"char_enc"**, where *char_enc* is the character encoding you want for your XML document **(Figure B.1)**.

Character Encodings

- **ASCII:** In 1963, the *American Standard Code for Information Interchange* was published. It mapped the English alphabet, digits, punctuation, and other symbols (including a set of non-printable characters) to the values from 0 to 127. This enabled ASCII encoding to be stored in seven bits of a byte of computer memory.
- **ANSI:** The *American National Standards Institute* code standard extended ASCII with European language characters. Note: Windows "ANSI" refers to a Microsoft character set, not an ANSI standard.
- **ISO-8859-1:** The *International Organization for Standardization*, together with the *International Electrotechnical Commission*, also extended ASCII with additional characters. The standard is divided into different parts representing different language groups such as ISO-8859-1 (Latin-1/Western European), ISO-8859-5 (Latin/Cyrillic), ISO-8859-8 (Latin/Hebrew), and others.
- **UTF-8:** The 8-bit *Unicode Transformation Format* is a character encoding that can represent any character in the Unicode character set by using one to four bytes, as necessary. Note: **UTF-16** also represents any character in the Unicode character set, except that it uses 16-bit "words" instead.

```
xml
<?xml version="1.0" encoding="UTF-8"?>
<ancient_wonders>
 <wonder>
```

Figure B.1 *I have now specified that this XML document's character encoding is* UTF-8.

Specifying the Character Encoding

```
x m l
<?xml version="1.0"
  encoding="ISO-8859-1"?>
<?xml-stylesheet type="text/xsl"
  href="wonders-master.xsl"?>
<ancient_wonders>
 <wonder>
  <name language="English">
    Colossus of Rhodes</name>
  <name language="Greek">
    &#922;&#959;&#955;&#959;&#963;
    &#963;&#972;&#962;
    &#964;&#951;&#962;
    &#929;&#972;&#948;&#959;&#965;
  </name>
  <location>Rhodes, Greece</location>
...
```

Figure B.2 *I have replaced* Κολοσσός της Ρόδου *with the corresponding Unicode code points. Notice also that I have specified an* ISO-8859-1 *character encoding instead of UTF-8 or UTF-16. This is to prove a point illustrated in the figure below.*

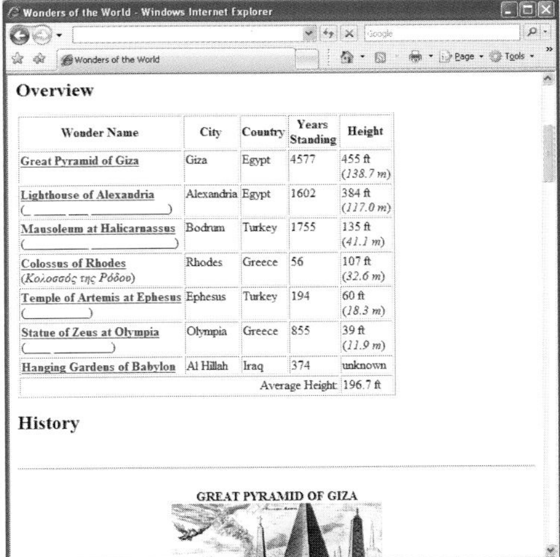

Overview

Wonder Name	City	Country	Years Standing	Height
Great Pyramid of Giza	Giza	Egypt	4577	455 ft (138.7 m)
Lighthouse of Alexandria ( )	Alexandria	Egypt	1602	384 ft (117.0 m)
Mausoleum at Halicarnassus ( )	Bodrum	Turkey	1755	135 ft (41.1 m)
Colossus of Rhodes (Κολοσσός της Ρόδου)	Rhodes	Greece	56	107 ft (32.6 m)
Temple of Artemis at Ephesus ( )	Ephesus	Turkey	194	60 ft (18.3 m)
Statue of Zeus at Olympia ( )	Olympia	Greece	855	39 ft (11.9 m)
Hanging Gardens of Babylon	Al Hillah	Iraq	374	unknown
			Average Height	196.7 ft

History

GREAT PYRAMID OF GIZA

Figure B.3 *The Greek characters typed into the XML document don't display properly because of the conflict between the ISO-8859-1 character encoding and Unicode. However, the Colossus of Rhodes Greek characters, which used NCRs, display just fine.*

Using Numeric Character References

By design, Unicode shares its first 127 characters with ASCII. This means that any ASCII character can be typed directly into your XML document from the keyboard of any system.

Any Unicode character beyond 128 may also be typed, but then you may run into character encoding problems. Instead, you can use a numeric character reference to put that character into your document.

To use a (decimal) numeric character reference:

1. Type **&#**.
2. Then, type **n;**, where *n* is the *decimal* number that corresponds to the desired Unicode character **(Figure B.2)**. (See Tip below for a list of all Unicode characters.)

To use a (hexadecimal) numeric character reference:

1. Type **&#x**. (Note the addition of the "x".)
2. Then, type **h;**, where *h* is the *hexadecimal* number that corresponds to the desired Unicode character.

✔ Tips

- NCRs will translate into their underlying Unicode numbers (also called *code points*), regardless of the XML document's character encoding setting **(Figure B.3)**.
- For a list of every Unicode character's code point, go to: *www.unicode.org/charts*.
- Consult the table on for a list of the Unicode code points corresponding to some common European language characters, along with some common symbols.
- To convert a decimal NCR back into Unicode, you can type it into Google's search field and simply click "Search."

Using Entity References

XML has five predefined entities for characters that have specific meanings. They are:

- & (for an ampersand character: &)
- < (for a less than sign: <)
- > (for a greater than sign: >)
- " (for a double quotation mark: ")
- ' (for a single quotation mark or apostrophe: ').

Without these entities, the intended use of each character in an XML document could be easily misconstrued.

You can also declare you own entities using DTDs, as discussed in Chapter 7. Moreover, you can use the set of entities defined for HTML and XHTML by using a public DTD reference, or by downloading the files from *www.w3.org/TR/xhtml11/#h-A2* and incorporating them into your DTD **(Figure B.4)**.

To use an entity reference:

1. Type **&**.
2. Then, type **ent_name;**, where *ent_name* is the name of the entity that corresponds with the desired Unicode character **(Figure B.5)**.

✔ Tips

- Entity references will translate into their underlying Unicode code points, regardless of the XML document's character encoding setting **(Figure B.6)**.
- Public DTD references are not supported in all browsers.
- Although the set of HTML / XHTML entities is large, it is not nearly large enough to represent the entire Unicode character set.

```
dtd
<!ENTITY % HTMLsymbol SYSTEM
  "xhtml-symbol.ent">
%HTMLsymbol;

<!ELEMENT ancient_wonders (wonder+)>
...
```

Figure B.4 *After downloading* xhtml-symbol.ent *from the W3C, I have incorporated it into my DTD.*

```
xml
<?xml version="1.0"?>
<!DOCTYPE ancient_wonders
  SYSTEM "B-03.dtd">
<ancient_wonders>
 <wonder>
  <name language="English">
    Colossus of Rhodes</name>
  <name language="Greek">
    &Kappa;&omicron;&lambda;&omicron;
     &sigma;&sigma;&#972;&sigmaf;
    &tau;&eta;&sigmaf;
    &Rho;&#972;&delta;&omicron;
     &upsilon;
  </name>
  <location>Rhodes, Greece</location>
...
```

Figure B.5 *In this XML excerpt, I used XHTML entities for most of the characters in the Colossus of Rhodes' Greek name. However, there are no entities defined for the ό character (omicron with tonos), so I used the numeric character reference* ό *instead.*

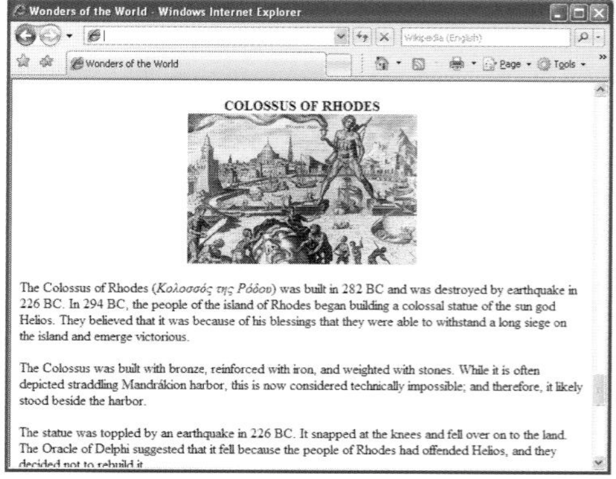

Figure B.6 *There is no character encoding specified in the XML document in Figure B.5. In that case, the XML processor sets the character encoding based on its own configuration. Regardless, the entity references display just fine.*

Unicode Characters

Here is a table of some interesting Unicode characters, their numeric character references (NCRs), and their XHTML entity references. This table shows only a fraction of the total XHTML entity references, and less than one-tenth of one percent of the total Unicode character set. A set of PDF charts covering the entire Unicode character set can be found at *www.unicode.org/charts/*.

Unicode Character	NCR (Decimal)	NCR (Hexadecimal)	Entity Reference
à	à	à	à
á	á	á	á
â	â	â	â
ã	ã	ã	ã
ä	ä	ä	ä
å	å	å	å
æ	æ	æ	æ
ç	ç	ç	ç
è	è	è	è
é	é	é	é
ê	ê	ê	ê
ë	ë	ë	ë
ì	ì	ì	ì
í	í	í	í
î	î	î	î
ï	ï	ï	ï
ñ	ñ	ñ	ñ
ò	ò	ò	ò
ó	ó	ó	ó
ô	ô	ô	ô
õ	õ	õ	õ
ö	ö	ö	ö
ø	ø	ø	ø
ù	ù	ù	ù
ú	ú	ú	ú
û	û	û	û
ü	ü	ü	ü
œ	œ	œ	œ
§	§	§	§

Unicode Character	NCR (Decimal)	NCR (Hexadecimal)	Entity Reference
α	α	α	α
β	β	β	β
γ	γ	γ	γ
δ	δ	δ	δ
ε	ε	ε	ε
ζ	ζ	ζ	ζ
η	η	η	η
θ	θ	θ	θ
ι	ι	ι	ι
κ	κ	κ	κ
λ	λ	λ	λ
μ	μ	μ	μ
ν	ν	ν	ν
ξ	ξ	ξ	ξ
ο	ο	ο	ο
π	π	π	π
ρ	ρ	ρ	ρ
σ	σ	σ	σ
τ	τ	τ	τ
υ	υ	υ	υ
φ	φ	φ	φ
χ	χ	χ	χ
ψ	ψ	ψ	ψ
ω	ω	ω	ω
™	™	™	™
©	©	©	©
¢	¢	¢	¢
£	£	£	£
¥	¥	¥	¥

INDEX

The elements and attributes of the XML languages defined throughout the book are listed alphabetically for easy reference. We have chosen to leave off the namespace prefixes (`xsl:`, `xsd:`, etc.) so that the elements and attributes can be easily found alphabetized by name. For example, you'll find the `xsl:apply-templates` element under the letter "A," listed as `apply-templates`. We made this choice because (although there are standard prefixes) the namespace prefixes that people use may not necessarily be the same, or may not be used at all *(see Part 5)*.

B

C

D

E

Index

F

Index

G

H

I

J

K

L

M

N

O

S

T

X

Y

Z